SAINTS SEAWAYS AND SETTLEMENTS IN THE CELTIC LANDS

SAINTS, SEAWAYS AND SETTLEMENTS IN THE CELTIC LANDS

BY

E. G. BOWEN

CARDIFF
UNIVERSITY OF WALES PRESS
1977

First edition 1969
Reprinted 1977
(with revised plates and second preface)

SBN 900768 30 4

First edition printed by Estate Printers Limited, Treforest
Reprinted by South Western Printers Limited, Caerphilly.

PREFACE

This book is in many ways an expansion of a smaller work published in 1954 entitled 'The Settlements of the Celtic Saints in Wales.' It seeks primarily to interpret the dedication distribution patterns associated with particular Celtic Saints and to seek correlations between such patterns and others derived from earlier cultures, more particularly those of the native Iron Age in Britain. The earlier work studied such correlations as they appeared in Wales, while the horizons of the present volume are considerably widened and attempt to embrace the whole of the Celtic Lands. Ireland, Scotland, Wales, the Isle of Man, the South-West Peninsula and Brittany are all included, while the story at times is extended to include Iceland in the north and the Spanish See of Britoña in the south. The author is fully aware of all the problems, historical, literary and etymological associated with the use of dedication distribution patterns and makes no attempt to claim that dedications to a particular Saint are in any way necessarily contemporary with the individuals so honoured. What is claimed is merely that this study attempts to look at the Age of the Saints from a specialist angle—that of the historical geographer. It so happens that the historical geographer working in the Celtic Lands is, of necessity, working in areas where the continuity of tradition is a predominant cultural feature. He is, therefore, not concerned with the fact that a particular dedication to St. David, or to any other Celtic Saint, was established by a visit of the Saint in question (or one of his immediate followers) to the site that now bears his name, but with the fact that the distribution of dedications to a particular Saint marks his or her 'patria'—a specific territory in which a revival of the Saint's cult might have taken place many times and over many centuries. The important fact is that the region in which such an occurrence takes place is a distinctive one, and one, we think, which possessed a long tradition of cultural unity centuries and, even millennia in some cases, before the Age of the Saints. Frequently, such territories have been invaded by rival cults, but such intrusive influences can easily be detected. The tripartite title of this book is designed to emphasize that it does not seek to be a history of the Celtic Church or of the individual saints whose *Lives* are mentioned in it—it attempts to deal only with the sphere of influence of the various saints, and to demonstrate how the great activity known to be associated with the seas of the Atlantic margins of Europe in prehistoric times continued to be of outstanding significance in the diffusion of Celtic Christianity in proto-historic times. It is for this reason that comparisons with distributions reflecting earlier movements along these sea-ways are so easy to demonstrate. The present volume includes a section on the settlements established by the wandering monks, as far as we are able to reconstruct them at the present time. The treatment of this essentially geographical problem is somewhat different in the present volume from that adopted in 'The Settlements of the Celtic Saints in Wales' in 1954. In brief, the difference is that in the present volume an attempt is made to examine the type of settlement established in the Dark Ages rather than to follow up the subsequent history (if any) of the site originally established at this period, as was attempted in the earlier volume.

The original study attracted considerable attention among historical geographers, historians, literary and linguistic specialists, archaeologists and prehistorians, as well as theologians and students of early church history. For this reason I felt encouraged to proceed to this extended examination of the problem.

I am deeply grateful for the very generous grant made to me by the Leverhulme Trustees with the special object of furthering this work. I am greatly indebted also to Emeritus Professor H. J. Fleure, D.Sc., F.R.S. and to Miss Ethel R. Payne, M.Sc. of the School of Education of the University of Birmingham, who have read the whole work and have offered valuable criticisms and suggestions which have been adopted in the text. Miss Payne also kindly undertook the preparation of the index, for which I am very grateful. Professor D. A. Binchy, D.Litt., the Director of the Irish School of Advanced Studies and Professor J. E. Caerwyn Williams, D.Litt., the Professor of Irish at the University College of Wales, Aberystwyth have both read the Chapter on Ireland, while Emeritus Professor R. H. Kinvig, M.A. of the University of Birmingham read that on the Isle of Man. The three gentlemen have offered the most valuable suggestions for which I am deeply grateful. I have also received great encouragement and direct assistance from numerous other distinguished workers in this field, including the late Canon G. H. Doble of Truro, and the late Dr. V. E. Nash-Williams, Keeper of Archaeology at the National Museum of Wales, Cardiff. Others who have given valuable assistance and whose opinions I value greatly are Dr. G. MacNiocaill, Assistant Librarian in the National Library at Dublin, Dr. Liam de Paor, and Mr. Neville Hadock all well-known authorities on Early Christianity in Ireland as well as Professor T. Jones-Hughes M.A. of the Department of Geography at University College, Dublin; while in Britain Miss L. F. Chitty, M.A., F.S.A., Vice-President of the Cambrian Archaeological Association, Dr. Nora K. Chadwick F.B.A. of Newnham College, Cambridge, Mr. G. R. J. Jones, M.A., of the University of Leeds, together with Professor W. H. Davies, M.A., Head of the Classics Department and Professor Harold Carter, M.A., of the Department of Geography at the University College of Wales, Aberystwyth have been most helpful at all times in the discussion of the many problems and difficulties involved in this work.

The spelling of all place names in Wales follows the official list prepared by the University Board of Celtic Studies first published in 1956, but it is more difficult to be consistent with spellings of the names of the various saints. A general rule would be to adopt the spellings used in the saint's native land, but so many of the prominent saints are known today by the anglicized form of their names that these spellings have frequently been adopted for the sake of clarity. Special care, however, has been taken (as with Welsh place names) that when a Breton, Welsh or Irish form is used that it is spelt correctly in the language concerned. I am also most grateful for the courtesy and attention given to me by the staff of the British Museum and the National Libraries in which I have worked, and naturally I am particularly indebted to the administrative, secretarial and technical staff of the Department of Geography of the University College of Wales, Aberystwyth. In particular, I would wish to thank Mr. A. J. Bird, the Map Curator, for invaluable assistance at all times; Mr. Morlais Hughes, the Chief Cartographer, and Mr. D. D. Griffiths, the Senior Photographer. Likewise, Mr. Michael Gelly Jones and Mrs. Margaret Woolley of the Cartographical Department have also helped greatly in the preparation of this work. In addition, I have been ably assisted by Mr. Brinley Jones, who typed the manuscript, and by my secretary, Miss Hilda Edwards, at every stage in the progress of the work.

Grateful acknowledgement is made to the Ordnance Survey: many maps included in this volume are based on existing Ordnance Survey maps. Permission has been granted to use these maps by the Controller of Her Majesty's Stationery Office.

Since this study was written, several important works have appeared bearing on Early Christianity in the British Isles. Many of them deal with matters directly related to the Celtic Church. The more important works include Professor R. P. C. Hanson's *"Saint Patrick: his origin and career"* and T. O'Raifeartaigh's commentary on this work in Irish Historical Studies (1968) entitled *"The Life of St. Patrick: a new approach."* Special mention must also be made of Dr. John Morris' *"Dates of the Celtic Saints"* in the Journal of Theological Studies, and possibly, most important of all, the publication under the general title of *"Christianity in Britain,* 300-700 *A.D."* (edited by M. W. Barley and R. P. C. Hanson) of the papers presented to the Conference on Christianity in Roman and Sub-Roman Britain held at the University of Nottingham in April 1967. A careful perusal of these and other recently published works does not appear to necessitate any change in the views put forward in this book.

Finally, I would like to add my gratitude to the University of Wales Press Board for undertaking the publication of this book, and to the printers for the skill and attention they have bestowed on the volume at every stage in its production. In particular, my special thanks are due to Dr. R. Brinley Jones, of the University of Wales Press Board, not only for his constant courtesy, but also for his expert advice so generously and freely given to me at all times.

St. David's Day, 1969. E. G. BOWEN.

PREFACE TO REVISED EDITION

The production of a paper-back edition of *Saints, Seaways and Settlements in the Celtic Lands* was called for when the first edition became exhausted after a lapse of six years. During this short period much supplementary work has appeared in this and allied fields, with the result that a clearer picture of the origins and nature of Celtic Christianity in western Britain is slowly emerging. Nevertheless, with the exception of one or two matters of general interest, the additional literature now available did not appear to necessitate any considerable re-writing of the original text, so that it could, therefore, be reproduced cheaply by photo-lithography. At the same time, the inclusion of a second preface could be used to draw attention to relevant matters which seem to be receiving increasing attention at the present time.

In recent work more emphasis is placed on the existence in Britain in the fourth century of a Christian Church organized on a territorial diocesan basis not only in south-eastern England but also in western, and parts of northern Britain as well. The argument depends largely on Dr. John Mann's study of the delegates present from Britain at the Council of Arles in 314 and particularly the territories or dioceses from which they may have come. Professor Charles Thomas has followed up this work by suggesting that here we may have a basis for certain arguments as to the nature of British Christianity in sub-Roman times as well. He has examined the situation in some detail in southern Scotland between the walls in the fifth and sixth centuries suggesting that this territory included several dioceses each under its own bishop, and each bearing a territorial relationship to the contemporary native Kingdoms. There could well have been a diocese based on Carlisle with another at Whithorn covering the native Kingdom of Reged, while one on the southern shores of the Forth could have served the old native Kingdom of Gododdin. Likewise, there may well have been a sixth century diocese centered on what is now Glasgow, and associated with St. Kentigern (Mungo). This would correspond to the Celtic Kingdom of Strathclyde. A diocese in the Tweed Valley around Peebles could have served part, at least, of the old British principality which became known in later times as Bernicia; while Abercorn (west of Edinburgh) and Old Melrose (Mailros) could easily (like Whithorn) be diocesan seats of sub-Roman bishoprics. Since these suggestions of Professor Thomas do not appear in this book, even when reprinted, they must be taken into account by the reader as implying a much stronger carry-over of the diocesan structure and, indeed, of the Christianity of the Roman Occupation period, into the formative phases of the Celtic Christianity in the West than the present text indicates.

Professor Thomas appreciates the implications of his arguments, based on southern Scotland, as far as the other Celtic Lands of Western Britain are concerned, but they have not, as yet, ever been developed in detail. In sub-Roman Wales and Cornwall and indeed, in those parts of England that escaped the full influence of the Anglo-Saxon invasions, the assumption must be that Bishops and Dioceses continued. In these areas, in the absence of fixed Roman Provincial divisions, and for the most part of Roman towns, it is likely, in Professor Thomas's view, that the diocesan unit, as in southern Scotland, bore some relationship to the native Kingdom if, indeed, to any definite territory. If, therefore, we were to revise what is said in this text in the light of the preceding arguments we would most certainly have to consider St. Dubricius more and more as a territorial bishop in the sub-Roman sense rather than a Celtic Saint. He could well have been Bishop of the little Celtic Kingdom of Ercic or Erging (Archenfeld) which drew its name from the Romano-British town of Ariconium, with his seat at Hentland nearby. Alternatively, he could have had a wider diocese involving Gwent as well as Erging. In the twelfth century, at any rate, he was believed to have possessed land near the Roman legionary fortress at Caerleon. His appearance at the great monastic school at Llanilltyd Fawr to ordain the future St. Samson (a reference to which is found in the very early *Life* of the Saint) might, using Professor Thomas's reasoning, have added significance. Anyway, here in south-east Wales was a thoroughly Romanized area, having even greater claims for the survival of Roman traditions than is the case with southern Scotland in the sub-Roman period. Our present thinking, therefore, would be that while Dubricius was certainly not the founder of the See of Llandaf, he certainly exercised episcopal jurisdiction in the area that afterwards became the territory of the diocese of Llandaf, although he might not have been the first bishop to do so.

If we attempt to apply Professor Thomas's thesis to North Wales a certain change of emphasis in the present text is also indicated. Nearly half a century ago Sir Mortimer Wheeler showed that before the Romans left North Wales their important station at Segontium had grown into a civil as well as a military centre. There is growing evidence of some civil Roman life surviving in the North-West into the sub-Roman period. We have inscriptions referring to a *magistratus*, a *medicus* and a *civis* respectively. It is very likely, therefore, on the parallels already cited, that there could have been a diocesan bishopric here, with probably no precise boundaries, but covering most of what is now Môn, Llŷn and Arfon. A situation of this kind might even have been strengthened by the coming of the Sons of Cunedda from exactly the same territory in southern Scotland as Professor Thomas has suggested sub-Roman bishoprics may have existed. St. Deiniol of Bangor is the outstanding Celtic Saint in this area, (except where parts of it yielded to St. Beuno). St. Deiniol has always been claimed, with little authority, to have been the first bishop of Bangor; but if we postulate a sub-Roman See of Gwynedd, on the Scottish model, Deiniol's claim as first bishop of the north-western diocese becomes very uncertain. What is, however, important is the contrast between north-west Wales and south-east Wales at this time. Diocesan bishops appear to succeed one another in Bangor, but in the south-east Dubricius's distinguished successors in these parts were men like Cadoc and Illtud, but they never appear in an Episcopal (to say nothing of a Diocesan) context. We have to await the coming of the Normans before the See of Llandaf is established.

It may well be, therefore, that the existing text has, by emphasizing the importance of the western Seaways, at the same time slightly overemphasized the contribution of Gallo-Roman Christianity as compared with the Romano-British contribution to the development of Celtic Christianity as we know it. If we sought to restore the balance somewhat, it is clear that more emphasis should be placed in the light of present research on the possible survival in many parts of western Britain of a Roman diocesan episcopal structure into sub-Roman times and that Celtic Christianity owed much to this foundation.

Since a number of pages at the beginning and end of this reprint have to be reset, the University of Wales Press very kindly undertook the improvement of the halftone plates. Where the old blocks appeared to be satisfactory they have been retained, but in other cases new halftone illustrations have been prepared and some different subjects selected.

E. G. Bowen Michaelmas 1976

CONTENTS

LIST OF MAPS AND DIAGRAMS

LIST OF PLATES
(at rear of volume)

Plate

CHAPTER I

THE WESTERN SEAWAYS

ONE of Britain's most distinguished geographers in the opening years of the present century described the North Channel separating South-west Scotland from Ulster as completing "the insulation of Ireland". Mackinder[1] was presumably surveying the contemporary scene, and thinking for the moment in terms of physical geography alone, but if he had chosen to glance backwards into history he would have felt more convinced than ever that the strongly worded phrase he had used was fully justified. There would be several reasons for this. First of all, the classical tradition in scholarship in the age in which Mackinder wrote carried with it a deep admiration for the greatest land-based Empire the world had ever seen. Historians and historical geographers alike were steeped in the classics. They knew how the Roman Empire had been based on its network of roads - the roads that united its vast territories and were the foundations of its military, political and economic greatness. While the Romans certainly possessed a fleet, it was with the legions that the glory rested. It was only natural, therefore, that the ancient authors concentrated on the land, and rarely described events at sea. The sea divides and the land unites was their motto. Very little was known, and little said by the classical geographers of the local sea traffic that went on beyond the Roman frontiers. Writers made a passing reference to the spectacular - adventurers like the Greek astronomer, mathematician and geographer - Pytheas of Massilia, who voyaged into the British seas and beyond, but of the regular trade routes and activities on these seas there is little comment. Strabo,[2] it is true, noted that vessels sailed to Britain from the estuaries of both the Loire

(1) Mackinder, H. J., *Britain and the British Seas*, Oxford, 1902, p. 21.

(2) Strabo, *Geog.*, IV, 199.

and the Garonne, while Diodorus Siculus tells of merchants travelling from Cornwall to the mouth of the Rhône and crossing overland from the Atlantic to the Mediterranean coasts of France in the process.[1] Caesar gives a further sidelight on this trade by indicating the part played by the Veneti—the powerful seafaring people who occupied south-western Brittany in the last century B.C.[2] Nevertheless, all this appears to be somewhat incidental. There was nothing to be derived from classical sources to suggest that on the outer fringes of Europe movement by sea was more important than movement by land. In light of the evidence available to him at the time, therefore, Mackinder would have seen little reason for changing his point of view. Here the matter rested for a while. In the nineteenth century there were no means of extending our knowledge of the past other than by the study and careful scrutiny of the literary sources.

It was the rise of prehistoric archaeology as a science in its own right during the present century that revolutionized the whole picture. It is important to realise that our increased knowledge of the Western seaways in remote antiquity has been acquired not so much from archaeological excavation as by the careful mapping of the locations of archaeological finds and sites on an extensive scale. It is the cartographical representation of archaeological material that has made it essential for the student of prehistory to assume the existence of important marine highways on the seas off western Britain, involving not only the ocean itself, but its many arms, which reach far into the land, and the connecting routes across the peninsulas which bound its bays. It is in this way that we are able to build up a picture of the intense maritime activity that characterized these sea-lanes in remote antiquity. Traffic along these routes goes back to the Mesolithic at least, and we now possess abundant evidence that they were extensively used throughout the three millennia which preceded the Christian era. The traffic carried along them tended to unite the shorelands of the Irish Sea (and often the whole of the

(1) Diodorus Siculus, *V*, 22 and 38.

(2) Caesar, *De Bello Gallico,* III, 8. See also Strabo, *Geog*., IV., 4, 1

Atlantic fringes of Europe from Caithness to Galicia) under a single cultural stimulus, so that historians can speak today of a Celtic Thalassocracy extending in early Christian times from Dalrida to Brittany and perhaps even to Spain.[1] Eminent archaeologists, likewise, have seen "the grey waters of the Irish Sea as bright with Neolithic argonauts as the Western Pacific is today."[2] Thus, over a period of half a century the wheel has turned full circle—no longer do we consider that in ancient times the sea divides and the land unites, but, on the contrary, that the sea unites and the land divides.

It would appear that the credit for first recognising the importance of the Western sea-routes in prehistoric times belongs to Dr. O. G. S. Crawford whose paper in the *Geographical Journal* in 1912 broke new ground.[3] In this work Crawford discussed the distribution of gold lunulae of Irish origin in Britain and elsewhere, and showed the existence of an isthmus road across Cornwall and North-west Wales at this period. It was well-known that early seamen disliked rounding stormy promontories. They preferred to disembark on one coast so that their goods could be transported overland to the opposite shore, where their cargo was re-embarked for the next stage of the journey. The early use of isthmus roads at Sybaris, Mycenae, Corinth and Troy was first discovered by Victor Bérard, himself an experienced navigator of small sailing ships, in the early years of this century.[4] Crawford's work showed how a similar procedure must have been in use in South-west Britain in the Bronze Age. He could have enforced his argument by drawing attention to the fact that the waters off the Land's End peninsula were, in any case, notoriously stormy. This early and important paper of Crawford is often overlooked, but it laid the foundations of later work both on the nature and the unquestionable significance of the seaways as lines of trade and communication in North-western Europe in ancient times.

(1) Lewis, A. R. *The Northern Seas,* Princeton, 1958, Chap. II, p. 64.

(2) Childe, V. G. *Scotland before the Scots,* London, 1946, p. 36.

(3) Crawford, O. G. S. *The distribution of Early Bronze Age Settlements in Britain,* Geog. Journ., XL, 1912, pp. 184 ff. and 304.

(4) Bérard, V., *Les Phéniciens et l'Odyssée,* Vol. 1 (1902), Bk. ii, Chap. 1.

During the First World War Professor H. J. Fleure at Aberystwyth was attempting a re-construction of the seaways further north, and was particularly interested in the distribution and spread of the Megalithic monuments of the Neolithic Age. In particular, he drew attention to the transpeninsular routes used at this time across the western peninsulas of Wales, in Llŷn and Pembrokeshire. An important paper published in 1915 entitled 'Archaeological problems of the west coast of Britain'[(1)] makes it clear that Fleure envisaged the great importance of the seaways and this prompted others to go into greater detail in this field.

After the war years, progress was rapid. In the pre-war years the Hon. John Abercromby had written about the most distinctive of all British prehistoric pottery - the Early Bronze Age Beaker, but, as yet, there was little corresponding study of the European Beaker. It was in Europe, obviously, that Beaker origins were to be sought. The distinguished Spanish archaeologist Bosch-Gimpera sought their origin in Spain and although few modern authorities on the subject would agree with his views today, we can not overlook the fact that Bosch-Gimpera drew attention to the importance of the Western seaways, and particularly to their connecting land routes across southern France in his conception of the origin and spread of Beaker pottery.[(2)]

About the same time E. T. Leeds returned to a problem similar to that envisaged by Crawford in 1912. Leeds[(3)] was concerned with the distribution of a particular Late Bronze Age socketed axe, square in cross section. The cartographical evidence showed this to be concentrated in Brittany, particularly in the western part of the country, with a sporadic distribution along the south coast of England, indicating that Breton traders in the Late Bronze Age frequented ports along the whole coast of southern Britain as did the Veneti from the same harbours some five centuries later. A detailed knowledge

(1) Fleure, H. J. and Roberts, E. J., *Archaeologia Cambrensis,* Vol. 70, 1915, pp. 405-20.

(2) See general discussion in Peake, H. and Fleure, H. J., *Corridors of Time VI, The Way of the Sea,* London. 1929, pp. 46-78.

(3) Leeds, E. T., *Archaeologia* XXVI, 1927, pp. 223-35.

of the southern sea-routes was beginning to emerge, and the long standing sea-links between Brittany (and possibly north-western Spain) and South-western Britain were now clearly

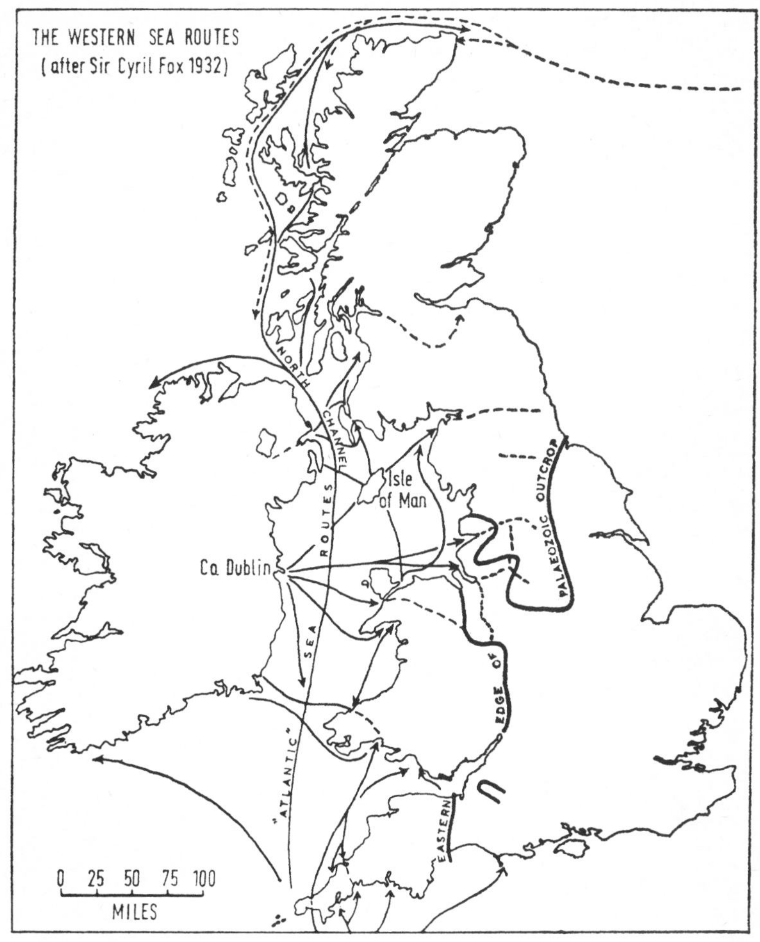

Fig. 1

envisaged and generally accepted, while much was also known of the use of the seaways further north. The time was ripe for a comprehensive statement, and this came in 1932 with the publication of Sir Cyril Fox's *Personality of Britain.*(1) Fox adopted the geographer's approach. The book is fully illustrated with distribution maps of archaeological finds and monuments covering the whole range of British pre- and proto-history. The text discusses the relationship of these distributions to the physical geography of our islands, more particularly to its two major physiographical provinces called by Fox the Highland Zone and the Lowland Zone. From the accumulated evidence thus portrayed, Fox was able to construct an overall map of the major routeways in the Western Seas, whose existence he considered vital to the interpretation of his archaeological distributions in the Highland Zone. Here, then, was the first attempt to map the sea-routes as such (Fig. 1). A number of interesting points emerge.

Fox considered that the sea-routes off Western Europe fell into three sections. There was a southern section where the early navigators who followed the Atlantic coasts of Portugal, Spain and Biscayan France would pass by Brittany and the western end of the English Channel and so enter the Irish Sea Approaches. The major routeway would, of course, send off several branches. With the Irish Sea Approaches a second section begins. The Irish Sea and the St. George's Channel form basin-like structures and provide numerous natural harbours and estuaries to attract primitive navigators on all sides. The first landfall in Britain would be Cornwall, and beyond this the major sea-route would split into three sections, one section would branch off to the southern Irish harbours, another would proceed northwards into St. George's Channel, while a third would enter the Severn Sea Basin. The main route lying in the St. George's Channel sent off numerous branches to the coasts of Wales and Ireland before proceeding into the North Irish Sea Basin with the Isle of Man in a central position. Here numerous further offshoots can be traced. For the third major part of its course the main Atlantic sea-route

(1) Fox, C., *The Personality of Britain,* National Museum of Wales, Cardiff, 1st Edition 1932. There have been three further editions, the last of which (4th Edition, 2nd impression) appeared in 1947. There is substantially very little change made in the map showing the distribution of the sea routes and the limits of Highland and Lowland Britain in this, the latest edition.

would pass through the North Channel and follow the deep water channel which skirts the Western Isles of Scotland and provides a convenient passage-way between Skye and the Hebridean Islands to the north-west. These islands provided a welcomed shelter from some of the worst storms and dangers of the open ocean. This northern section of the major seaway sent off branches into the Clyde estuary, along the Great Glen and among the islands of the North-West. It naturally passed around the stormy coastlands of Cape Wrath and included within its compass the Orkney and Shetland Islands. Fox makes the point that archaeological distributions frequently lie thickly in these islands and suggests that this may reflect some measure of their importance in the days of early navigation-as the last ports of call, to take in food and water, before voyaging further across the North Sea.

Fox pays particular attention to the part played by Ireland in pre-historic and proto-historic times. It received numerous cultures of southern and British origin by way of the sea-routes, but it always welded what it received into something new and characteristically its own, and then re-diffused the modified cultures into Britain and beyond. In this way it was by no means a sleeping partner of Great Britain culturally, it proved a very active partner indeed, diffusing Irish cultures by way of the sea-routes in all directions throughout the Highland Zone. Fox notes the importance of the shorter routes linking north-eastern Ireland with Galloway, the Clyde and the Isle of Man; other sea-routes linking Dublin Bay with the Isle of Man, the Mersey and the Ribble estuaries, Anglesey, the Llŷn peninsula, and the north-Pembroke coast. A third and very important route left the Wexford and Waterford harbours for north Pembrokeshire and the northern coasts of Cornwall.

A number of other points arise from a detailed perusal of Fox's map. The transpeninsular routes across Cornwall, and Dyfed (from the mouth of the Tâf in Carmarthenshire to the estuary of the Gwaun in north Pembrokeshire) and across the Llŷn peninsula in North Wales, and the Mull of Galloway in South-west Scotland are all clearly shown, and need little further comment. The position of the Isle of Man in the North

Irish Sea Basin as a focus of pre- and proto-historic sea-routes deserves further comment. The geographical position of the island is, of course, unique. On a clear day it can be seen from North Wales, Cumberland, South-western Scotland and North-eastern Ireland, and, in turn, the four countries are visible from the summit of Snaefell. Here was an obvious landmark for primitive navigators, and Fox's map shows that the island was in contact with the Carlingford Lough, the Mull of Galloway, the Solway Firth, Dublin Bay and the Menai Straits by way of the sea-routes in prehistoric and later times. The island's position in the midst of the sea is basic to an understanding of its cultural life in antiquity, and to the part it played as a focus of ancient seaways in the North Irish Sea Basin. It must also be noted that the map in the *Personality of Britain* attempts to show some of the landward links of the major routes, especially across the Highland Zone, into the South-eastern Lowlands. An important landward route into Northern Ireland is shown behind the Belfast Lough, while the map marks a routeway down the Clyde and across the Southern Uplands to the North-east coast of England. Another route utilized the Tyne Gap, connecting the Solway entry with the North-east coast. Routes left the Ribble and the Mersey for the Peak District and the Pennines and linked southwards down the Welsh Border. In the middle Borderland this routeway was joined by another which crossed the mountains of North Wales and was linked with the sea-routes using the Menai Straits and the Llŷn transpeninsular route. Further south no other land-link is marked, although it may be claimed that a continuation of the Pembrokeshire transpeninsular route overland beyond Carmarthen Bay across the coastlands of Glamorgan to the south-eastern margins of the Vale might have been added, as there is abundant evidence that such a route was used, and a shorter crossing of the Severn Sea thereby effected. Fox did not attempt to map anything south of Land's End and the mid-English Channel, the details of the southern section of the Western seaways had to wait until another attempt to map them as a whole was made by Crawford in 1936.[1] The additions south of Cornwall made by Crawford show branch routes off the main Atlantic stem striking across Brittany or encircling its shores. The very important overland links between the estuaries of the Loire and the Garonne and the Mediterranean coast of France are also shown (Fig. 2).

We cannot leave the fundamental contributions made by Fox and Crawford to the study of the Western sea-routes without mentioning an important corollary of the former's division of Britain into a Highland and a Lowland Zone. Fox was able to show that cultural and economic intercourse was most active along the Western seaways during those periods when the Lowland Zone was subjected to invasion from the Continent across the Narrow Seas.[2] Thus, it was, for example, during the so-called Dark Ages — a period with which we will be closely concerned in this volume—that the Anglo-Saxon invasions were affecting our south-eastern Lowlands and, as a corollary, the Western sea-ways were stimulated into an intense activity—the activity which is associated with the spread of Celtic Christianity in the Age of the Saints.

Further work on the archaeological side has served to confirm and amplify this basic picture. A long list of distinguished contributors may be mentioned including Miss L. F. Chitty, Sir Lindsay Scott, Dr. Glyn Daniel, Dr. Savory, Professor Hawkes, Professor Piggott, Dr. Mac White and Dr. Ralegh Radford. The work of Dr. Daniel, Miss Chitty and Dr. Ralegh Radford may be singled out for special comment—Dr. Daniel's work has emphasised the activity along the major Atlantic sea-routes during the Megalithic colonization of North-western Europe; Miss Chitty's cartographical work in the British area led to a more detailed knowledge of the activity associated with the minor sea-routes in the St. George's Channel and the Irish Sea Basin during the Bronze Age; while Dr. Ralegh Radford's studies of the distribution and cultural associations of the Dark Age 'Tintagel' pottery have indicated

(1) Crawford, O. G. S., *The Western Seaways* in *Custom is King*. Essays presented to R. R. Marett, London, 1936, p. 183.

(2) Fox, C. *The Personality of Britain*, Fourth Edition, 1947, pp. 38-41.

Iona
Strathclyde
Lindisfarne
Mailros
MARE
ORIENTALE
Hexham
Jarrow
Carlisle
Benchor
Nendrum
Sabul
Hwiterne
Etar
Hostium Dee
MARE OCCIDENTALE
Dair Inis
Miniu
Lan Ildut
Nant Carban
Pyrus
London
Carrum
Silchester
Richborough
Amfleat
Bononia
Quentawic
Docco
Fowey
MARE AUSTRUM
Sinus
Gallicus
Sargia
Pentale
Tréguier
Bréhat
Is.
Leon
Ushant
Lampaul
Dol
Rennes
Vannes
Redon
Ruis
Corbilo
Nantes
To Narbonne and Marseille
0
50
100
150
Miles
WESTERN SEAWAYS
After
O.G.S. CRAWFORD 1936

Fig. 2

very clearly the part played by the sea-routes in distributing a type of pottery that is known to be contemporary with the Age of the Saints.

Daniel's paper published in 1941 deals with the dual nature of the Megalithic colonization of north-western Europe.[1] He classifies the Megalithic tombs into two major groups on typological grounds, labelled Passage graves and Gallery graves respectively. It would appear that the Passage grave in its western and northern European form can be traced to the Almerian area in south-eastern Spain. From there the culture spread to the south-western coast of Portugal, and thence by way of the main Atlantic sea-route onto the Biscayan coast of France from the Gironde estuary to Finistère. Daniel shows that the main route carried the tomb builders thence into the Irish Sea Basin, as several important tombs are found in the valley of the Boyne. This is a clear example of a culture carried northwards by the main sea-route impinging on the coastlands bordering the Irish Sea. In Ireland itself the Passage Grave culture developed specialized local forms, of which the cruciform passage grave at New Grange is a typical example. The Boyne culture spread throughout Ireland, and, as we shall see later, was re-diffused by the shorter sea-routes onto the opposite British shores. Meanwhile, the main culture-spread can be traced northwards by way of the North Channel and the waters of the Western Isles around the extreme north of Scotland to the Moray Firth, where there is a well-marked concentration of this type of burial chamber. Many authorities such as Fox, Fleure and Daryll Forde think that the Northern European megaliths in Germany, Denmark and Sweden can be ascribed to migration across the North Sea from this north Scottish base. Here, then, is an excellent example of the main western sea-route in action. From this main current of movement branch routes stem in many directions. Daniel would derive the megalithic Passage Graves of the shorelands around the Gulf of St. Malo from those of southern Finistère. He is convinced that the St. Malo group is not an overland spread, but represents a sea-borne colon-

(1) Daniel, G. E. *The Dual Nature of the Megalithic Colonization of Prehistoric Europe,* Proc. Prehist. Soc., New Series, Vols. 6 and 7, 1940-41.

ization from south Brittany, influencing the Channel Islands as well as the coasts of the Gulf of St. Malo. Likewise, the Passage Graves in south-western Cornwall and the Scilly Isles mark a secondary offshoot (via a short sea-route) of the Biscayan culture of Finistère. Another branch route impinged on south-eastern Ireland from Brittany direct, for Passage Graves are found in Co. Waterford forming what is locally termed the Tramore culture. Some workers, notably de Valera, would wish to add a still more westerly route carrying the Megalithic culture directly from the continent to the shores of Western Ireland. The Boyne culture (which has already been noted) is based on the main landfall of the Passage Grave people in the Irish Sea Basin. This also sent out its offshoots. There is evidence of contact with the Isle of Man; with Anglesey; the Llŷn peninsula, as well as with western Pembrokeshire.

Daniel seeks the origin of his second major group of tombs—the Gallery Graves in the islands of the western Mediterranean—Sardinia, Corsica and the Balearics. These tombs are clearly marked in the Pyrenean area and in southern France generally, whence they can be traced along the famous Narbonne-Corbilo route to the mouth of the Loire. From the lower Loire the Gallery Graves spread into Brittany, and from here along the main Atlantic sea-route into the Irish Sea Basin making a major landfall again on the Irish coast, but this time in the Carlingford Lough region, to the north of the Boyne settlers. In brief, the route followed by the Passage Grave people is repeated except for the section across France. As was the case with the Passage Grave culture offshoots from the main routes are numerous and re-diffusion from the Carlingford Lough area into Western Britain particularly well-marked. A major offshoot stems from the Lower Loire along the valley into the Paris Basin. This is really a land route and does not concern us here, except to note that it is possibly by this route that the Gallery Graves reached North-western Germany and the Baltic Lands. More significant for our present theme is the fact that in the Loire area, or nearby, a subsidiary type of tomb evolved. This is known as the Transceptal Gallery Grave and it was from this area that settlers embarked and colonized the shores of the

Bristol Channel in South-eastern Wales, Somerset and South-western Gloucestershire. Here is a Brittany-Severn Sea linkage by the sea-routes.

The branch routes by which the cultural rebound from Ireland was carried include those linking the Carlingford Lough with the Arran, Bute and Loch Fyne area. These settlers established the Clyde group of tombs. Other routes linked the Carlingford Lough with Galloway, the southern Ayrshire coast and the Solway entry. Cashtal-yn-Ard, a famous tomb in the Isle of Man, belongs to this group and shows north-east Ireland-Isle of Man sea-connections at this period. Other routes which led across the seas to the estuaries of the Ribble and the Mersey carried Gallery Graves ultimately into the southern Peak District, Anglesey and Llŷn, as well as into Denbighshire and Merioneth. This culture spread also into Carmarthenshire as well as south-south-eastwards into Cornwall, Devon and Somerset. The Penwith group of tombs in Cornwall belong to the Gallery Grave tradition, and, like the other groups mentioned, contain numerous examples of all the Irish types of Gallery Grave. The overall impression left from Daniel's analysis of cultural migrations in these remote days is that the Irish Sea and the waterways to the north and south represent a very busy intersection of sea-routes.

Mention must now be made of the work done by Miss L. F. Chitty following the publication of the first edition of the *Personality of Britain,* as she, more than most archaeologists and prehistorians has concentrated on the *mapping* of archaeological finds and sites. Her maps showing the distribution of Bronze Age objects are extremely important (many were used by Fox in later editions of the *Personality of Britain*). Her map of the flat and hammer-flanged Bronze Age axes which are known to be of Irish origin(1) reveals very clearly a network of traffic lanes over the Irish Sea by which these objects must have reached a wide range of ports in western Britain and spread thence by many trackways over the Highlands into most parts of the country. What is basic to our present thesis is that the sea-

(1) Plate VI in C. Fox, *Personality of Britain,* Fourth Edition (2nd impression), Cardiff. 1947.

routes would appear to be very much the same as those postulated by Daniel in his analysis of the Passage and Gallery grave cultures. The routes from Northern Ireland to the Clyde and the Galloway peninsula as well as to the Isle of Man and to the Ribble estuary, and hence by way of the Aire gap to Yorkshire, are clearly indicated. From a base in Dublin Bay the sea routes to Anglesey and the Menai Straits led on to land trackways across North Wales and down the Borderland to the Cotswolds, while another entrê-port must have been located at the mouth of the Mersey. From Southern Ireland the seaways to north Pembrokeshire and South Wales were obviously used by some of the Bronze Age merchants, while others seem to have sailed from the south-eastern Irish estuaries directly to Cornwall at this time.

Ralegh Radford's analysis of the archaeological material found at the Celtic monastery at Tintagel in Cornwall has demonstrated very clearly the activity along the sea-routes in the Age of the Saints in the 5th and 6th centuries A.D.[(1)] Various types of pottery, not unlike Roman Samian ware in character, including sherds stamped with Christian symbols; the remains of amphorae used for importing wine and oil, together with several glass fragments are recorded and analysed. Radford notes the parallel between some of the Tintagel sherds and similar pieces from Egypt—similar, but not identical, pottery is common in Tunisia and in North Africa, while a sherd stamped with a cross like one from Tintagel has been found at St. Blaise, near Marseilles and is of 5th century date. Similar pottery occurs at Bordeaux and Toulouse, while vessels from the Palace of St. Pierre at Nantes, near to the mouth of the Loire may well indicate the route by which this pottery reached Britain. Another type of pottery found at Tintagel can be shown to be linked with southern Gaul. It is found again at St. Blaise, and probably reached Tintagel by a similar route. D. B. Harden says of the five glass fragments found in the same layers as the imported pottery associated with the Celtic monastery at Tintagel, that one piece is of western manufacture

(1) Radford, C. A. R., *Imported Pottery found at Tintagel, Cornwall. Dark Age Britain* (Ed. D. B. Harden), London, 1956, pp. 59-70.

and four are almost certainly eastern. He suggests an Egyptian origin in the late 3rd to 5th centuries A.D. for these four, although with such small fragments precision is impossible.[1] It is when we turn to examine the distribution of the Tintagel red pottery and associated forms in the British area as a whole that we realize the full implications of the Western sea-routes at this time. The distribution of this material is definitely western and exclusive of Roman Britain. It is certainly not found anywhere in Lowland Britain which corresponds roughly with the Roman civil zone in Imperial times. All this suggests very clearly that it belongs to an age when trade was once more flowing northwards along the Atlantic seaways and avoiding the shores of the Narrow Seas which had, by the 5th and 6th centuries, been blocked by the barbarian conquests. We have already noted how the southern section of the sea-route, including the Atlantic-Mediterranean crossing of Southern France, is clearly involved in any study of the origins of the pottery at Tintagel. This applies equally to similar material found at Padstow, the monastery of St. Petroc, and at Castle Dore in the same county. The major sea-route to the North is indicated by the presence of pottery of this kind at St. Mochaoi's monastery at Nendrum on Strangford Lough, and at the great hill-fort (occupied after Roman times) known as Dinas Emrys in Caernarvonshire (Fig. 3). As with the megalithic tomb-builders who used this route over three thousand years before, these sites represent typical landfalls on the margins of the Irish Sea Basin. Fragments of this pottery occur again at Dunadd in western Scotland indicating that the merchants had penetrated into the northern sections of the sea-route via the narrow North Channel. Land connections had been established with Elie in Fife and with Catterick in northern Yorkshire, where further finds of this type of ware have been recorded. Nor have the branch routes been inactive. Tintagel pottery has been recovered from the well-known hill-fort at Dinas Powys near Cardiff, in Glamorgan,[2] indicating that the Severn Sea branch was active, while even more important, as far as our main thesis

(1) Radford, C. A. R. *op. cit.* see Appendix by D. B. Harden. p.70.

(2) Alcock, L., *Dinas Powys,* Univ. of Wales Press, Cardiff, 1963, pp. 125 ff.

is concerned, is the occurrence of this pottery on several sites in

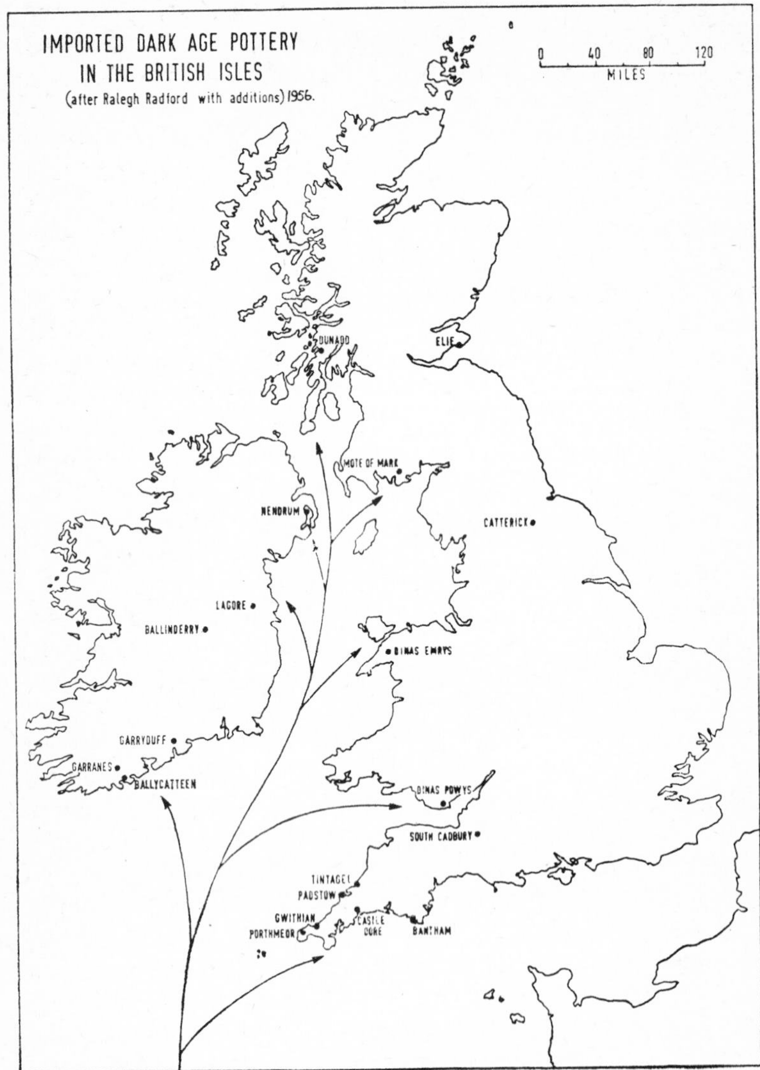

Fig. 3

southern Ireland, Garranes; Garryduff, in County Cork, where some Egyptian glass has also been recorded; Ballycatteen and

Lagore. All this strongly suggests that the harbours of Southern Ireland at this time were the terminals of an important western branch of the Atlantic sea-route, placing them, almost certainly, in direct contact with ports at the mouth of the Loire and of the Garonne in western France.

Several other aspects of the sea-routes have received the attention of scholars in recent years. Dr. Margaret Davies has sought to relate them to the physical background of winds, currents and tides and to coastal morphology generally.[1] This is clearly a matter of geographical importance. Dr. Davies assumes that the tidal circulation of the Irish Sea basin has not changed greatly since Megalithic times and that the configuration of the coast has been only slightly altered over the intervening five thousand years. One would assume that mariners who were at the mercy of the winds and the tides would, with experience, learn where the major tidal eddies and sand banks were located and attempt to avoid sailing into them. Likewise, in time, they would learn to await favourable stages of the tide so that they could use strong tidal currents to their advantage. The distribution of archaeological remains is, however, the only indication we possesss of the way the ancient mariners went. Such patterns would appear to indicate that the tides and currents associated with the surface waters, as well as the landmarks formed by "mountains arising from the sea" had much to do with the routes they took. There would be, for example, a marked southern ingoing current closely correlated with the southern section of the main northward running sea-route. This current would carry small craft at good speed past the Pembrokeshire coast and across Cardigan Bay towards Llŷn. Thus, the inner side of Cardigan Bay with strong winds, but weak tidal currents need not be navigated by seafarers passing northwards. This, in turn, gives added importance to the westward projecting peninsulas of Wales. Once across the Llŷn peninsula primitive navigators would most likely use the Menai Straits on their northward journey to avoid the tide

(1) Davies, Margaret, *"The diffusion and distribution pattern of the Megalithic Monuments of the Irish Sea and North Channel Coastlands"*. Antiquaries Journal, 1946, Vol. XXVI, Nos. 1 & 2, pp. 38 ff.

races around the Skerries to the north-west of Anglesey, but should they have proceeded across the island and climbed up to Holyhead mountain, they would see on a clear day the northern basin of the Irish Sea ringed round as if with islands—the Wicklow Hills, the Mountains of Mourne, Snaefell in Man, and the Fells of the Lake District in the distance. They would set sail for such objectives and so avoid the sandy, lowlying shores of Lancashire and Cheshire.

On the opposite side of St. George's Channel the incoming current travels northwards at a good speed. The rate of flow increases until it is travelling at nearly four knots off Wicklow Head. North of this it continues as a fairly rapid flowing stream towards Dublin Bay. The speed then slackens northwards along the coast of Meath, giving slack water and suitable landings at the mouth of the Boyne, Dundalk Bay and Carlingford Lough. There are no tidal streams in this part of the Irish Sea except very close inshore. We have already noted these areas as major landfalls in Megalithic times. Further north, the main sea-route encounters the difficulties of the northern incoming tide, entering the Irish Sea Basin through the narrow North Channel. Thus, off Rathlin Island and Tow Head tidal eddies and whirlpools abound, and the greatest speeds of tidal flow in British western waters are encountered. On the Irish side the flow slackens more quickly as the channel opens out into the Irish Sea, but off the Mull of Galloway the tidal current still maintains a six knots flow. It is for this reason that the transpeninsular route from Luce Bay to Loch Ryan assumed such importance. Once across this isthmus road the voyagers would make for the Firth of Clyde where there would be many islands and peninsulas to beckon them onwards. They would certainly make for Arran rather than sail near the low shores of central Ayrshire. Thence, taking advantage of the sheltered sea-lanes among the Western Isles they would enter Hebridean waters—the Little Minch and the North Minch, so as to obtain the fullest protection from the long skerry guard of the Outer Hebrides on their voyage northward. Others, possibly less venturesome, would sail via the Sound of Sleat and the Inner Sound east of Raasay, so as to obtain double protection from the open ocean afforded by the Outer Hebrides and Skye.

We know little concerning the type of boat that sailed these stormy seas in prehistoric times. No archaeological evidence survives. We have thus to depend on written records to obtain some idea of the nature of these primitive craft. Pliny, quoting the 4th century B.C. writer Timaeus, says that the people of Britain sailed abroad in vessels of wickerwork covered with hide, and Avienus also mentions vessels of this type. These are clearly vessels of the coracle or curragh type.[(1)] In spite of their frailty it is said that such craft were able to withstand seas that would be fatal to boats of a more solid construction. From an early time there was undoubtedly a larger boat of this kind possessing a wicker framework and covered by many thicknesses of hide. It would be capable of transporting a crew of twenty men and carrying a mast. Such large craft were certainly known in Ireland in later times, for in the ninth century A.D. Dicuil speaks of large seafaring coracles sailing to Iceland.[(2)] Vessels of even stronger build were certainly known in Ireland towards the close of the Iron Age, as is indicated by the elaborate gold ship-model from Broighter in Co. Derry. This had nine benches for rowers, eighteen oars in all, besides a steering oar, mast, yard, three booms, a punting hole and an anchor. Such a ship is certainly reminiscent of the large ocean-going ships of the Veneti in southern Brittany as described by Caesar.[(3)] When he arrived in Gaul he found two types of ship in use along the whole Atlantic coastlands from Spain to Norway. These were the *curraghs* described above, and the *Ponto*, employed by the Veneti. The latter was a large carvel built, flat-bottomed, ocean-going ship, with a high poop and stern, leather sails and iron anchors. In these ships, Caesar says, the Veneti navigated to Britain and beyond. Dr. H. O'Neill Hencken is of the opinion that large substantial ships of this kind may have been in use along the Atlantic coastlands of Europe for many centuries before the time of Caesar. He

(1) Hornell, J., *The curraghs of Ireland,* Mariners Mirror, XIII, 1937, pp. 75-93.

(2) Dicuil, *De memoria orbis terrae,* VII, 17, Ed. Parthney, p. 44.

(3) Caesar, *De Bello Gallico,* III, 13.

sums up our existing knowledge of this subject by saying that although Breton and Irish ships of some size, as well as the much lighter coracles, are known to have frequented the sea-routes towards the close of the prehistoric period, it is probable that quite large vessels were used for long distance trade by the natives of Atlantic Europe at a much earlier date.(1)

What these vessels carried in the earliest days of the sea-routes we shall never know. Indeed, we shall never know why they put to sea at all. There may have been economic causes in their homelands why they should have left in search of some precious metal or commodity. On the contrary, we may have to fall back on Childe's suggestion that the Megalithic colonists of Atlantic Britain were merely "boatloads of voyagers driven against their will by winds and currents to the remote solitudes of Britain and Northern Europe".(2) Whatever the reason or motive, the archaeological evidence makes it abundantly clear that maritime activity was intense at this time. The activity continued throughout the Early Bronze Age to slacken a little in the Middle Bronze Age, when the archaeological evidence points to the use of the continental trade routes across Europe. In the Late Bronze Age and throughout the Iron Age the Atlantic seaways flourished again with the increasing demand for Cornish tin. Indeed, it can be said that Cornish tin was one of the most famous products of Ancient Britain, and one of the most romantic to be carried along the ancient sea-routes. For the people of the Classical World the tin trade had a certain glamour about it, reaching out as it did into the western ocean that lay beyond the realms of the then known world. It must be remembered, too, that tin deposits are relatively rare, and as tin was a necessary constituent of bronze—the hallmark of the Bronze Age—the trade routes leading to these deposits acquired a great importance. When the Carthagenians in the sixth century B.C. closed the Straits of Gibraltar to Greek merchants, alternative routes to the Western Ocean had to be found. It was at this time that the southern section of the

(1) Hencken, H. O'N., *The archaeology of Cornwall and Scilly*, Methuen 1932, pp. 184-5.

(2) Childe, V. G., *The Prehistory of Scotland*, London 1935, p. 56.

ancient western sea route became prominent once again. The Greek trade route now crossed southern Gaul from Massilia to the Atlantic coasts and thence ships sailed to Cornwall for supplies of tin. It was from the traffic along this route that the Ancient Greeks obtained their knowledge of Western Europe. For the next five hundred years this route held the monopoly of the Greek and Roman markets for tin in the western Mediterranean. The student of historical geography would stress the importance of the fact that the two main transpeninsular routes across Cornwall, from Harlyn Bay to the Fowey, and from St. Ives to St. Michael's Mount happen to pass through the most important centres of prehistoric tin streaming in the peninsula and, consequently, are located where they would be most needed to transport the tin to the coasts for shipment. Hencken who has made a special study of this trade[(1)] discusses the sea-route from the Cornish harbours direct to Corbilo at the mouth of the Loire, and refers to a clear account by Diodorus Siculus of convoys of pack animals laden with ingots of Cornish tin plying between the Atlantic and the Mediterranean coasts of France. Diodorus says that the cross-country journey took about thirty days at the beginning of the first century B.C. A further indication of the significance of the part played by the Cornish tin trade in the development and consolidation of the western sea-routes is to be found in the fact that the western English Channel was called *Muir'n Icht* or Mare Austrum in ancient times. It was called the Sea of Icht after Ictis, St. Michael's Mount, famous as a depôt for Cornish tin. The other name, the 'southern sea' was still used in the fifteenth and sixteenth centuries to distinguish it from the 'North Se', an alternative name for the more usual 'Severn Se'. The 'North Se' and the 'Southern Sea' emphasize the isthmus character of Cornwall and help to place in perspective the significance of the transpeninsular routes. It would be unwise to overemphasize the importance of the Cornish tin trade (significant and well-known though it undoubtedly was) for other commodities must have travelled southwards along these

(1) Hencken, H. O'N, *The Prehistoric Tin Trade, Chap. V Cornwall and Scilly,* The County Archaeologies, London, 1932, pp. 174-75.

routes from Ireland—copper and gold may be mentioned, while dogs, slaves and hides are known to have travelled this way as well. Moving in the opposite direction would be wine, oil and luxury goods and possibly wheat — all of which were available in the Mediterranean lands, and much sought after in the Celtic north-west.

The spread of Roman power in the last century B.C. and the first century A.D. resulted in the temporary weakening of the western routes. The Romans discovered new supplies of tin in Spain in the last century B.C. and by the mid-century, Caesar had smashed the power of the Veneti, thereby dealing a fatal blow to the most vigorous centre of the western sea trade. The Roman conquest of Gaul, and particularly the territory of the Belgae, helped towards the opening up of South-eastern Britain in Iron Age times, leading to its final conquest by Rome in the next century. The spread of Roman power, therefore, stabilized the eastern land routes and traffic flowed more and more to the continent across the Narrow Seas. The Western sea routes were not to regain their vitality until the Lowlands of south-eastern Britain were once again submerged by barbarian invasions. The renewed activity along the Atlantic sea-routes in the Dark Ages was associated with the rise and spread of Celtic Christianity—a theme central to the interests of this book. Before we can consider this in detail we need to examine the major pre-Christian culture areas of Atlantic Europe which developed in association with the sea routes. It is, therefore, convenient to close this chapter by setting out in summary form the main routeways discussed therein (see also Fig. 4).

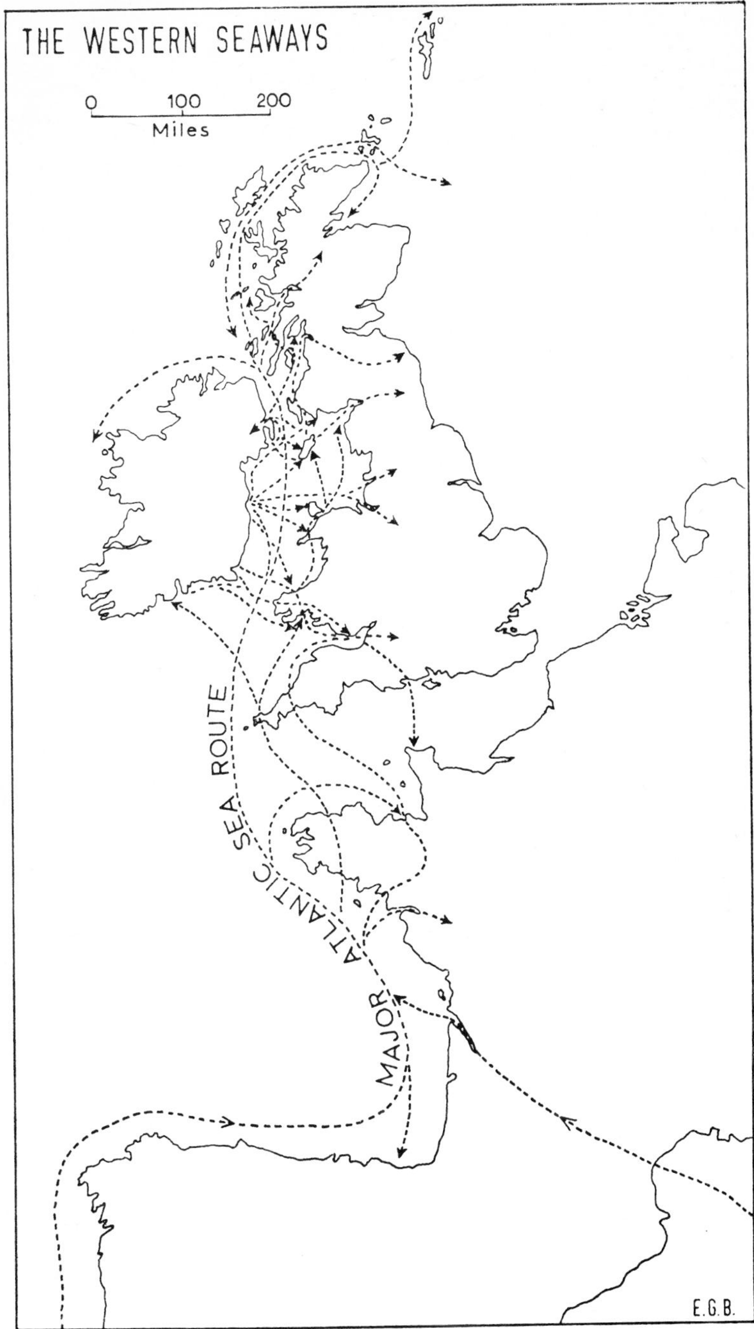
THE WESTERN SEAWAYS
0
100
200
Miles
MAJOR ATLANTIC SEA ROUTE
E.G.B.

Fig. 4

I. SOUTHERN SECTION: MAIN ROUTES

A. Atlantic coasts of Spain/Portugal, Biscayan France, past Brittany to Western Approaches of Britain (Mare Austrum).

B. Western Mediterranean—Narbonne/Marseilles overland to estuary of the Garonne and thence past Brittany to Western Approaches of Britain.

BRANCH ROUTES

(i) into estuary of the Loire. Corbilo-Nantes.

(ii) into estuaries of southern Brittany and thence overland via Redon, Rennes to Dol, and Bréhat Is., thence across the Padstow-Fowey crossing of Cornwall via the Somerset coast to S.E. Wales and the Severn Sea.

(iii) around Brittany by sea to the St. Malo area.

(iv) via Finistère to western crossing of Cornwall—St. Ives—St. Michael's Mount.

II. MIDDLE SECTION: MAIN ROUTES

A. Continuing I. A.B. above from Western approaches of Britain northward into the St. George's Channel.

B. Possibly continuing I. A.B. westward and northward around to western Ireland.

BRANCH ROUTES A (1) Eastern

(a) via St. Ives-St. Michael's Mount crossing of Cornwall, thence across Severn Sea to

(b) Carmarthen Bay and transpeninsular route across S.W. Wales to Cardigan Bay, thence to

(c) Llŷn and Anglesey and thence via Menai Straits to

(d) Isle of Man and the Solway Firth.

(e) Isle of Man to Luce Bay-Loch Ryan crossing of Galloway peninsula.

(2) Western (a) to Southern Ireland harbours especially Waterford & Wexford

(b) Dublin Bay

(c) Boyne River

(d) Carlingford Lough

(e) Strangford Lough

(f) Belfast Lough

CROSS ROUTES (i) Belfast Lough to (a) Clyde estuary, thence Strathclyde — Mailros— Lindisfarne or via Crinan Isthmus to Firth of Lorne and Iona.

(b) Luce Bay, Whithorn, Solway Firth, and thence by Tyne Gap to Tynemouth.

	(c) Isle of Man
(ii) Strangford Lough to	(a) Luce Bay and Whithorn
	(b) Isle of Man
(iii) Dublin Bay to	(a) Isle of Man
	(b) Mersey and Ribble estuaries and thence to Peak District and southwards by Midland Gap.
	(c) Anglesey and Llŷn
	(d) North Pembrokeshire
(iv) Wexford and Waterford Harbours to	(a) North Pembrokeshire and thence by transpeninsular route to Carmarthen Bay and South-east Wales.
	(b) around Southern Pembrokeshire to the South Wales coast.
	(c) Western Cornwall—St. Ives—St. Michael's Mount crossing.

III. NORTHERN SECTION: MAIN ROUTE	A.	Continuing I. A.B. & II.A via North Channel, Inner Hebrides, Little Minch, North Minch, Cape Wrath, Pentland Firth, Moray Firth. Orkney and Shetland Islands, and North Sea.
BRANCH ROUTES	(i)	around North coast of Ireland, possibly to islands of West coast.
	(ii)	via Sound of Jura, Firth of Lorne to the Great Glen.
	(iii)	via Sound of Sleat, Kyle of Lochalsh into the North Minch.

CHAPTER II

THE SEAWAYS AND CULTURE AREAS IN PRE-CHRISTIAN TIMES.

THE intense activity which characterized the Western sea-routes throughout pre-historic times obviously had a profound influence on the way of life and cultural associations of the neighbouring shorelands. Indeed, the territories lying behind the long established landfalls tended to become culture areas of their own, that is, regions where the manifestations of a particular pattern of living in both its material and non-material aspects are sufficiently characteristic to distinguish the area from its neighbours. The concept of the culture area has long been familar to the social anthropologist and the human geographer(1) while in recent years it has been successfully employed by the archaeologist as well.(2) The usual procedure is to select a number of indices from either the material or the non-material culture of a people and map their occurrence, drawing a rough boundary around the area where the selected indices occur. It is obvious that there are several difficulties encountered straightaway. For example, the weakest part of any region is precisely where it is made on the map to appear most significant by drawing a boundary or a frontier-line between it and another area. Such a line should, in fact, be a zone of transition. Likewise, it is difficult to select an appropriate index of the culture whose area it is intended to delineate, as all the traits of a given culture cannot be plotted simultaneously, and even when a selection is made the patterns resulting from the plotting of the various traits hardly ever coincide, so that the distinction between the core and the periphery of the region

(1) See, for example, Herskovits, M. J., *The Culture Areas of Africa, AFRICA,* Vol. III, 1930, p. 59 ff; Unstead, J. F., *A Systematic Regional Geography,* Vol. I, British Isles, Vol. II, Europe, London 1935, 1939.

(2) Hawkes, C. F. C., *The ABC of the British Iron Age, Antiquity,* XXXIII, 1959, p. 170 ff.

would in this way be further accentuated. Further restrictions in the use of the concept arise when the archaeologist attempts to delimit culture areas. He is perforce restricted in his choice of an index to elements of material culture, while the social anthropologist and human geographer can select indices from either the material or the non-material culture of the people whose culture area they wish to delineate. Anyway, in spite of these limitations in the use of the concept it has yielded important results when the culture areas of Western Britain in prehistoric times are studied in relation to movements along the sea-routes. A significant point is the continuity of the major culture areas themselves throughout the whole of prehistoric times. It would be possible to trace this continuity of pattern in Western Britain from Neolithic times to the Age of the Saints,[(1)] but since one of the aims of this work is to concentrate on the latter period it should be sufficient for our purpose to indicate the major culture areas as they existed in the pre-Roman Iron Age, which itself, survived in Western Britain throughout the Roman Occupation into the Dark Ages.

Before embarking on this task there remains one further matter for general consideration. Thus far, we have been using a loose geographical term, namely Western Britain, for the area influenced by the cultures brought by the western sea-routes. There is need for greater precision. Instinctively the historical geographer and the archaeologist turn to the nomenclature used by Sir Cyril Fox in his well known *Personality of Britain.* Here the country is divided into a Highland and a Lowland Zone and it is expressly stated that continental cultures impinge on the south-eastern Lowland Zone, while 'Atlantic', or western sea-derived cultures, impinge on Highland Britain. It would, therefore, be more appropriate to speak of Highland Britain rather than Western Britain. There remains, however, the difficulty of using physiographical terminology for what are, in fact, two major cultural areas, and, indeed, few would wish to imply a close correlation between relief and culture. Recently, A. Downes[(2)] has looked at this problem anew and

(1) Bowen, E. G., *'The Travels of the Celtic Saints'. Antiquity,* Vol. XVIII, 1944.
(2) Downes, A., *The Prehistoric and Proto-Historic Culture Areas of Britain.* M. A. thesis, University of Wales, 1961. Unpublished.

has attempted to avoid the oversimplified generalizations as well as the terminological confusion involved in Fox's thesis. He has suggested three major culture areas for prehistoric Britain which he has re-named Inner, Intermediate and Outer respectively. The Inner or Metropolitan province[(1)] comprises most of South-eastern England with a curvilinear boundary reaching from Dorset to the Wash. Throughout the prehistoric ages this area received most of its cultures from across the Narrow Seas. The Intermediate area, reaching from Eastern Yorkshire towards Somerset and Gloucestershire, received (particularly at its north-eastern and south-western ends) cultures deriving from the Metropolitan area, on the one hand and from the western sea-routes on the other. Beyond the borders of the Intermediate area Downes shows that Metropolitan influences markedly decline and local developments, rising in the main (but not always) from Westerly influences are much stronger. This extensive area involving nearly two-thirds of Britain and including Ireland may well be considered culturally as the Outer Province. (Fig. 5).

The cultural characteristics of Fox's Lowland and Highland Britain can be transferred with little modification to Downes' Metropolitan and Outer Provinces respectively, provided we take cognisance of the Intermediate area. We shall, therefore, in this chapter be concerned with the delimitation of cultural provinces in Outer Britain in Iron Age times, although it will be necessary to envisage a further extension of the Outer Province beyond the limits of our islands so as to include Brittany, an area which had the closest cultural contacts with Outer Britain in both Iron Age and Dark Age times.

The Iron Age invasions of Britain began in the middle of the sixth century B.C. with the spread of Hallstatt culture into the Metropolitan areas of South-eastern Britain. This movement was followed some three centuries later by the spread of La Tène culture into Outer Britain by way of the western sea-routes. There is abundant evidence that this

(1) This term was borrowed by Downes from Sir H. J. Mackinder's *Britain and the British Seas* (1902). Mackinder used the term in a strictly economic rather than in a broad cultural sense to distinguish this South-eastern area, tributary to London, from industrial Britain.

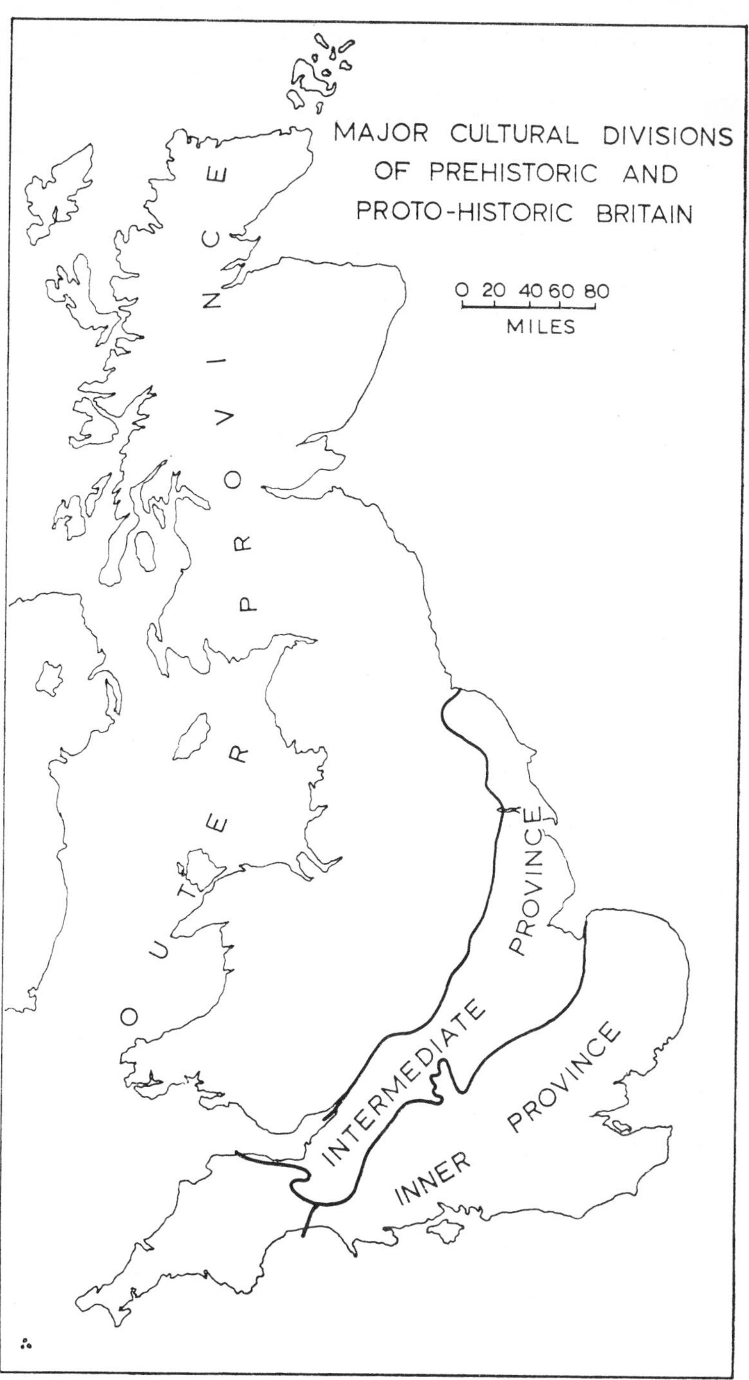
MAJOR CULTURAL DIVISIONS
OF PREHISTORIC AND
PROTO-HISTORIC BRITAIN
0 20 40 60 80
MILES
OUTER PROVINCE
INTERMEDIATE PROVINCE
INNER PROVINCE
After Downes 1961

Fig. 5

culture was based on Western France and passed over into Cornwall and the South-west Peninsula possibly associated with the Cornish tin trade. It spread across the Bristol Channel to the coasts of South Wales and thence up the eastern Borderlands into Powys and North Wales. A coastwise expansion from Cornwall can be traced further westwards into Pembrokeshire and presumably along the west coast of Wales and beyond. An independent invasion of chieftains from the valley of the Marne in France associated with this culture, seems to have impinged on the coastlands of North-east Yorkshire. By the beginning of the first century B.C., if not before, the Metropolitan culture and that of the Outer Province were in contact with one another in the Intermediate culture area to which reference has already been made. This last century B.C. saw still further invasions, particularly of Belgic culture into the Metropolitan area. The first invasions can be dated to about 75 B.C., affecting mainly south-eastern areas, while a second invasion occurred in the Wessex area a quarter of a century or so later, following upon Caesar's pacification of Gaul. Since 1931 it has become customary for archaeologists to adopt Hawkes' nomenclature for the British Iron Age cultures. Those arising from the Hallstatt invasions of south-eastern Britain are termed Iron Age A; those arising from La Tène movements along the western seaways—Iron Age B; and the Belgic cultures are referred to as Iron Age C.(1)

We must now direct our attention in greater detail to the British Outer Province if we are to obtain a clear picture of the cultural sub-divisions that emerged there in the age which preceded the coming of Christianity into these parts. The details of the picture are provided by the considerable movement of peoples that followed upon the unsettled conditions both in Britain itself and in Gaul as the menace of Roman arms advanced gradually, but surely, north-westward in Europe in the last century B.C. and the first century A.D. The situation developing in southern Britain had marked repercussions in

(1) Hawkes, C. F. C., *The British Hill-Forts, Antiquity* V, 1931, p. 60.

far distant Scotland and throughout the whole of Outer Britain.

Considerable uneasiness and much local disturbance prevailed following upon the Belgic invasions and Caesar's raids of 55 and 54 B.C. The full realization of the Roman power in Gaul made itself felt in the courts of the British chieftains. In this atmosphere a situation was created in which many groups felt that the time had come to set out northwards hoping, at least, for a respite. Indeed, there is abundant archaeological material indicative of such action, pointing at the same time to the fact that the great confederacy of the Brigantes stretching from sea to sea south of the Tyne-Solway line at first prevented the passage of refugees through its boundaries, so that access to the northern lands was possible only by sea.[(1)] It would appear that the first and most formidable of the resultant Celtic intrusions into the North reached central and eastern Scotland by the North Sea route. This was the Abernethy culture characterized by its large hill-forts with their strong ramparts interlaced with timber structures which were either accidentally or deliberately burnt so as to give a vitrified mass of stone. They are known, in consequence, as vitrified forts. Caesar refers to such walls which he had seen in Gaul as *murus gallicus.* The culture of the vitrified fort people is closely linked with the British Iron Age A and ultimately with the continental Hallstatt. In Scotland these people clearly occupied the best land and, at the same time, their forts appear to guard the main maritime entries and inland routes. After the Roman advance they would certainly have lost their territories south of the Antonine Wall, but much remained to the north of it, especially the eastern highlands and coastal plains between the Moray Firth and the Forth (Fig. 6b). This area appears to have been the centre of their power, and it is in this region that the Picts emerge in post-Roman times. A second movement from southern Britain utilizing the North Sea routes is indicated by the presence in south-eastern Scotland between the Forth and the Tweed of

(1) Piggott, Stuart, *South-east Scotland—Prehistoric Settlement.* Brit. Assoc. Handbook, Edinburgh meeting 1951, pp. 45-60.

a large number of small hill-forts, very different in structure from the vitrified forts. Their main concentration appears to

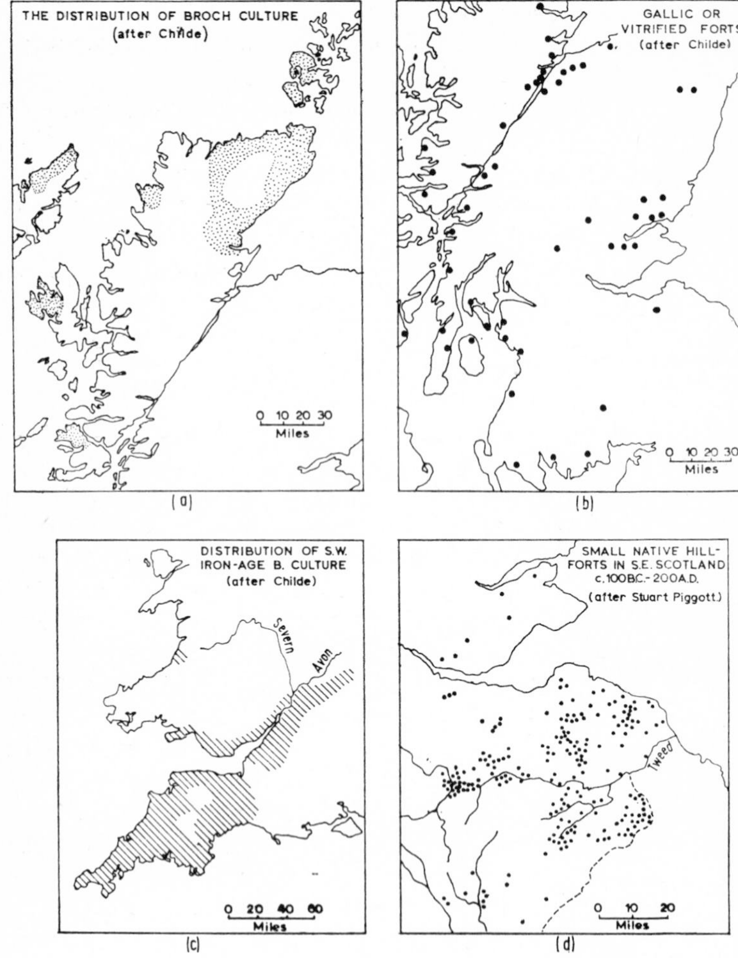

Fig. 6
Selected Distributions of British Iron Age Cultures

be in the hill-country overlooking the drainage system of the Tweed, but they appear to have moved in westwards as there are notable concentrations around Peebles and towards

Lanark. This westward extension (which is a matter of considerable interest) might well be correlated with the congestion resulting from the powerful 'Pictish' barrier to the north and the ever increasing power of the Roman arms to the south. When the large number of small hill-forts in south-western Scotland are excavated the westward extension of this culture might be shown to have been more marked than our present evidence allows us to prove. Stuart Piggott is forced to the conclusion that these forts in the Tweed Basin, and their extensions, represent the presence of Celtic refugees from England who fled northward either before or just after the Conquest of 43 A.D., hoping to obtain at least a generation's respite from the disaster which had overtaken the Celtic Iron Age aristocracy in Gaul.[(1)] On the western side of the country, at a period contemporary with, or a little later than, the North Sea movements just described, we have clear evidence of the spread northwards of settlers who made a special type of pottery, and had an elaborate weaving technique and built a special style of house, indicating that they were participating in a more complete migration than that which affected the Tweed Basin. Whole families appeared to be taking the road to the Isles; to the Hebrides, and thence around to Caithness and to the Orkneys and Shetlands. They settled in considerable numbers in these northern parts where their presence is marked by their defensive circular-tower houses known as Brochs. All the evidence points to the cultural origins of the Broch culture being sought for in the Iron Age B settlements of south-western Britain. The movements of the Broch builders can be understood only as a reaction to the disturbed conditions in south-eastern England and on the continent at this time.[(2)] It may well be, too, that the strongly held central part of Scotland in the hands of the vitrified fort people was the reason why these colonists had to move so far to the north to find an area for re-habilitation.

We can now turn our attention to the southern end of the Outer Province. La Tène (Iron Age B) culture entered this

(1) Piggott, Stuart, op. cit., p. 52.

(2) Scott, Sir Lindsay, *The Problem of the Brochs,* Proc. Prehist. Soc., Vol. XIII, 1947, p. 26.

area by way of the western sea-routes—a movement associated with the Cornish tin trade. In immediate pre-Roman times this trade was in the hands of the Veneti.[1] This powerful tribe were not only experienced seamen; they were also skilled in the arts of war. They seem to have been responsible for the building of hill-forts and cliff castles with multiple lines of defence and for the introduction of sling fighting with a range up to approximately 100 yards. Sir Mortimer Wheeler maintains that it is reasonable to ascribe the widespread use of sling stones and multiple defences in the hill-forts and cliff-castles of south-western Britain to Venetic colonization or influence.[2] The distribution of Iron Age hill-forts and cliff-castles with two or more lines of entrenchment provides in turn, a convenient basis for the subdivision of the southern section of Outer Britain (together with Brittany) into major cultural regions at this time.

The south-western coastal zone of Brittany including southern Finistère and Le Morbihan has a series of cliff-castles and other earthworks representing headland fortresses described by Caesar as normal to the Veneti in those parts. Here then is the central area of Venetic economic and cultural influence, and it is of interest to note the expansion of Venetic power, with control of the sea, from the home zone around the Morbihan north-westward along the coast of Finistère. The cultural associations of Le Morbihan seem to have been different from those of Finistère and Côtes du Nord throughout prehistoric times, although on the eve of the Roman Occupation we seem to have two cultural areas in Brittany—Venetic Le Morbihan with southern Finistère, on the one hand, and northern Finistère and Côtes du Nord, on the other.

The cliff-castles of the Scilly Isles and the Cornish peninsula have slingstones and multiple defences. The construction of the defences of the cliff-castle at Gurnards Head in Penwith (western Cornwall) very closely resembles that of the small multiple fortresses of Kercaradoc and Penhars near Quimper,

(1) Caesar, De Bello Gallico III, 8.

(2) Wheeler, R. E. M., '*Hill Forts of Northern France—a Note on the Expedition to Normandy* 1939'', Antiquaries Journal. Vol. XXI, p. 268.

while the cliff-castles of Castel Coz and Castel Mow on the Finistère coast, between Douarnenez and Le Ponte du Rez, are identical in character with the cliff-castles of Cornwall.

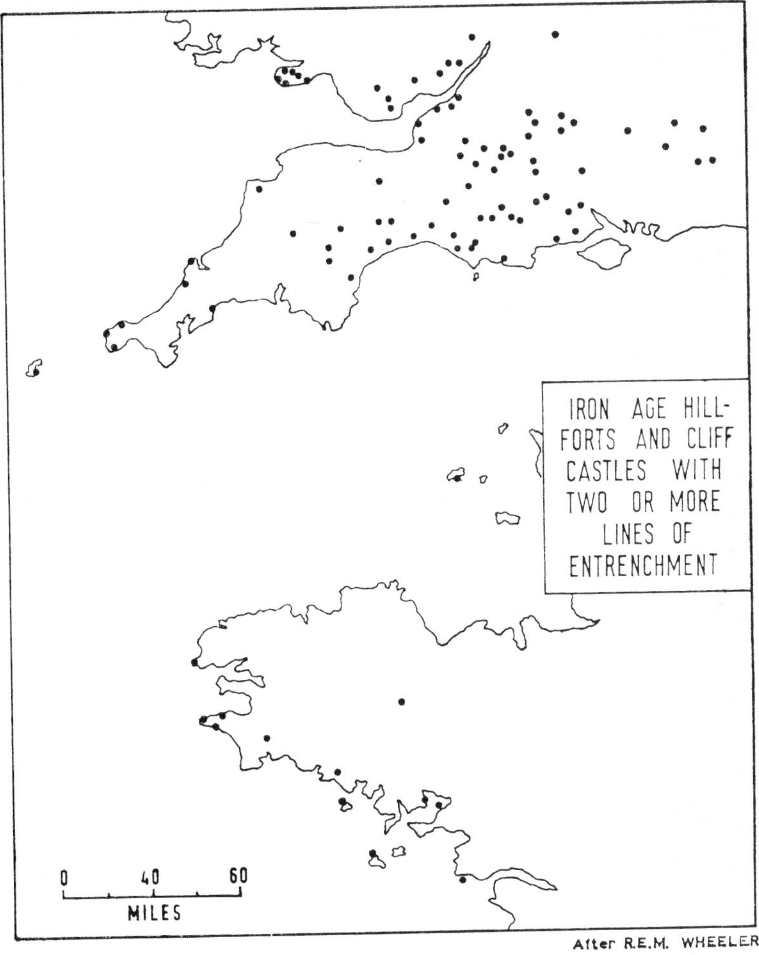

Fig. 7

Wheeler is convinced that the cliff-castles of Cornwall and the Scilly Isles are the product of Venetic activity before the time of Julius Caesar. We can, therefore, demarcate this furthermost peninsula of Outer Britain as a Venetic colony at this time.

Outside the metalliferous area of Cornwall and its approaches, the map (Fig. 7) shows a considerable number of hill-forts and cliff-castles with two or more lines of entrenchment in Devon, Somerset, Dorset, and throughout the Wessex country generally. Wheeler has shown, especially with reference to Maiden Castle, that the presence of such multiple defences was often a later addition to the hill-forts and linked with sling fighting and with the immigration of a small number of experts in the art of war. He attributes these influences, not as in Cornwall, to Venetic traders, but to Venetic refugees following upon the catastrophic events in their homeland in 56 B.C. Here, then, is a division of the South-west peninsula into two unequal cultural sub-provinces, an extensive area of Venetic influence in the east, and a longer established economic region, partly colonized by the Veneti, in the south-west.

As had so frequently happened throughout pre-historic times, influences that affected the south-western peninsula spread across the Bristol Channel to affect South Wales. Fig. 7 shows the unmistakable importance of the south-eastern Borderlands of Wales as a distinct sub-province at this time. Hill-forts and cliff-castles of the pattern described are found from the Gower peninsula in the west, through the Vales of Glamorgan and Gwent into the lands immediately west of the Severn. All workers recognize this sub-province. Childe says that beyond the Bristol Channel, the coasts of South Wales, and presumably the iron mines of the hinterland, became "a transmarine province of the South-western culture",[1] while more recent workers refer to it as the "Western Third B province," distinguished by its 'duck pottery' from the stroke design found in Iron Age forts east of the river. The distinction between south-eastern Wales with its multiple rampart forts and ultimate Venetic influence and South-west Wales, where these features are not in evidence, is clearly

(1) Childe, V. G., *The Prehistoric Communities of the British Isles,* London 1947, p. 241, Map p. 226.

brought out on Fig. 7. This contrast is vital for our subsequent argument, for here we have illustrated the fundamental distinction in South Wales between a south-eastern and a south-western province. The former is influenced by cultures emanating from the innermost parts of the Severn Sea as well as by cultures based on the Intermediate Province of Britain (Fig. 5), while the latter is influenced by cultures based essentially on those of the Irish Sea province. It would be absurd to think that such cultural provinces remained absolutely distinct and self-contained, or that there was anywhere a firm line of demarcation between them. Indeed, movement along the South Wales coastal plain and the northern shores of the Severn Sea would make this impossible, and considerable overlap inevitably occurred. We can instance in this connection the abundant evidence for the spread of certain elements of the South-western Iron Age B culture into the Irish Sea province especially on the British side. For example, a sherd of 'duck stamped' pottery was found in the reconstructed hill-fort at Pen Dinas, near Aberystwyth.[(1)] Further to the north there is evidence of the South-Western culture in Galloway and the Solway Firth, where a coin of Bodvoc found at Birkhill on the Dumfries-Selkirk border[(2)] may indicate distant contact with the Dobuni of the Cotswold and inner Severn Sea area. Still further to the north, as we have seen, archaeologists trace the remote influence of South-western Iron Age B culture in the Brochs of northern Scotland and the Isles. All this, however, must not be allowed to obscure our major thesis, namely the presence of distinctive south-eastern and south-western provinces on the northern shores of the Severn Sea in Iron Age times.

We can now redirect our attention, in summary, to the mainland of Britain where we have been able to distinguish in the Outer Zone three culture areas in the Scottish North and four in South-western Britain, (two in Cornwall and two in South Wales.) This leaves an extensive 'corridor zone' between

(1) Forde, C. D., *'Excavations on Pen Dinas Hill-Fort, Cardiganshire'*, Ant. Journ. 14 (1934) and 18 (1938).

(2) Evans, John, *Coins of the Ancient Britons*, London 1864, p. 135.

them, including much of the present North Wales, the middle and north Welsh Borderland, Lancastria, Cumbria, South-west Scotland and North-eastern England. As will be indicated presently, these lands apparently shared, in a somewhat diluted manner, the cultural characteristics of both the Northern and the South-western sub-areas. The vitrified fort technique is, for example, fully developed at Dinorben, a hill-fort near Corwen in north-eastern Wales,[1] while W. J. Varley has shown that the third version of the hill-fort at Almondbury in southern Lancashire was built in *murus gallicus* style. Likewise, the entrance and inner rampart at Maiden Castle, Bickerton, and the second stage at Castle Ditches, Eddisbury, in north-western Cheshire were similarly constructed. Varley concludes: "the *murus gallicus* provides us with a link with the forts of the Abernethy complex of Scotland and similar forts of Argyllshire."[2]

H. N. Savory,[3] discussing the distribution of some sub-Roman British brooches has recently emphasized the links in the opposite direction. He points out that in order to explain the presence of brooches with a geomorphic design, and made in all probability in the Welsh Border country, near Hadrian's Wall and elsewhere in the North, as well as in eastern and southern Wales in the sub-Roman period—it is necessary to recall, among other things, that the Romans had enrolled a Cohors I Cornoviorum for service on Hadrian's Wall.[4] This use of the Cornovii must be compared with the transfer of Cunedda and his Votadini from the North to North Wales in the last days of Roman Britain. Savory

(1) Childe, V. G., op. cit., p. 213.

(2) Varley, W. J., *Excavations at Almondbury, Maiden Castle, Bickerton and Eddisbury Camps.* Arch. Journ. 1948, pp. 220-60. Professor Piggott was so impressed with this evidence that he was for a time prepared to argue that the arrival of these fort builders in Scotland might have been by the west coast Atlantic route from a point near the Cheshire Dee, and that the East coast of Scotland examples are the result of subsequent movement up the Great Glen.

(3) Savory, H. N., *Sub-Romano-British Brooches from South Wales* in *Dark Age Britain* (Ed. D. B. Harden, London, 1956. pp. 40-58,

(4) The Cornovii were a mid-Welsh Borderland tribe centred on the Shropshire, Montgomery, Brecon-Radnor Borderland.

emphasizes that these two tribes were at opposite ends of a continuous zone of relatively unromanized, and for the most part, mountainous or forested territory, but were united by common cultural foundations in the Early Iron Age. This is suggested by the similar evolution of the hill-forts and the distribution of the first phase of insular Celtic art.[(1)] Such is the background against which the archaeologist should consider the survival alike on the Scottish and on the Welsh Border of native craftsmanship with common artistic traditions, and the arrival in forts near Hadrian's Wall of brooches made in all probability in the Welsh Border country. No stronger statement is necessary concerning the cultural nature of the long corridor which linked the more clearly defined cultural sub-areas of the northern and south-western portions of the Outer Province at this time. We shall have need to refer to this background later when we come to consider the cultural areas associated with the Age of the Saints.

Reference must now be made to two other areas lying outside the mainland of Britain but, nevertheless, intimately affected by the great sea-routes. These are Ireland and the Isle of Man.

Ireland in the Early Iron Age seems to have been somewhat of a backwater. It was not until the close of the Roman period in Britain that it became once again such an active partner in the affairs of Britain. It was at this period that Irish immigration into Britain began to assume considerable proportions. We shall have to devote special attention to this matter later, as the establishment of Irish colonies in Outer Britain frequently either created new culture areas, or modified those already existing. For the moment we must return to the pre-Roman Iron Age in the island. A great collection of bone work belongs to this period, but nothing that clearly belongs to the Iron Age A, or AB, textile industry as known elsewhere, has ever been found in Ireland. Likewise, there is no trace of the hill-forts of the type so commonly found in Britain at this time. No vitrified forts, no ramparts reveted with timber, no multivallate forts and no inturned entrances

(1) Leeds, E. T., *Celtic Ornament*, Oxford 1933, p. 5 ff.

have yet been described.[1] In their place we have the rath or cashel, clearly belonging to a different tradition. Nevertheless, there is evidence that Iron Age culture reached Northern Ireland, for in the Ulster region we find weapons and horse-trappings decorated in La Tène style. The ornamentation and the type of horse-bit found connects the invaders with the Arras charioteers who settled in eastern Yorkshire. Much of the archaeological evidence indicates that these invaders must have reached Northern Ireland from Galloway. This, of course, is the most ancient route taken by man into Ireland, and, as on many occasions in the past, invaders and cultures reaching Ireland from Northern Britain show a tendency to concentrate in Ulster, for the same reason that continental cultures show a tendency to concentrate in south-eastern Britain.[2] For the rest, Ireland shows little trace of invaders in Early Iron Age times. Late Bronze Age Urn–folk and builders of crannogs and souterrains survived into a period contemporary with the large-scale Iron Age invasions of Britain. In this way two culture areas stand out—a north-eastern area with a veneer of intrusive Iron Age B culture, and a larger southern and western area of cultural survival. Some archaeologists have noticed that in the latter area stone pebbles have been found decorated with La Tène motifs. It is agreed that these have come from Brittany rather than Britain and although their importance must not be exaggerated in Early Iron Age times, they do serve to show that this southern area of Ireland maintained direct contact with the Continent, however slight, at this time. In the Age of the Saints this contact of southern Ireland with western Gaul was to become very much more important.

The Isle of Man is of the greatest interest, for by its insular character it forms an obvious natural region, and by its location in the midst of the Irish Sea it occupies an unique position not only in relation to the major sea routes but also in relation to the larger units of the British Isles which surround it. The

(1) Bowen, E. G., *The Seas of Western Britain: Studies in Historical Geography. Geography at Aberystwyth* Jubilee Volume, 1968, pp. 157-59.

(2) Fox, C., op. cit., p. 42.

island is placed at an equal distance between the coasts of Ireland and of Cumberland. A short sea-voyage of some sixteen miles separates the north of the island from the coast of south-western Scotland, while a distance of forty-four miles separates its extreme southern point from Anglesey in North Wales. Indeed, anyone who climbs Snaefell, the highest peak in the island, can see on a clear day England, Scotland, Ireland and Wales in one sweep. Two important points follow; cultural influences borne by the sea-routes can thus approach the island from all directions, yet it is sufficiently large in size and sufficiently isolated to allow of many local cultural developments. The interaction of British and Irish influences impinging on the 'south side' and the 'north side' of the island respectively, together with occasional insular developments are the chief features of the pre- and proto-history of the island.(1)

It would appear that in Iron Age times we are witnessing one of the periods of insular development as was the case in Ireland. There is little evidence of the great Iron Age hill-forts that characterized the contemporary culture of South Wales and the South-west Peninsula of England. The great hill-forts spread along the Severn valley and into North Wales. This, however, was a landward extension of the South-western Iron Age B culture, and there is very little evidence that it was taken further north by the sea-routes. Modifications of Iron Age B culture were certainly taken northwards by the sea-routes—this is clear from an analysis of the Broch culture, but there is no evidence of this culture in the Isle of Man. The island has many promontory forts which probably date from the pre-Viking period, but Dr. G. Bersu has shown in recent years that the most distinctive feature of Manx Iron Age culture is the large round Celtic homestead representing the dwelling place of a chieftain and his family.(2) These houses are entirely unfortified, suggesting that a prosperous

(1) Grahame Clark, *The Prehistory of the Isle of Man.* Proceedings of the Prehistoric Society, 1935, pp. 70-92, also Kinvig R. H., *A History of the Isle of Man.* 2 Edit. Liverpool, 1950, and Bowen E. G., *Current Archaeology* 8. 1968. pp. 203-4.

(2) Bersu, Gerhard, *"Celtic Homesteads in the Isle of Man"*, Journ. of the Manx Museum, V, 1945-6.

family was able to live in peace at this time without special protection, despite the fact that they lived on an island set in the midst of a busy sea.

It should, however, be noted that similar types of homestead occur in Ireland, where they are usually referred to as 'Raths'. In Scotland, too, the small 'duns' are very similar and it would seem that in other parts of Outer Britain, including Wales, social conditions prevailed in Iron Age times which were closely comparable with those in Man. As would be expected, therefore, the Island showed the major cultural elements characteristic of the surrounding territories at this time.

The dating of these Celtic homesteads is difficult, but they are known to have been in existence in the early centuries of the Christian era and so would have been contemporary with the Roman occupation of the British mainland. A certain amount of trading, or perhaps of mere raiding, must have taken place between Roman Britain and the Island, as happened between Britain and Ireland. Nevertheless, the only Roman finds so far discovered in the Isle of Man are five coins, of which three were found in Castletown, one in the parish of Santan and one in Onchan parish.[(1)] In spite of the paucity of this material, here at least is a clear 'south side' distribution, as one would expect to result from material emanating from British bases.

Into the overall cultural picture thus emerging must be set the Irish infiltrations that were such a marked feature of the Age when the Empire was dying in Britain. Irish settlements were being established along almost the whole length of the Outer Province from Cornwall to Argyll, but they appear to be more extensive and clearly marked in some areas than in others, and it is to such areas that we must direct our attention in this study, for the important reason that these areas became culturally distinct as a result of their deep Irish infusion. Many of these Irish infiltrations are well attested historically and traditionally, but this is not always the case archaeologically. The absence of recognizable domestic pottery from most of Ireland at this epoch removes at once the

(1) Kinvig, R. H., *A History of the Isle of Man*, Univ. of Liverpool Press 1950, p. 32.

easiest way of confirming such an expansion through excavation. Nevertheless, the most clearly marked new province to emerge in the North was the kingdom of Argyll, established by the migration of the Scotti from the coast of Antrim in the late fifth century. This would appear to be simply an expansion of its royal house— a peaceful penetration of a relatively empty land without leaving any clearly marked evidence for the archaeologist. Here, at any rate, is an added culture area in Scotland.

A different situation is found further south, in south-west Wales, where it would appear that a second major concentration of Irish settlers was located.(1) The Deisi from the Waterford district came over in the 4th century A.D. and maintained a close relationship with their homeland for several centuries. Their presence is mentioned in a number of early Irish texts and in later Welsh genealogy. Nennius mentions the Ui Liathaim, another southern Irish tribe, as having settled not only in Pembrokeshire, but also in the region of Gower and Cydweli as well. Archaeologically, this movement seems to be well attested by the distribution of the Ogham inscribed stones and by certain personal names recorded on these inscriptions. The Ogham alphabet consists of consonants and vowels represented by a number of long and short strokes which can easily be cut upon the edges of roughly square stone pillars. This form of writing seems specially adapted for memorial stones and seems to have been invented in southern Ireland during the period of the Roman occupation of Britain by someone who knew the Latin alphabet as well as Irish.

(1) The emphasis placed on Irish settlement in Argyll, South-west Wales and Cornwall must not be thought of as ignoring in any way contemporary Irish settlement in either Galloway, Cumbria, the Isle of Man, Lancastria, North Wales or even Brittany. In some of these areas, especially in North Wales, there is considerable traditional evidence for their presence. Nennius, for example, mentioned settlers from Ireland joining their commrades in North Wales and there is the well-known account of the sons Cunedda and their mission to drive out the Irishmen from these parts, Nevertheless, a survey of all the evidence at our disposal suggests that the Irish were less important in North Wales than in South-west Wales and hence the emphasis placed on the latter area. The importance of this area is confirmed also by the survival of a very large number of Irish place names and farm names at the present time, (see Melville Richards, *Irish Settlements in S.W. Wales,* Journ, Roy. Soc. Ant. Ireland XC part ii, 1960, p. 148).

The language employed by those who used the Ogham script was an early form of Gaelic or Old Irish. Ogham writing was chiefly employed in southern Ireland whence it spread to South Wales, Cornwall and Devon with the Irish emigrations described above (Fig. 8). The inscriptions date from the fifth to the seventh centuries A.D. In Ireland Ogham inscriptions generally occur alone on the memorial stones giving the name of the deceased in the genitive case followed by the name of the father, thus: "the stone of So and So, the son (daughter) of So and So"; but in Britain it is common to have a brief epitaph in Latin written in Roman capitals with an attempt to reproduce all or part of it in Old Irish, written in Ogham letters, on the same stone. Recently, Professor Melville Richards[(1)] has analysed the personal names indicated in this way and argues that they refer to the ruling class and not to raiders. In other words, here we have the intrusion of a settled aristocracy. This south-west Wales colony seems to have had an outlier in what is now southern Breconshire, for we hear of a semi-legendary eponymous king of Brecon whose name appears to be the Irish Broca or Brocagnus, whose traditional territory possesses several Ogham inscribed stones. We can say, therefore, that the Irish infiltration into south-west Wales helps to distinguish it still further from south-east Wales, while its Breconshire overspill serves to distinguish the mountain land of south-east Wales centred on Brecon, from the southern coastal plain, which (as we have seen) is the real core of the south-eastern cultural province. The fact that these territories were culturally distinct before the Age of the Saints is a matter of considerable significance for our general thesis.

The South-west Peninsula deserves consideration as a third area of major Irish infiltration in the post-Roman period. Recent work indicates that there have been two distinct infusions.[(2)] The earlier one which affected north-eastern Cornwall, east of the Padstow-Camel estuary is marked by

(1) Richards, Melville, *Journ. Roy. Soc. of Antiquaries of Ireland,* Vol. XC, Pt. II, 1960. pp. 132-162.

(2) Thomas, Charles, *'Archaeology in Cornwall* 1933-58', Twenty-fifth Anniversary Number, Proceedings of West Cornwall Field Club, Vol. 2, No. 2, 1957-58, pp. 64-68.

the presence of Ogham inscribed stones and other memorials

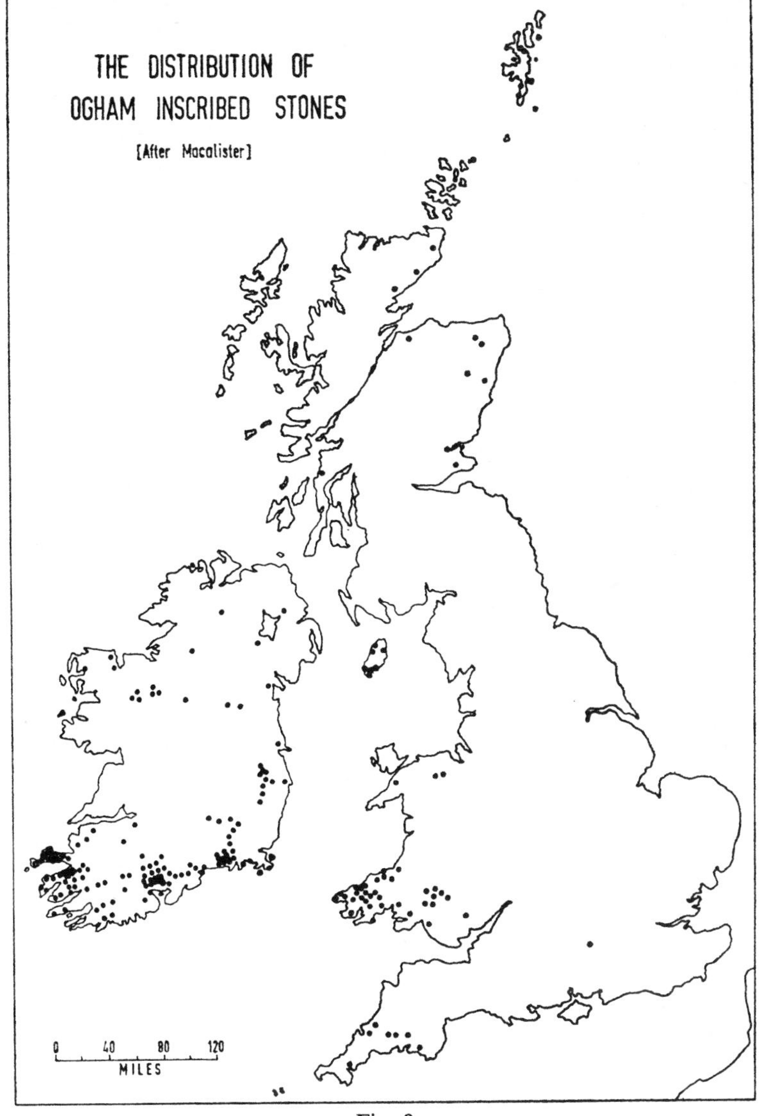

Fig. 8

bearing Irish names. All the evidence points to this movement being a movement not from Ireland itself, but of Irish settlers coming from South Wales. West of a line from New Quay to Truro there is evidence in western Cornwall of a slightly later Irish infiltration which, on the contrary, is better attested on archaeological rather than on literary evidence. Recent excavations in western Cornwall have shown distinct pottery links between this area and the coasts of Down, Antrim and Londonderry in Northern Ireland from whence it is assumed that the Irish in this part of Cornwall ultimately derive.[(1)]

We are thus left with the addition of an Argyll province in the North–something distinctive and new, while the already existing culture area in south-west Wales has been given a strong Irish acculturation; simultaneously, the two already clearly marked culture provinces in the South-west Peninsula have received Irish immigrants from two distinct areas around the margins of the Irish Sea. The overall view of present scholars concerning Irish immigration into Outer Britain at this period tends to emphasize its significance more and more. Mrs. Nora K. Chadwick, for example, maintains that Irish expansions onto the west coast of Wales had already been extensive in the Roman period, and from the fifth century onwards reached a pressure second only to that of the Teutonic peoples in the east and south of Britain.[(2)] In her view the influence of this Irish pressure from the west and the contemporary Saxon pressure from the east was to result, among other things, in the migration of many refugees from South Wales and Cornwall into Brittany in the Age of the Saints—a matter to which more attention will be given in a later chapter.

It is appropriate to conclude this chapter by listing again, and also by summarising in map form (see Fig. 9), the major culture areas and their subdivisions on the margins of the Western Seas in pre-Christian times, much in the same way as was done in the previous chapter for the sea-routes.

(1) Thomas, Charles, op. cit., p. 67.

(2) Chadwick, N. K., *Celtic Britain,* Ancient Peoples and Places, London, 1963, p. 69.

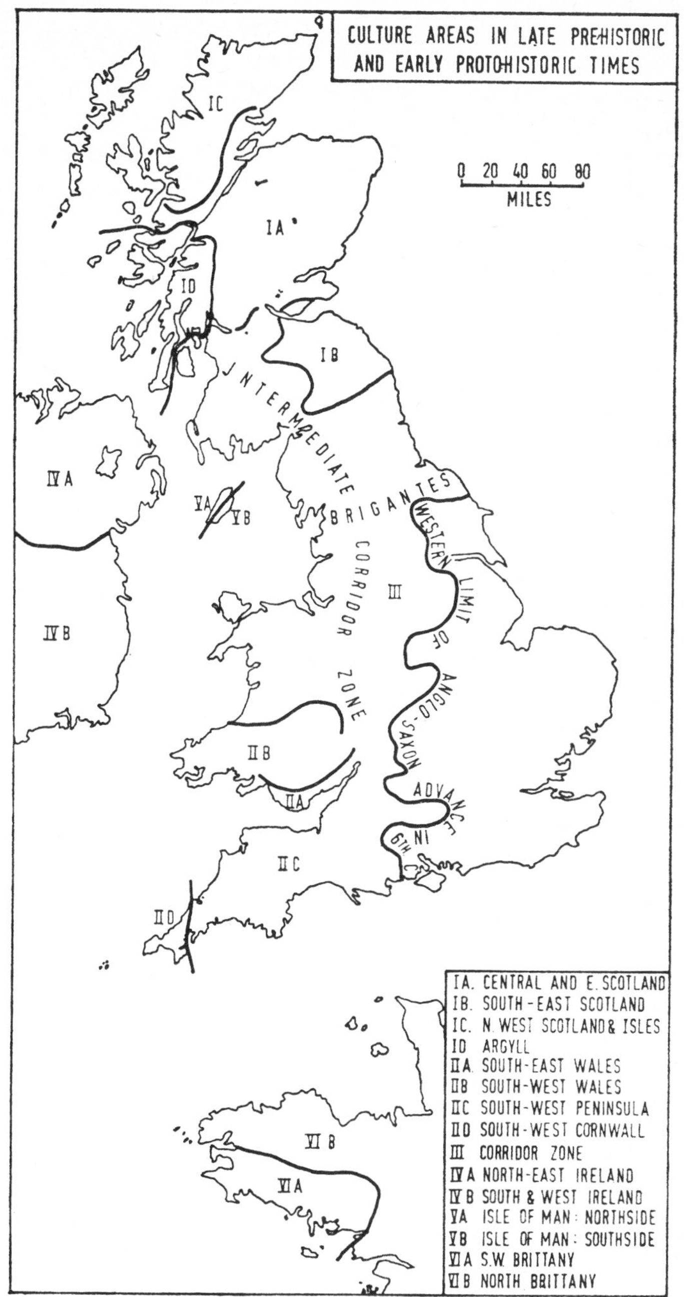
CULTURE AREAS IN LATE PREHISTORIC AND EARLY PROTOHISTORIC TIMES
0 20 40 60 80
MILES
IC
IA
ID
IB
INTERMEDIATE
BRIGANTES
CORRIDOR ZONE
III
WESTERN LIMIT OF ANGLO-SAXON ADVANCE IN 6TH C.
IVA
VA
VB
IVB
IIB
IIA
IIC
IID
VIB
VIA
IA. CENTRAL AND E. SCOTLAND
IB. SOUTH-EAST SCOTLAND
IC. N. WEST SCOTLAND & ISLES
ID ARGYLL
IIA. SOUTH-EAST WALES
IIB SOUTH-WEST WALES
IIC SOUTH-WEST PENINSULA
IID SOUTH-WEST CORNWALL
III CORRIDOR ZONE
IVA NORTH-EAST IRELAND
IVB SOUTH & WEST IRELAND
VA ISLE OF MAN: NORTHSIDE
VB ISLE OF MAN: SOUTHSIDE
VIA S.W. BRITTANY
VIB NORTH BRITTANY

Fig. 9

Culture areas associated with the Western Seaways in Iron Age and Proto-Historic Times

I. NORTH BRITISH GROUP:	(a) Central and Eastern Scotland
	(b) South-eastern Scotland
	(c) North-western Scotland and the Isles
	(d) Argyll
II. SOUTH-WESTERN BRITISH GROUP:	(a) South-eastern Wales
	(b) South-western Wales
	(c) The South-west Peninsula
	(d) Penwith area of Cornwall
III. INTERMEDIATE ZONE ON BRITISH MAINLAND:	(This includes North Wales; the Middle and North-west Borderland, Lancastria, Cumbria, Galloway and North-eastern England).
IV. IRELAND:	(a) The North-east
	(b) Southern and Western Ireland
V. THE ISLE OF MAN:	(a) The 'North side'
	(b) The 'South side'
VI. BRITTANY:	(a) Le Morbihan with Southern Finistère
	(b) Northern Finistère with Côtes du Nord.

CHAPTER III.

THE SAINTS AND THE SEAWAYS

THERE can, obviously, be no precise date following the withdrawal of Roman protection when the crossing of the Narrow Seas became too dangerous and had to be abandoned, and when contact with the Continent returned once more to the western sea-routes. This was bound to be a gradual and, inevitably, an intermittent process. Anyway, when Vortigern in south-eastern Britain engaged the Saxon fleet as mercenaries in 426 the change-over could hardly be far from complete, and this action implied that a Roman channel fleet giving protection to the crossing of the Narrow Seas no longer existed. As the Barbarian invasions resulted in disturbed conditions in Lowland Britain and north-eastern Gaul, the corollary of Fox's famous dictum became apparent, and intense activity returned to the western sea-routes.

The southern section of the major sea-route soon became active with particular emphasis on the links between south-western France and northern Spain with Ireland. Refugees from Aquitaine made their way across the seas to southern Ireland taking with them their culture and the last echoes of classical learning. These were the *alumni* of Bordeaux and other cities of south-western Gaul recorded by an anonymous author as leaving their homeland early in the 5th century. Literary experts have been able to detect the influence of the continental rhetorical style among the earliest Leinster poets, and there seems to be no difficulty in accepting the derivation of this style from the continental *literati* of the 5th century. It is thought that many of the rhetoricians of Gaul attached themselves to the native princes of southern Ireland and Britain at this time, but more particularly to the Irish chieftains, because Ireland was a safer refuge.(1) They

(1) Chadwick, N. K., *Intellectual contacts between Britain and Gaul in the Fifth Century.* Studies in Early British History, Cambridge, 1954, p. 243.

might even be responsible for the introduction of the Christianity that was known to have existed in southern Ireland in pre-Patrician times. The links of Ireland with Spain seem to be equally clear. Orosius writing in the early 5th century speaks of a city in Galicia, which he calls Brigantia, as having some kind of direct relationship with Ireland.(1) Modern authors stress the presence in Ireland at this time of specialized art motives, like the marigold design, which must have reached the island by the same route from Spain or southern France. This motive is usually considered to be the most characteristic feature of Visigothic art. It is found all over Spain and again in Lisbon, while occasional examples occur in France from Poitiers southwards.(2)

When we turn to the inner branches of the sea-route, that is those emanating from south-western France and establishing contact with the western peninsulas of Britain, we witness an equally intense activity. It would appear that Gallo-Roman Christians leaving the traditional homeland of Gallic Christianity in the Lyon-Vienne area migrated in large numbers by way of the sea-routes to northern lands. This movement which is thoroughly well documented archaeologically was, most likely, but another result of the increasingly disturbed conditions in this part of Western Europe from the 5th to the 7th centuries. The archaeological evidence for these migrations is to be found in the numerous rough stone slabs bearing a funerary inscription in Roman letters, which these early Christians apparently raised as memorials to their dead. It is presumed, therefore, that originally they were associated with a churchyard or burial ground. Their Christian character is clearly indicated by the formulae employed. The numerous examples occurring in Wales have been exhaustively studied by Nash-Williams.(3) It will be necessary to expand a little with reference to this movement, not only to indicate the fullness of activity associated with the sea-routes but also because this movement

(1) Orosius, *Operae*, Book I, Cap. ii.
(2) Clapham, A. W., *The origins of Hiberno-Saxon Art*, Antiquity VIII, 1934, p. 50.
(3) Nash-Williams, V. E., *The Early Christian Monuments of Wales*, Cardiff, 1950.

is ultimately connected with the final emergence of the Celtic Church and the Age of the Saints.

The epigraphical evidence for the origin of these immigrants will first be considered and, subsequently, their chief areas of settlement in Britain will be listed.

Sometimes the evidence locating the origin and date of this diffusion from southern Gaul is direct, while at other times it can be inferred from the type of funerary formula employed. One of these memorials set up at Penmachno in Caernarvonshire states that it was erected "in the time of Justinus the Consul".(1) Justinus was consul in 540 A.D. and the use of his name was limited on the Continent to monuments in the Lyon-Vienne area. He was the last consul whose name appears on inscriptions in the Western World. Here then is precise evidence for both the origin of the person commemorated and the date of the erection of the memorial. A frequently occurring formula is HIC IACET.(2) This specifically Christian formula originated in Italy in the late 4th century and came into fashion in Gaul in the first half of the 5th century, particularly in the Lyon-Vienne area, and in the Rhineland. It was much used at Trèves—a centre known to have associations with Magnus Maximus, who in turn led Roman troops out of Wales in the late 4th century in his bid for the Imperial purple. In Trèves, too, there are traditions concerning the links of this family with St. Martin of Tours, while medieval Welsh legends tell of the return of Helena—wife of Maximus—to Wales in a Christian context after the death of her husband. Similarly, another formula IN HOC TUMULO, frequently found on early Christian inscribed stones in western Britain is especially characteristic of Gallic Christianity in the 5th century and later; and, likewise, yet another formula used, IN PACE, derives mainly from Southern Gaul. Since we are primarily concerned with origins and the use of the sea-routes we should remember that there are other formulae found in western Britain suggestive of early Christian settlers

(1) Nash-Williams, V. E., *op. cit.*, No. 104. See Plate 3.

(2) In Western Britain the customary form of the verb is IACIT with I replacing the E as in vulgar Latin.

from even further afield, in fact, using the extreme southern portion of the major sea-route which reached not only to

Fig. 10

Spain but through the Straits of Gibraltar to the North African shores. The MEMORIA formula, which is rare in Gaul, is well known in North Africa. It occurs at Yarrowick in Scotland and at Lewanick in Cornwall. The PINACI NOMENA inscription found at St. David's in Pembrokeshire may also derive from a North African source.[1] We should recall that some of the contemporary pottery described by Ralegh Radford and referred to in a previous chapter came from a similar source.

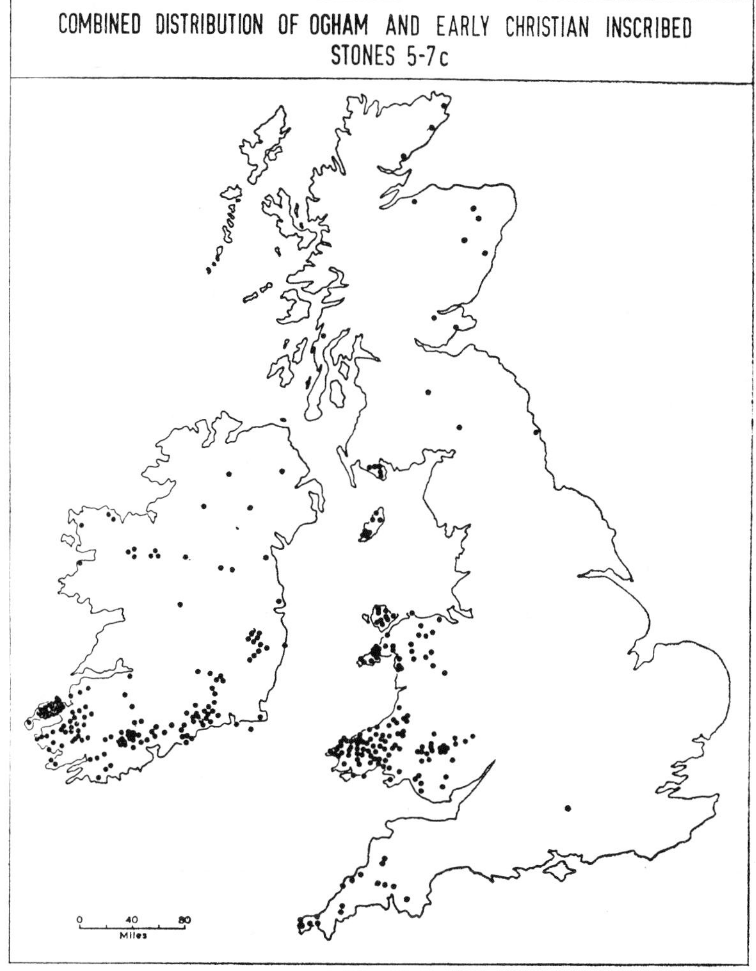

Fig. 11

With the sea-routes thus in full operation one would expect

(1) Nash-Williams, V. E., *op. cit.*, No. 370.

to find large numbers of these Early Christian memorial stones in southern Ireland, but this is not the case (Fig. 10). A special consideration operated in Ireland. The island lay outside the territories of the Roman Empire and Latin was not generally known or understood. Yet we recollect that southern Ireland has about three hundred stone slab memorials of this type with a funerary inscription in Ogham. It is clear that despite differences of script and language these monuments reflect a common cultural tradition of raising inscribed memorials to the dead. As we have seen, in Western Britain there are very many instances of both languages appearing on the same stone—Latin and Ogham. There is, therefore, everything to be said for considering the distribution of Early Christian Inscribed Stones and Oghams together in this book (see Fig. 11). This should not imply that the monolingual inscriptions in Ireland were necessarily used in the first instance in a Christian context—all we are concerned with here is that their combined distribution shows the spread of a particular culture complex, possibly Roman in origin, propagated by the sea-routes and revealing not only a spread from the Continent, but, in the case of the British Oghams, both monolingual and bilingual, a characteristic reflex movement from Ireland.

We can now look in some detail at the overall distribution. The monolingual Ogham inscriptions in Ireland are heavily concentrated in the southern counties of Kerry, Cork, Wicklow and Kildare (Fig. 11). In Cornwall, Devon and Somerset there are over thirty inscriptions of this period, of which about a fifth are bilingual and the remainder in Latin alone. In South Wales there are over ninety memorials of this kind, of which about one-third are in Latin as well as Ogham. Of this total, thirty-six inscriptions, including sixteen in Ogham are in Pembrokeshire, showing the dominance of a westerly location. There are forty inscriptions of this period in the three north-western counties of Wales—Anglesey, Caernarvon and Merioneth, but in spite of their westerly location in this case there are only two with Ogham inscriptions. The Isle of Man has three stones with Latin inscriptions and four (including one of the former) with Ogham. In Scotland, between the Walls, the surviving material of this age is not great, but two monuments appear to occur in early Christian cemeteries—the Catstone at Kirkliston near Edinburgh, and the Yarrowkirk stone in Selkirkshire. The chief concentration, however, is in the Galloway peninsula. Three stones at Kirkmadrine in the Rinns of Galloway and two at Whithorn are clearly Christian memorials ranging from the 5th to the 7th centuries. Further to the north and west Latin inscriptions, obviously do not occur, but a few Irish derived Oghams (non-Pictish) occur. The two in Argyll are worthy of note as reference has already been made to an Irish colony established in these parts.

In summary, therefore, the main sea-routes from the south have brought the Gallic, Spanish and even the North African world into contact with southern Ireland, Cornwall and Devon, south-west Wales, north-west Wales, the Isle of Man, the Galloway peninsula and the Solway area. Reflex movements from Ireland show sea connections between Ireland and Argyll, Ireland and south-west Scotland; Ireland and the Isle of Man; Ireland and North Wales: Ireland and south-west Wales; Ireland and Cornwall. Whichever way we look at the mass of evidence before us we find that every single one of the sea-routes listed in the previous chapter was in action at this time.

An obvious corollary of the use of the sea-routes by these Gallo-Roman Christians and Irish invaders of Britain is the markedly western location of their memorials (Fig. 11). A detailed plotting of these inscribed stones would, however, indicate that in certain areas there was considerable penetration inland, and nowhere is this more marked than in South Wales. The reasons are likely to be partly physical and partly historical. If we look at the other coastal areas where groups of these memorials occur, we find that in south-western Scotland penetration inland is not very difficult from the physical point of view, but the number of these inscribed stones is very small, indicating possibly only a small number of immigrants. Even-so, one of the western sea-derived memorials actually occurs in Northumberland. An eastward movement from North-west Wales was fraught with considerable physical difficulty, as the

Snowdonian massif must have been a formidable barrier, and even those who sought to overcome this difficulty found themselves in, what was then, the heavily forested lowlands of the Cheshire plain. Those landing in the extreme south-western peninsula of Britain would find it easier to cross the peninsula by the isthmus roads than to negotiate an eastward penetration either across or around Dartmoor. From South-west Wales, however, inland movement was much easier. There were no really difficult physical obstacles, while coastal lowland and wide valley-ways abound. Ease of penetration in the physical sense is not the only matter to be considered. Far more important is it to note that inland penetration followed what remained of the Roman roads, and it must be remembered, as Crawford has pointed out,[(1)] that during the Roman Occupation the main route from Ireland to Rome lay across South Wales. Most likely this followed track-ways from Porth Glais, near St. David's, running south of Mynydd Presely by way of Meidrim to Carmarthen (Moridunum) and thence along the coastal plain of South Wales, crossing the Severn to Abona, at the mouth of the Bristol Avon, and thence by way of Bath, Marlborough, Silchester, London and Canterbury to Richborough. Indeed, one persistent Irish immigrant must have used what remained of this route early in the Dark Ages and got as far as Silchester, where his memorial, in Ogham, was discovered many years ago while digging out an ancient well.[(2)] In addition, we must not overlook the fact that there was a very important section of this ancient route branching north-eastwards. It stemmed from the coastal route near Carmarthen and then followed the Roman road, up the wide valley of the Tywi to Llansefin near Llangadog, and thence across to Llan-faes, near Brecon, giving access in this way to the valleys of the Usk and the Wye and the south-eastern borderland of Wales generally. The Ogham inscribed stones of Breconshire also bear witness to the use of this route

(1) Crawford, O. G. S., *Western Seaways* in *Custom is King*, London, 1936, pp. 188-9.

(2) *Archaeologia* LIV, 223 and 241, also *Victoria County History, Hants*, Vol. I 1900, p. 279.

inland from western Pembrokeshire (see Fig. 8). There is an interesting description of movement in the reverse direction in a narrative occurring in the *De Situ Brecheniauc* (a 12th century manuscript preserving much older traditions). This account tells of Marchell, daughter of Tewdrig and mother of Brychan Brycheiniog proceeding this way from the territory that is now Breconshire to Ireland to marry Amlach-an Irish prince.(1) The early post-Roman kingdom of Brycheiniog had in this way very strong Irish associations and its semi-legendary king—Brychan not only gave his name to the modern county of Breconshire, but is reputed in Welsh hagiology to be the father of a prodigiously large family of saints-both male and female. We shall have occasion to refer to them several times later in this book.

For the purposes of our present argument what is most significant about the eastward penetration of these sea-derived immigrants in South Wales is not the extent of their penetration (which is more marked here than in many other areas), but the fact that it brought them ultimately into contact with refugees moving in the opposite direction from the Christian communities known to have existed in the Gloucester-Cirencester-Bath area in the late stages of the Roman Occupation. The Christianity characteristic of Britain during the period of the Roman Occupation was, of course, similar to that which had developed in the late Empire on the Continent—a church ruled by Bishops from their metropolitan sees—a church with a marked provincial ecclesiastical administration.(2) It was essentially an urban church—a matter for the dwellers in the Roman towns and villas and not something markedly associated with the army of occupation. It may be well to stress in this context the clearly marked south-eastern distribution of Roman towns and villas in Britain; for the most part they lie south-east of a line from the Humber to the Severn. Fig. 12 shows this important distribution abstracted from the Ordnance Survey map of Roman Britain which also brings out the marked con-

(1) Crawford, O. G. S., *op. cit.*, p. 190.

(2) We hear of three bishops of this church attending the Council of Arles in 314 (see Williams, H., *Early Christianity in Britain*, Oxford, 1912, p. 139).

centration of civil Roman life in the lower Severn-Cotswold region. In addition, it is not so much the concentration of

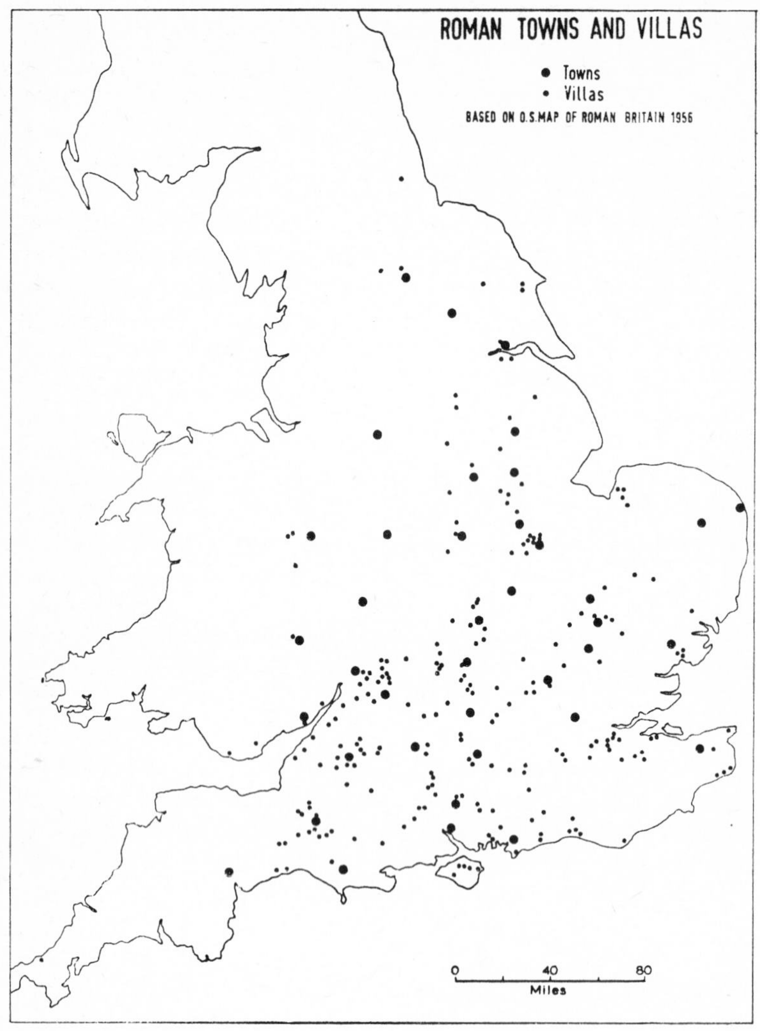

Fig. 12

civil life in this area, as the fact that we have considerable archaeological evidence indicating its long survival here as well.

It seems to have lingered on long after the withdrawal of the Roman troops from Britain and thus constitutes an important 'growth point' for many of the hybrid cultures of Western Britain in the Dark Ages. As conditions deteriorated, however, the area where some local Romanized civilization continued steadily shrunk in size until only at two places, at Bourton-on-the-Water in Gloucestershire and at Lydney on the Welsh side of the Severn do we find any remaining *minimissimi*—those symbols of continuing Roman economic traditions.[(1)] There is also evidence of the survival of Christianity from Imperial days, and some fairly clear indications of its late spread (still in a sub-Roman context) into the western extensions of the region in the Vales of Gwent and Glamorgan. It is in such a context that we must recall the small Christian church found in the Roman town of Caerwent in Monmouthshire whose foundations lie in a debris layer one foot above the ruins of a Roman bath.[(2)] Not far away at a Roman villa near Llantwit Major in the Vale of Glamorgan later excavations have shown that the burials discovered in 1888 were orientated in the Christian manner, and that the graves were cut through the mosaic floor of the building, indicating that we have a Christian cemetery of late 5th century date on the site of a ruined villa, and not the massacred remains of the last Romano-British inhabitants.[(3)] The incoming Gallo-Roman Christians from southern Gaul arriving in Britain by the western sea-routes thus came into contact with what remained of the life of the Roman civil zone somewhere in this south-east Wales-Herefordshire-Gloucester borderland. There was little opportunity for contact with this protracted Roman culture (with its strong Christian component) from any other landfall in western Britain, whether it be Cornwall, North-west Wales or the Solway Firth. The absence of Christian inscribed stones of early date from south-eastern Wales (Fig. 10) suggests that the culture contact was, as we have described, overland from Pembroke-

(1) Lewis, A. R., *op. cit.*, (1958), p. 100.

(2) Nash-Williams, V. E., "*Further Excavations at Caerwent, Monmouthshire 1922-25*," *Archaeologia* LXXX (1930), p. 235.

(3) Nash-Williams, V. E., "*Excavations of the Roman Villa at Llantwit Major, Glamorgan*, 1938," *Archaeologia Cambrensis* (1938), p. 255.

shire and not coastwise along the Severn Sea.

We can turn aside at this point from the consideration of the strictly distributional evidence (which is the first concern of the geographer) to describe in the briefest outline the type of Christianity most likely to be associated with these recent arrivals by way of the western seas. We know, for example, that at this time new influences were entering the provincial episcopal church of Gaul. They emanated from the East. The fame of the Desert Fathers of Egypt and the hermits of Cyrenaica had already reached southern Italy, and before the close of the 4th century had spread into southern Gaul. Many Christians sought to emulate the aesetics. The emergence of St. Martin and his election as Bishop of Tours was something new in Gaulish ecclesiastical tradition. Previously, the great sees had remained in the hands of territorial bishops, the successors of the Roman administrative system. The new spirit in religion which St. Martin introduced — the mysticism characteristic of the East, combined with the asceticism and the urge to seek some 'desert' place for solitary contemplation and worship, was something previously unknown in the West. That it took deep root and flourished in southern Gaul is well known. A poem (anonymously written about 415-16 A.D., but often attributed to Prosper of Aquitaine) tells of the sufferings of the solitaries — those "who had no other occupation in their caves and caverns than to praise God day and night"—when the Barbarian invasions fell upon them.[(1)] Contemporary writers such as Gregory of Tours refer to the solitaries who occupied, in the late 5th and early 6th centuries, the mountains and forests of the Jura, Le Pêrche and the Auvergne and other parts of southern France. Those who accepted the new ideas and put them into practice found a spirit of marked hostility growing up towards them in Gaulish episcopal circles. This is abundantly clear from the contemporary writings of Sulpicius Severus. Such hostility was, of course, well-known both in Italy and the East. There can be little doubt, therefore, that the Gallo-Roman Christians im-

(1) Polanque, J. R. and Le Labriolle, P., *The Church in the Christian Roman Empire*, Vol. ii, London, 1952, p. 488.

pinging on the western shores of Britain "in the time of Justinus the Consul" brought with them a strong eremitical element — an urge "to seek the desert" — some cavern or mountain-top — so desired by the solitaries. Indeed, the whole movement out of Gaul may have had such a religious impetus behind it. We should, therefore, be careful not to over-emphasize the fact that the immigrants were merely escaping from the Barbarian invasions. Nash-Williams who made such an exhaustive study of the geographical, archaeological and epigraphical evidence in Britain came to a similar conclusion when he suggested that the newcomers might be participating in a deliberate evangelization by the Gaulish church directed at Cornwall, Wales and South-western Scotland.[(1)]

We have already argued that the Irish colonists, especially in South-west Wales should be considered as closely associated with the newcomers from Gaul. J. D. Bu'lock[(2)] has recently made a most interesting suggestion bearing upon the religious background of the Irish. His arguments are based on a geographical analysis of the Latin and Ogham formulae used on the memorial stones found in different parts of western Britain. He distinguishes between those memorials that use the HIC IACIT formula, with its derivative forms such as HIC IN TUMULO IACIT, followed by the name of the deceased person, and those memorials that record the fact (implied) that this is the memorial of So and So, the son (or daughter) of So and So stated as X filius Y, or, in Ogham as X maqi Y. We know that the early Christians gave up the former Roman pagan custom of naming the deceased's parents, as they recognised but one Father — their Heavenly Father[(3)], and considered their earthly parentage to be the source of original sin. Yet on 77% of the 5th to the 7th century early Christian memorials in Carmarthenshire, for example, this injunction was ignored by the use of either the X filius Y formula, or the X maqi Y, or both, on the memorial stones (Figs. 13 and 14).

(1) Nash-Williams, V. E., *op. cit.*, p. 4.

(2) Bu'lock, J. D., *"Early Christian Memorial Formulae," Archaeologia Cambrensis,* Vol. CV 1956, pp. 133-141.

(3) Mathew xxiii, v.9 "Call no man your father on the earth."

This rejection of the doctrine of original sin was exactly what the followers of Pelagius were accused of doing at this time. After showing that the percentage of memorials using the

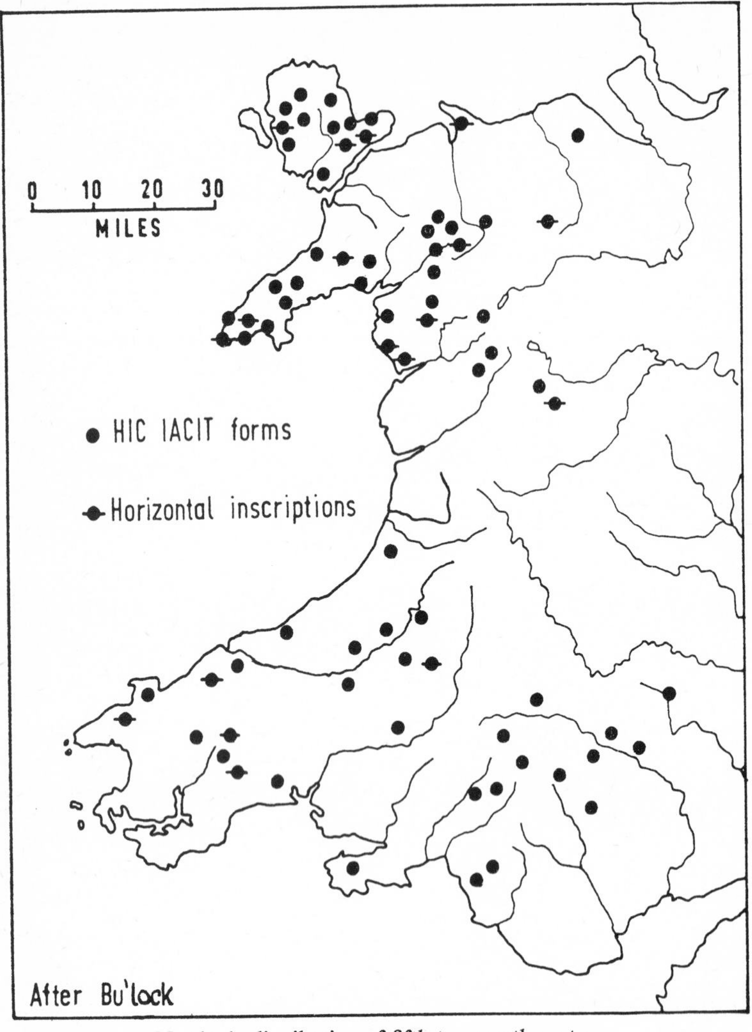

Northerly distribution of fifth to seventh century inscriptions with Gaulish features

Fig. 13

FILIUS/MAQI formula rather than the HIC IACIT type is considerably less in the other important areas of Gallo-Roman settlement in Britain (Anglesey only 8%; southern Scotland

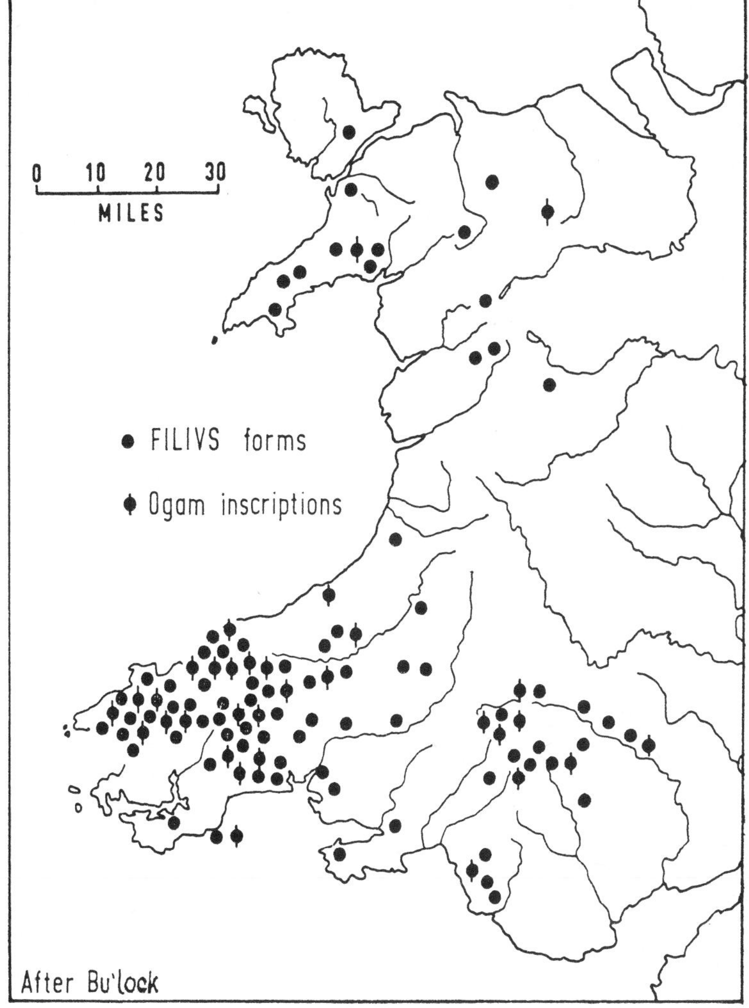

Southerly distribution of fifth to seventh century inscriptions with Goidelic features

Fig. 14

20% — (representing but two memorials where in each case the FILIUS formula is combined with HIC IACIT); Cornwall and Devon, (which derived much of its culture from South-west Wales at this time: 67%), Bu'lock concludes that the use of this parental formula is something clearly related to the presence of a large number of Southern Irish settlers in South-west Wales. Anyway, the practice of defining a man's name by adding that of his father's is well-known in all Celtic lands. In arguing, therefore, solely on epigraphical grounds, that there was more than a dash of Pelagianism in the theological 'climate' of southern Wales at this time, we must not overlook the fact that contemporary writings testify to the hold this heresy secured on early British Christianity and to the interesting fact that Pelagius himself was a Celt and most probably an Irishman.(1) Whatever happened, it is extremely unlikely that the Pelagian heresy could ever have acquired its great prestige in Britain without strong support from the governing classes. Many scholars are now of the opinion that such a function appertained to the court of the notorious Vortigern, who was Prince of much of the Welsh Borderland at this time. Such a suggestion would help to explain the bitter hostility towards Vortigern, and the disreputable character ascribed to him by St. Germanus, who is said to have made two visits to Britain in the years 429 and 447 respectively, to combat the Pelagian heresy. Unfortunately, we do not know his exact destinations in Britain and much of the inferential evidence would appear to locate him, certainly during his first visit, in the South-East. Modern opinion, more particularly with reference to the second visit in 447 is inclined to see him in the capacity of a military commander, using the western approaches to our islands by way of Cornwall and west Britain into the Welsh Border country. Crawford(2) mentions this, commenting on the apparent ease with which such a journey could be undertaken in these western regions

(1) Chadwick, N. K., *The Age of the Saints in the Early Celtic Church,* London, 1961, p. 15.

(2) Crawford, O. G. S., *op. cit.,* p. 187. It is interesting to note that P. Grosjean also mentions the westward movement of trade in the English Channel before the second visit of St. Germanus (*An. Boll.* LXXV, (1957), 161-177).

as late as the year 447. It is tempting to associate the many churches dedicated to St. Garmon in Powysland with the great St. Germanus, but, however attractive the association may be both geographically and hagiologically, there are serious philological difficulties which we can not ignore.[1]

We are now in a position to re-state our major argument which is that in the early years of the fifth century at least three facets of contemporary Christianity were converging on the South-eastern Borderlands of Wales. There were Christian refugees from Roman Britain carrying with them regional episcopal traditions in church government. There were the Gallo-Roman Christians spreading inland from the west, heavily tinged with ascetic and eremitical ideas, and finally there were those with ultimate Irish affinities, strongly inclined, it would appear, to Pelagianism. Celtic Christianity in the Age of the Saints resulted from the fusion of these subcultures in the territories now known as Monmouthshire, Breconshire and Herefordshire. The whole situation is complicated by the intervention of St. Germanus. In due course, the Celtic Church evolved in Wales along lines similar to those of Ireland at a somewhat later stage. There arose three orders of Saints or Holy Men. First, those who were Bishops. They possessed a roving, rather than a territorial, commission and were possibly the earliest of the brethren. Then came the Second Order of Saints, the Holy Men in charge of the great monastic houses, where the monks were trained, and finally the Third Order — the most numerous of all — the wandering saints — the *peregrini,* roaming the lands and seas on pilgrimage, seeking some 'desert', or lonely place, wherein to abide and spend their lives in prayer, praise and meditation.

There is considerable evidence for suggesting that St. Dubricius (Dyfrig) was a saint of the First Order in the South-eastern Borderlands of Wales.[2] We have little information about him that can be considered in any way contemporary. Fortunately, an early cross-reference mentions him in the *Life*

(1) Williams, Ifor. *Hen Chwedlau.* Trans. Hon. Soc. Cymrod. 1946-47.

(2) Bowen, E. G., *"The Settlements of the Celtic Saints in Wales,"* Cardiff, (1954), p. 37.

of St. Samson of Dol, one of the earliest *Lives* of the Saints we possess,[1] said to have been written by a nephew of St. Samson himself. The picture of Dubricius that emerges in this very early text is that of a saint carrying with him many of the attributes of an ecclesiastic of the provincial Roman Order. He is actually referred to in this early text as *Dubricio episcopo,* and sometimes as *Dubricio papa,* while with two exceptions (interesting in themselves) all the churches dedicated to him are gathered in a group in an area in South-western Herefordshire, which itself inherits something of a civil Roman character. Equally interesting is the fact that Dubricius is said traditionally to have been a pupil of St. Germanus.

The two outstanding saints of the Second Order at this early stage are Illtud and Cadoc — the heads, respectively, of the great monasteries of Llanilltud Fawr and Llancarfan, in the Vale of Glamorgan. Both these saints have elaborately written *Lives,* compiled for them in the Middle Ages, some six hundred years after they are supposed to have lived.[2] These compilations are filled with hagiological material to such an extent as to make them well-nigh worthless historically, and it is only by the most careful sifting that a few grains of presumably historical data emerge. It would appear that St. Cadoc has a genuine local parentage, linking him with a princeling of Gwent, and there is much that appertains to a classical Roman setting in what is said about him in this late *Life*. Much the same can be said of St. Illtud who is reputed to be Breton by birth. But more important in the eyes of most experts is the fact that he, too, is said to be a disciple of St. Germanus, and with Dubricius, the first of the great Christian teachers of Wales from whom the others derive.[3]

The Third Order of Saints embraces many hundreds whose names have survived, and possibly hundreds more who

(1) Fawtier, R., *La Vie de Saint Sampson. Bibl.* de l'École des Hautes Études, Paris, 1912. See also Taylor, T., *Life of St. Sampson,* London, 1925.

(2) See Doble, G. H., *St Cadoc in Cornwall and Brittany,* Cornish Saints Series, No. 40, Truro, 1937. and by the same author, *St. Illtut.* University of Wales Press, Cardiff, 1944.

(3) Collingwood, R. G. and Myres, J. N. L., *Roman Britain and the English Settlements,* 1936, p. 312, writing of Illtud alone.

have 'vanished as though they had never been.' It would appear that these *peregrini* wandered over the countryside, sometimes alone, and sometimes with a small band of followers. At certain spots they would set up one or two beehive cells and possibly a wooden preaching cross. The spot where the holy man had dwelt became sanctified, and in time, a little church would grow up on the site of his cell, first in wattle and daub, then in timber, and, if the site proved really attractive, ultimately a stone building would be erected. The church would retain the name of its original founder, or, frequently, that of the founder's patron, and ultimately become one of our parish churches of today. The wandering monk would move on, establishing more settlements on his journeys until in the end he would retire to 'a remote place' and remain engaged in praise and prayer and in working miracles until his death. After death miracles were worked from his tomb. It is obvious that by plotting the distribution of churches bearing the names of these saints we can get some idea of their respective 'spheres of influence' and the regions through which they travelled. But, as has been repeatedly shown, it would be absurd to think that the present-day dedications to Celtic saints are all originally associated with the saint concerned, or that they can always be taken to indicate either his own travels or those of his immediate followers. The subject has to be treated with the greatest caution.(1) However, from the point of view of this chapter, maps showing the distribution of ancient churches dedicated to the *peregrini* — the Third Order of Saints — are likely to produce the best indication of how the seaways were, in fact, actually used in the Dark Ages. It was the *peregrini* who, at this time, spread furthest afield, and propagated Celtic Christianity far and wide. They were the relatively insignificant and humbler men whose fame during their lifetime was local. Their cult was unlikely to be revived in the Middle Ages to such an extent that later dedications were made in their name. This cannot

(1) The whole of this problem is fully discussed in Bowen, E. G., *"The Settlements of the Celtic Saints in Wales,"* Cardiff, 1954, pp. 6-12; Chadwick, Owen, The evidence of dedications in the early History of the Welsh Church, *Studies in Early British History,* Cambridge 1954, pp. 193-188 and also Hughes, K., *Irish Historical Studies,* 1956-57, pp. 238-242.

be said of the 'greater' saints — the men and women of the First and Second Orders — saints such as St. Brigid, St. Columba, St. Patrick, St. Illtud, St. Cadoc, St. David, St. Ninian or St. Kentigern.

We can look first of all at a group of *peregrini* using the southern portions of the western sea-routes which linked Ireland and Wales to Cornwall, Devon and Brittany. Doble was the first to show that a group of saints commemorated in the New Quay, Padstow and Bodmin area of Mid-Cornwall are all in some way connected with each other.(1) The list includes SS. Petroc, Congar, Cadoc, Maugan, Hernin, Carantoc, Brioc, Gwbert and Collen. Their provenance is, however, not confined to Mid-Cornwall. There are churches dedicated to all of them in Wales and to most of them in Brittany. It is convenient to select three of the more prominent *peregrini* in this list — Brioc, Carantoc and Petroc, as examples. These saints, or their cults seem to have originated in Wales and to have spread across the channel to Cornwall, where we find their churches in the hinterland of the Camel estuary. From here they, and their followers passed across the transpeninsular route to the Fowey and so by sea to Brittany. Dedications to St. Brioc at St. Brivaels in Gloucestershire, near the head of the Severn estuary, and to St. Petroc at Timberscombe near Watchet in north Somerset suggest that some of the *peregrini* may have taken the shorter crossings further up the Bristol Channel and then moved south-westward along the northern coasts of Somerset and Devon into Cornwall. Of the three examples chosen the pattern revealed by the dedications to St. Petroc is possibly the most representative (Fig. 15). Churches bearing his name are found at Llanbedrog in the Llŷn peninsula in North Wales, at Verwig near the estuary of the Teifi, at St. Petrox in south Pembrokeshire, at Timberscombe and Anstey West in Somerset, followed by seventeen dedications in Devon and six more in Cornwall. In Brittany St. Petroc has eight churches and chapels dedicated to him. They are mainly in the north of the peninsula. St. Brioc's churches follow very much the same pattern. Llandyfriog in south Cardiganshire

(1) Doble, G. H., *St. Carantoc. Cornish Saints Series*, No. 20, 1937, p. 25.

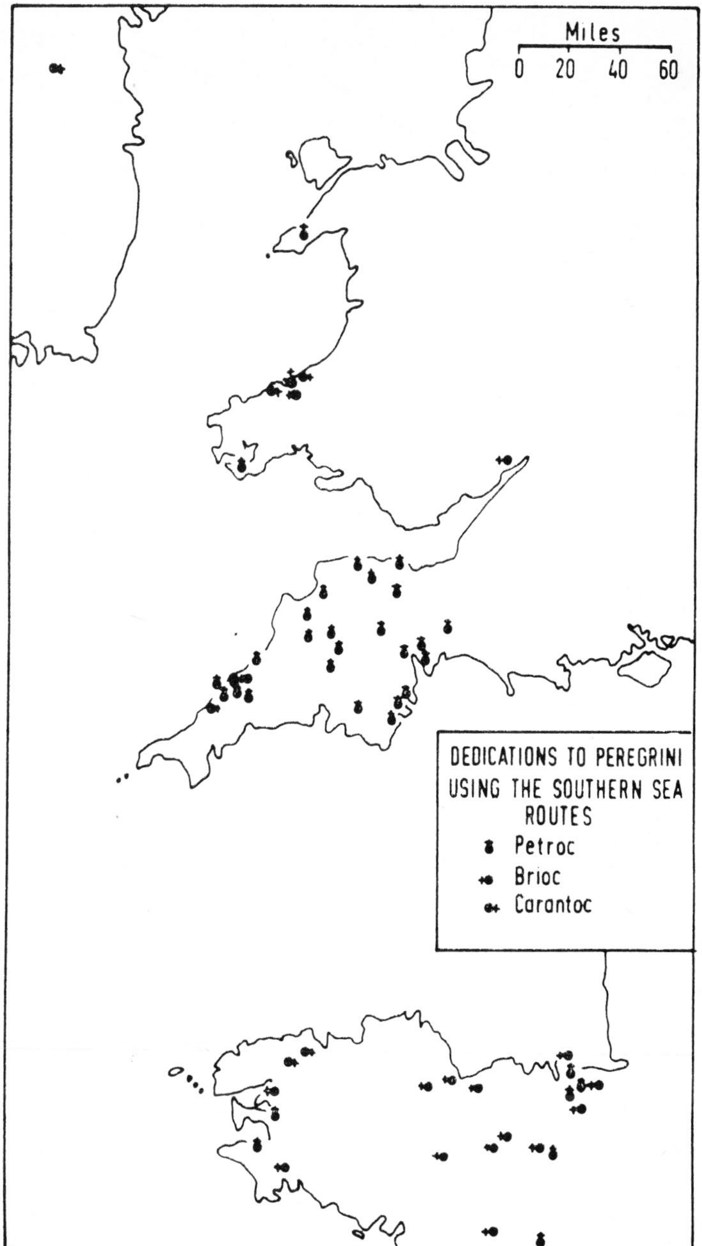
Miles
0 20 40 60
DEDICATIONS TO PEREGRINI
USING THE SOUTHERN SEA
ROUTES
Petroc
Brioc
Carantoc

Fig. 15

(about one and a half miles E.N.E. of Newcastle Emlyn) is dedicated to him, in close association with the churches of Petroc and Carantoc. Then there is St. Brivaels, already mentioned, together with St. Breoke some seven miles north-west of Bodmin in Cornwall. He was very popular in Brittany with thirteen surviving dedications in his name. They occur in the Morbihan area as well as in the northern parts of Brittany. It is almost certain that Carantoc is patron of Dulane in County Meath under his Irish name of Cairnach. He appears on the Cardiganshire coast at Llangrannog, and in association with a former chapel in the parish of Llandudoch in the extreme north-east of Pembrokeshire. In Cornwall he is culted at Crantock, seven and a half miles north-east of St. Agnes, while in Brittany he has churches dedicated to him at Carantec near Quimper and at Trègarantec south-east of Lesneven. Several other examples can be listed. There is the famous group of Irish saints led by St. Breaca[(1)] who seem to have originated in north-eastern Ireland in territories now known as Leinster and Ulster. They appear to have landed on the extreme south-western peninsula of Cornwall where several churches are dedicated to St. Breaca and her companions. There is no evidence of this group elsewhere in Britain, but there are churches dedicated to several members of this saintly company in Brittany.[(2)] No claim is made for the argument that these saints and others associated with them were contemporaries, or that they used the same sea-routes at the same time, or that they necessarily moved in the same direction. All that is stressed is that most of the churches which carry the names of these wandering monks are located within easy access of the coast, and it is obvious that either these saints themselves, or some of their immediate followers (desirous of honouring their names) did use the sea-routes, linking Ireland, Wales, Cornwall and Brittany to propagate their cults (Fig. 15).

In recent years interesting work has been done on what may be called the middle portion of the western seaways

(1) Bowen, E. G., *The Travels of the Celtic Saints. Antiquity,* March, 1944, pp. 16 ff.

(2) See Fig. 44.

which can roughly be described as the Solway Province encircled by Galloway, Cumbria, the Isle of Man and north-eastern Ireland with an important exit by way of the North Channel. An important study[1] seeks to show that the famous monastery of Nendrum in N.E. Ireland was originally orientated towards Candida Casa (Whithorn) rather than towards Armagh. This, of course, is in keeping with modern ideas concerning the origins of the cult of St. Patrick, which will be discussed later. It is even suggested that the famous monastery of Nendrum was originally founded by St. Ninian, or whoever the leader of the Whithorn mission was, early in the fifth century, and then ruled from the middle of the century to its close by St. Machaoi who is generally considered to be the original founder. E. G. Towill has been able to examine in some detail the distribution of the cult of St. Machaoi. He bases his study on the earlier work of E. A. F. Knight[2] who mentions eleven sites traditionally associated with the saint. The eleven have been examined in detail and six are accepted as being almost certainly genuine, and Towill has added a number of others. The resultant distribution pattern is shown on Fig. 16. It brings out very clearly the close inter-relationship that must have existed at this time, by way of the sea-routes, between the lands bordering the Solway Province. Towill rightly points out that the sea is not a separating but an unifying factor in the Age of the Saints, and argues that it is unbelievable that the evangelization of Galloway and Ulidia was not carried out without the closest co-operation between the missionaries concerned. The sea-routes alone can explain how the Galloway peninsula, the Isle of Man, north-east Ireland and Kintyre, and the lands bordering the estuary of the Clyde could be united at this time within a single cultural stimulus.

The seaways were used by other *peregrini* still further to the north. An interesting example is provided by the distribution of ancient churches and chapels dedicated to St. Donnan the Great. He is also associated with Candida Casa and has been

(1) Towill, E. G., *St. Machaoi of Nendrum. Ulster Journal of Archaeology* 3rd Series, Vol. 27, 1964, p. 159 ff.

(2) Knight, E. A. F. *Archaeological light on the Christianizing of Scotland,* London, 1933.

claimed by some "to have followed in the footsteps of St. Ninian" and consolidated his work.[1] Whatever his early locale, after many wanderings he established a monastery on the island of Eigg and there met his death at the hands of pirates in the year 618. Kenneth Jackson in reviewing W. D. Simpson's work points out, perfectly correctly, that a map of

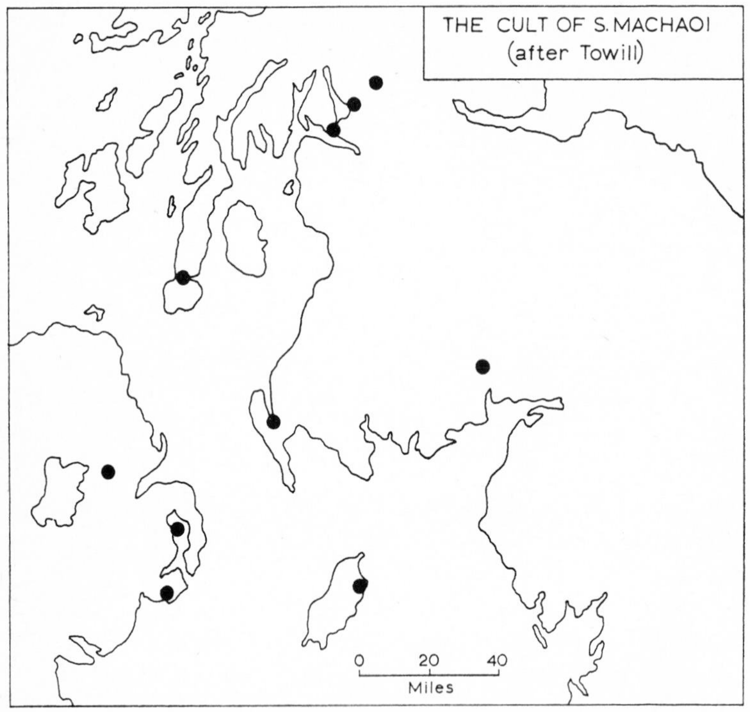

Fig. 16

his dedications (Fig. 17) far from showing that Donnan "followed in the steps of St. Ninian," merely shows that with the exception of an isolated excursion across the Great Glen, Donnan moved almost exclusively by sea.[2] His chapels in eastern Sutherland and in north-eastern Aberdeenshire might

(1) Simpson, W. D., *The Celtic Church in Scotland,* Aberdeen Univ. Studies, No. 111, 1935, Fig. 9.

(2) Jackson, K. H., *Antiquity,* Vol. IX, 1935, p. 493.

equally well have been reached by a sea voyage around northern Scotland and by way of the Moray Firth—following a route well-known from megalithic times. In brief, we can say that the distribution pattern does show an association with the Whithorn

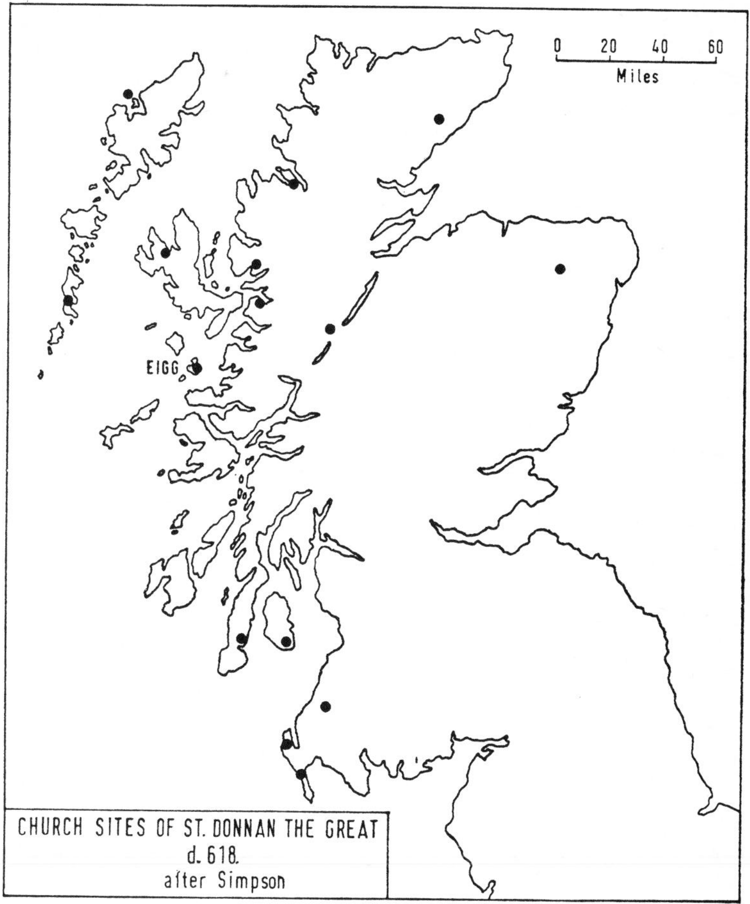

Fig. 17

sphere of influence, and even more clearly with the fullest use of the northern routes from island to island and from inlet to inlet along the much indented western coast of Scotland. It is clear that the group of ancient chapels bearing his name in the

Western Isles appears to have been established from his base at Eigg, making the fullest use of the sea-lanes.

We have now surveyed in general terms and, with the aid of a few examples, shown the use of the western seaways by *peregrini* from Sutherland to Finistère. The story would be incomplete, however, if we were not to mention the voyages of the *peregrini* far beyond these limits into the dark and stormy waters of the North, on the one hand, and into the sunnier and warmer lands of the South, on the other. We will examine the southern end of the great sea-route first of all. We have already indicated that the southern terminals of the Western sea-routes reached, in prehistoric times, to the western basin of the Mediterranean, including even the North African coasts. The major routes used the Straits of Gibraltar as well as the Narbonne-Carcassonne land-crossing. There is abundant evidence for the use of these routes in Megalithic times, and, indeed, as we have seen, the importation of luxury goods and sub-Roman pottery into Ireland and western Britain in the Dark Ages indicates that they continued in use right down to the Age of the Saints. Likewise, the contacts of Galicia with Ireland have been clearly demonstrated and there is direct evidence of the expansion of the Celtic Church into North-west Spain. It is well attested by the presence of the Celtic monastery of Santa Maria de Bretoña near Mondoñedo in Galicia. No one knows exactly when it was established or by whom, or whether the stimulus came from Ireland or Britain directly, or by way of Brittany. All we know is that this church and monastery were included in the episcopate of Britoña in a list dating from Suevic times, and that one of their bishops was named Mailoc, — sufficient evidence, if necessary, of direct Celtic associations.[(1)] It is worth adding that this Galician area is an ancient Celtic one in which the Teutonic Severi had established themselves early in the migration period. How long the links between the Celtic church of Galicia and the major centres in north-western Europe lasted, we do not know. They could not, in any case, have survived the Arab conquest of North

(1) Chadwick, N. K., *op. cit.* (1961) pp. 58-59.

Africa and Spain in the late seventh and early eighth centuries. The Arab conquest of Bordeaux and Aquitaine, though less lasting, must have severed completely the old connections of this area with the Celtic lands. The Arab conquests meant virtually the cutting off of the southern section of the great sea-route. It is true, however, that with the recession of the Arab tide direct relations between north-western Spain and south-western France and the Celtic lands to the north once more took shape, but they never again assumed the dominant rôle they played in the Early Christian period.[1] While the southern portions of the western sea-routes were cut off by the spread of Islam, the northern sections remained unmolested until the coming of the Vikings. Thus, in the eighth and ninth centuries, in particular, British, and especially Irish, *peregrini* moved into the stormy, empty waters of the Far North. They reached not only the Orkneys and Shetlands but succeeded in establishing their primitive Christian settlements in the Faroes, and in far distant Iceland as well.

These movements are well attested. We recollect that during the famous visit of St. Columba to the court of King Brude near Inverness, the King, at the Saint's request, was able to give instructions for the safety of Cormac and other ecclesiastics sailing in northern waters. As things turned out these instructions saved Cormac's life, when he landed in the Orkneys. St. Columba's biographer, Adamnan, tells of another voyage of Cormac in which he was under full sail before a southerly wind for fourteen summer days and nights, holding a straight course towards the north, until he seemed to pass beyond the limits of human journeying and beyond the hope of return.[2] It is possible that on this occasion Cormac visited the Shetlands, perhaps the Faroes and, possibly, Iceland itself.

It is, however, often difficult to distinguish fact from fiction in the *Lives* of the Celtic saints and never more so than when the saints are Irish. This is unfortunate because in their *Imrama,* or travel tales, there occur many passages which seem to reflect experiences in high latitudes with blowing whales and

(1) Ralegh Radford, C. A., *op. cit.* (1956), p. 69.

(2) Adamnan, *Vita Sancti Columbae* II, Chap. 42.

volcanoes belching fire and smoke. The best known of the Irish *Imrama* records the travels of St. Brendan.[1] In his *Vita* we see the transition from the wanderer in search of a secluded spot in the midst of the ocean (where he could pursue his devotions undisturbed) to a later conception of a voyage in search of the ideal earthly Paradise or Land of Promise—a type of narrative that most scholars feel must rest on some historical basis. We can, however, dispense with the *Imrama* of the saints and turn to more reliable literary evidence which shows that the Irish *peregrini* not only knew of Iceland and the Faroes, but actually lived in these islands for sixty or seventy years before their discovery by the Northmen. We obtain our information from a well-known source—the *Liber de Mensura orbis Terrae*, written in the year 825 by an Irish monk named Dicuil, in which he sets down information about the islands that lie north of Britain, based on first hand evidence of some of the *peregrini* themselves. In a famous passage Dicuil says "There are many other islands in the ocean to the north of Britain....on these islands hermits who have sailed from our Scotia (Ireland) have lived for roughly a hundred years. But even as they have been constantly uninhabited since the world's beginning, so now, because of Norse pirates they are empty of anchorites, but full of innumerable sheep and a great many different kinds of sea fowl. I have never found these islands mentioned in the books of scholars." It is generally accepted that Dicuil is here speaking of the Faroes which appear to have been discovered by the Irish saints about the year 700 A.D., and lived in by them until about the second decade of the ninth century. There can, however, be little doubt that towards the end of the eighth century Irishmen (among whom were the *peregrini*) reached Iceland also. The *Islandingabok* and the *Landnamabok,* as well as the Norwegian *History of Theodericus* record that when the first Norse settlers arrived in Iceland there were already Irishmen resident there. They were Christians, and they refused to live with the heathen Vikings, so they moved off, leaving behind their Irish books, bells and croziers

(1) Selmer, O. O., *Navigatio Sancti Brendani,* Notre Dame, 1959, p. 64.

by which their nationality and character were established. These were the *papar* — the monks and anchorites. From place-name evidence it is clear that there was a sprinkling of these *papar* over much of the south-eastern part of the island, which is the most likely landfall for ships coming from the south.[1]

In summary, therefore, we find that with the renewal of activity along the western sea-routes in the post-Roman centuries there emerged what may be termed a great Celtic Christian Thalassocracy which extended from Iceland to Spain. Its influence persisted longer in the north than in the south where its power was disrupted by the conquests of Islam. This Celtic maritime empire may have owed much to the surviving Roman tradition in western Europe, but it owed more to the great tradition of the western seas from prehistoric times. Professor Gordon Childe has made this matter absolutely clear in a famous passage where he stresses the closest parallels between the spread of the Megalithic culture along the Western sea-routes (now dated to the first half of the third millennium B.C.) and that of our Celtic saints approximately three thousand years later.[2] "Are not the Megalithic tombs of Britain the counterparts of the Celtic chapels founded by the Welsh and Irish saints in much the same parts of the British Isles? If so, their founders might be called 'megalithic' saints and owe their authority and status to spiritual prestige rather than to temporal power. In this way missionaries from the South-west won the allegiance of a British Neolithic peasantry by their reputation for sanctity or magic power.... It may be instructive to persue the analogy further. The Celtic saints were inspired by a faith that had originated in the Eastern Mediterranean as our Megalithic religion supposedly did, but the special version of that faith to which the Celtic saints gave expression (while owing much to Egyptian hermits) is believed to have assumed its distinctive form in the Western Medi-

(1) Jones, Gwyn, *The Norse Atlantic Saga,* Chap. I. London, 1964.

(2) Childe, V. G., *The Prehistory of European Society.* Penguin Books A415. 1958, pp. 128-9.

terranean and more precisely in south France, and it is with south France, rather than Portugal that the architecture of the British Megalithic tombs has most in common".

CHAPTER IV.

MAJOR CULTURAL AREAS IN THE AGE OF THE SAINTS

WE must now consider the problem of demarcating culture areas in the Age of the Saints. Superficially this would appear to be an easy task, especially if we were able to accept without question that an ancient church bearing the name of a Celtic saint was, in fact, established by the saint in question, or by one of his immediate followers. All that would then be necessary would be to plot all the churches bearing the saint's name and in this way delimit his 'patria', or sphere of influence, and hence his 'culture area'. We have already noted, however, that such a procedure would be open to a number of serious objections, particularly as it is far from certain that all churches with a Celtic dedication were established during the lifetime of the saint whose name they bear. A further objection which has particular reference to areal studies, such as those with which we are now concerned, has been made by Owen Chadwick who stresses the point that there was a marked tendency for many of the great cathedral churches both in Britain and on the Continent in the early Middle Ages to place under their own patron saint many of the churches in their dioceses or others over which they had legal control. He instances the situation in the Diocese of St. David's as a case in point, maintaining that as a result of the church policy outlined above, the dedications to St. David still surviving in the Welsh countryside tell us more about the property and power of the See of St. David's in the Middle Ages than they do about the movements and activities of St. David himself.[1] Therefore, to assume that the territorial limits of the medieval diocese of St. David's represents the 'patria' or sphere of influence of the saint during his lifetime (merely because it contains almost all the pre-Reformation dedications

(1) Chadwick, Owen. *The Evidence of Dedications in the Early History of the Welsh Church. Studies in Early British History,* Cambridge, 1954, p. 187

in his name found in Wales) would be absurd. It should be noted that throughout Chadwick's argument the emphasis is clearly that of the historian—the churches in the diocese which had been re-dedicated by the cathedral authorities, or the new ones built by them and dedicated to their patron, represent events many centuries later than the time in which the saint was supposed to have lived, and to use them as events contemporary with the life of the saint is historically fallacious. On the contrary, the time factor is not the prime concern of the geographer or the anthropologist attempting to delimit culture areas. They are concerned with spacial or areal considerations primarily, and in the case of the Diocese of St. David's what interests them most is the fact that this territory possessed a large measure of cultural unity long before the limits of the diocese were determined by the medieval bishops, or further dedications made to St. David. In Outer Britain several workers have stressed(1) that this is a land of 'the continuity of tradition'—areas such as that which ultimately became the Diocese of St. David's and which had a measure of cultural unity, based on the sea-routes and their landward connections in prehistoric times, continued to maintain this tradition throughout later ages. The 'adoption' by such an area of the cult of St. David is merely another aspect of the continuity of tradition on a territorial basis. Was not the area in South-west Wales which received the Ogham inscribed stones (with its annex, as it were, in Breconshire and Radnorshire and in parts of modern Herefordshire)—a precursor territorially of the medieval diocese of St. David's? Furthermore, what of the archaeological evidence we possess in the form of memorial crosses of the tenth century? Nash-Williams(2) has shown that one type of monument is found only in the vicinity of the St. David's peninsula, on the one hand, and again in south-western Herefordshire on the other. Here is a clear indication that the future cathedral area was in cultural contact with the most distant parts of the medieval diocese certainly two hundred years before

(1) See Fleure, H. J. in *Arch. Camb.* 1916, pp. 117-8; 1917, pp. 350-1 and 1923, p. 241. Also Fox, C. in *Personality of Britain* (1947), p. 40.

(2) Nash-Williams, V. E., *Early Christian Monuments of Wales,* Cardiff. 1950, Nos. 380-1, 393-4, 410.

the medieval diocese was delimited on a territorial basis with the coming of the Norman bishops. It is, therefore, clear that any revival or propagation of the saint's cult in the Middle Ages (which certainly did occur as Chadwick maintains) occurred in an area that had been culturally associated with St. David's long before the medieval diocese emerged. The prevalence of dedications to a particular saint in the later Middle Ages may indeed "have no relevance to the personality or worth of the saint himself", but, on the contrary, they tell us a great deal about the persistence of his cult and the areas over which it ultimately spread. It is in this context that we must proceed towards a further study of the spheres of influence of important Celtic saints in the culture provinces of Outer Britain.

(i)

Kenneth Jackson's careful studies in recent years have drawn considerable attention to St. Kentigern of Glasgow—probably the most important of all the northern saints of Britain. It would be useful to begin by examining the distribution of this saint's cult based on existing dedications, without reference, in the first instance, to his *Life* as written by Jocelyn of Furness c. 1180, or to Jackson's analysis of it, and its antecedents. On Fig. 18 we see an unmistakeable concentration of dedications in Lothian and south-eastern Scotland, then a trace across the Forth-Clyde isthmus; a secondary concentration in northern Cumberland and a few scattered dedications along the eastern side of Scotland, between the Forth and Moray Firths.[1] If we omit for the present the secondary concentration in Cumberland,

(1) There is a dedication to St. Kentigern in South-eastern Carmarthenshire at Llangyndeyrn in the valley of the Gwendraeth Fach. This dedication would appear to be out of context with others so far away to the northward. Baring-Gould and John Fisher (1913) were convinced that this dedication was to an otherwise unknown saint of the same name, yet with our much greater knowledge of movements by land and sea in the Dark Ages there is nothing whatsoever improbable in some wanderer taking the cult of this northern saint to these southern parts. After all, small pen-annular brooches of British zoomorphic design (which can be dated to the Dark Ages) have been found not many miles away from Llangyndeyrn along the South Wales coast and are known also from Mid-Lothian in the North (see Savory, H. N., *Some sub-Romano-British Brooches from South Wales*, Fig. 10 in *Dark Age Britain* (Ed. Harden, D. B., 1956)).

and the trace up the eastern side of Scotland, to which we shall return shortly, the bulk of the dedications would appear to indicate a pattern which is in some ways reminiscent of the

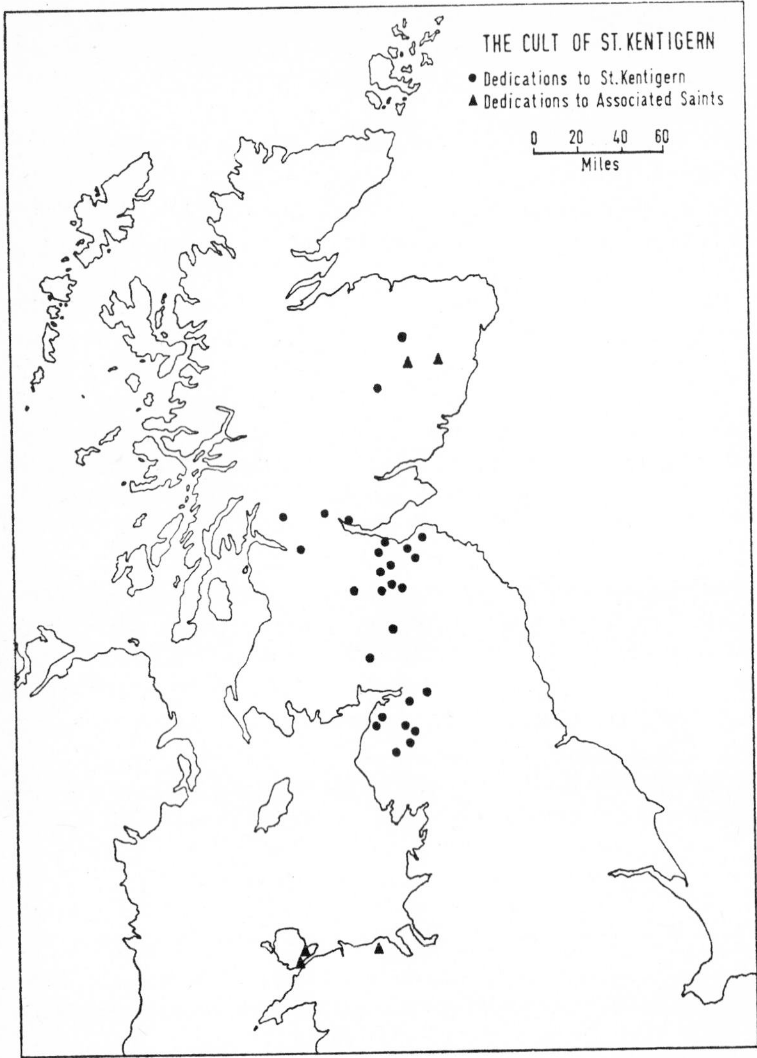

Fig. 18

South-east Scotland culture area as illustrated by the small Iron Age hill-forts of immediate pre-Roman times. The implications are, as was the case with the hill-forts, that the focal area of the cult of St. Kentigern is in Region IB (Fig. 9). and that there is a subsequent westerly spread. It is not without significance that Jackson comes to exactly the same conclusion by a careful and highly critical analysis of the literary sources.[1] He has shown clearly that the *Life* of the saint written by Jocelyn of Furness for his namesake Bishop Jocelyn of Glasgow (1175-1199) derives from several sources. Behind it is an anonymous *Life* written by a Norman priest (established by David I in Glasgow) some thirty years previously for Bishop Herbert (Bishop of Glasgow, 1147-1164) and referred to as the Herbertian *Life*. This, in turn, was based on oral tradition and on a more primitive Scottic *Life* of the mid-11th century, recording the miracles of the saint, and which itself, most likely, had antecedents. The interesting point is that the Herbertian *Life* contained a remarkable story of Kentigern's birth in the region of Lothian which was not found in the more primitive Scottic *Life,* and must have come, therefore, from the mass of oral tradition concerning the saint which the author of the Herbertian *Life* says he used. It is clear that behind the Herbertian author is a source with a detailed knowledge of Lothian—someone who knew the area well, together with all its geography and local religious legends. The whole clearly possesses a Celtic or even a Brittonic atmosphere. Jackson shows from the evidence of place-names that it is told by someone who knew Lothian when it had already been annexed by the Gaelic kingdom of the North, that is after the late 10th or 11th century, but the case for the survival of pockets of Brittonic speaking peasants possessing these legends is clearly demonstrated. It is here in Lothian, therefore, that according to ancient lore we must seek the beginnings of the Kentigern story. It may even be possible to tie down the legendary material to the neighbourhood of Loquharist, near the famous hill-fort of Trapain Law, as the Kentigern legend seems to have survived here from very early times. Loquharist

(1) Jackson, K. H., *"The Sources for the Life of St. Kentigern," Studies in the Early British Church,* Cambridge, 1958, pp. 273-357.

itself is very likely to be an early Kentigern dedication.

The next phase of the story is Kentigern's westward migration to Glasgow. On the way he is brought into association with St. Servanus. Apart from the desire of hagiological writers to associate the important saints of nearby districts, Jackson suggests that the fact that there was a chapel at Culross, Servanus' chief centre, dedicated to St. Kentigern, was all that was necessary to clinch the matter in the eyes of the medieval hagiologists. Here we are faced with the problem of the extent to which the text, as we have it, stimulated new dedications or, alternatively, the dedications were there first of all and the story built around them. Clearly, in this episode, Jackson is thinking of the latter—that the dedications are sometimes older than the *Lives*. After the Servanus contact Kentigern continued his journey to Glasgow. He follows the north bank of the Forth moving westward until he could cross the river possibly near Stirling. Here he turned south and moved by way of Bannockburn south-westwards to Glasgow. Subsequently, the story deals with material that has an entirely Cumbric or Welsh character.

Thus far the Kentigern legend and the distribution of the churches bearing his name would appear to form a pattern suggesting a reflection of Early Iron Age precedents in this culture area in southern Scotland. The next matter to engage our attention is the overspill of the Kentigern legend into the extensive corridor-area to the southward that linked Strathclyde with the borderlands of Wales. It would appear that this took place during the period 900-1092 when the Kingdom of Strathclyde was able to benefit from the weakness of Northumbria and the lack of unity between the Scandinavian and Norse settlers in Northern England. At this period the Princes of Strathclyde re-occupied Dumfriesshire and most of Cumberland as far as the Lake Hills and the Derwent, and up the Eden valley through north-eastern Westmorland to Stanmoor on the crest of the Pennines. They succeeded in holding this territory against both the English and the Scandinavians for over a century until it became merged in greater Scotland early in the 11th century. Although Strathclyde now lost its Celtic independence, the southern boundary of Scotland continued to reach as far south as the Derwent until William Rufus conquered Cumberland in 1092 and set the

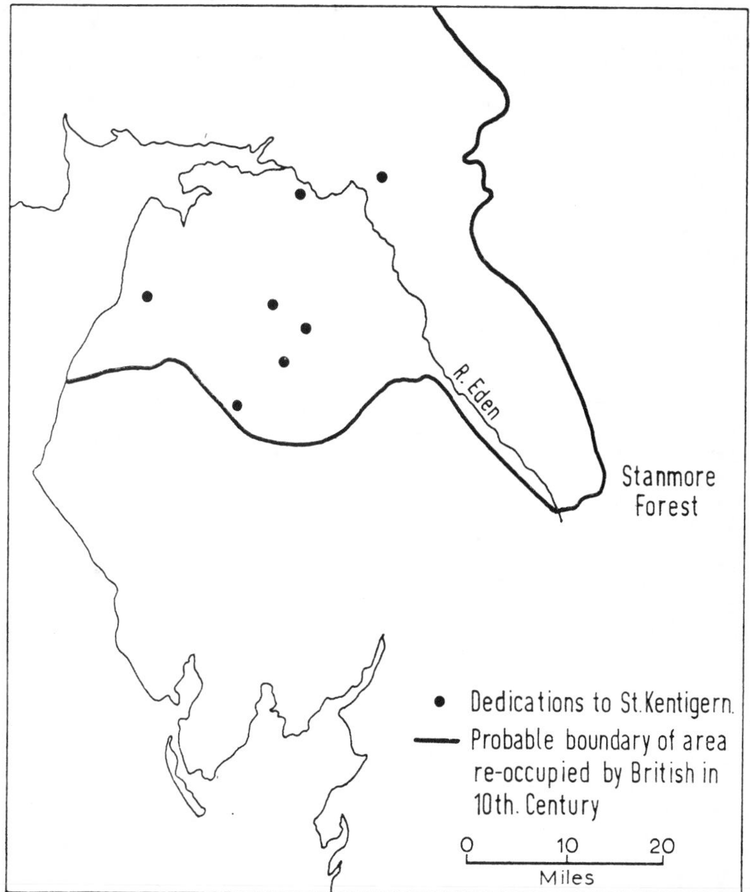

Fig. 19

Dedications to St. Kentigern in Cumberland

modern frontier where it is today. Recently, Jackson[1] has been able to show that the same area in northern Cumberland

(1) Jackson, K. H., *op. cit.*, p. 350.

contains the highest percentage of British village names. British names for villages are thought to indicate the survival of a British population more surely than British names for natural features such as rivers or hills. The situation is, of course, complicated in these parts by the presence of Norse names for villages. These may be either the names of new villages established by the Norsemen, or the result of the Norse re-naming existing British or English villages which they had occupied. In any case, with the re-occupation of this area by the Princes of Strathclyde the Cumbric language was re-introduced, and what Cumbric survived the English and Norse penetrations was in this way considerably strengthened, so that it might even have lingered on there until the beginning of the 12th century. In all this we are but underlining the general theme of this book, namely that tradition is deeply rooted in the lands of Western Britain and that a revival of interest in an ancient language, or point of view, is easily evoked. We should stress in this context a matter not previously noted, namely, that all dedications to St. Kentigern in the Diocese of Carlisle are located in exactly the same areas as British village names have survived in reasonably large numbers (Fig. 19). Presumably the re-occupation of this area by the Princes of Strathclyde in the 10th century led to a revival of interest in the saint's cult. By the 12th century, as we have seen, this had led to the production of two *Lives* of the saint and the dedication of many churches to him in Cumberland and South-west Scotland. It is important again for us to stress that some dedications, at any rate, preceded the actual publication of the *Lives*. Jocelyn himself records one when referring to Crosfield[1]—in which place 'a church built in modern times' is dedicated to St. Kentigern, on the strength of an alleged tradition that he had preached at this place. The dedications to the saint at Aspatria and Bromfield may also be earlier than the publication of either the Herbertian or Jocelyn's *Life*. The monuments associated with the churches indicate that they

(1) Quoted by Jackson, K. H., *op. cit.*, p. 313; see also Forbes, A. P., *Lives of St. Ninian and St. Kentigern. The Histories of Scotland,* Vol. V, Edinburgh, 1874.

are 10th century in date with a pronounced Norse influence.[1] They are the most westerly of the churches in this group and so nearest to the coast where Irish-Norse influence in the 10th century would be strongest. We know that the 10th century Norse dedicated their churches from the story of Orlyg dedicating a church to St. Columba far away to the north–in Iceland. We must remember, too, that the Cumbri played a great part under their King Owain as comrades of the new-come Norse in these parts, united in their joint opposition to the English.

The churches shown on Fig. 19 are only those in the present Diocese of Carlisle. The southward spread of the Kingdom of Strathclyde affected equally places in south-western Scotland on the other side of the Solway. There is much to suggest, for example, that there was a very early association of St. Kentigern with Hoddom in Dumfriesshire,[2]—a tradition possibly revived at this time by a new dedication. Whichever way we approach the matter there can be no doubt that there was a real tradition surviving into the tenth, eleventh and twelfth centuries among the Cumbri living in these parts of a mission of St. Kentigern in the area in the sixth.

We have now to deal with an even more difficult part of the Kentigern legend, namely his sojourn in north-east Wales as an exile during the ascendency of an anti-Christian party in Strathclyde and his subsequent recall with a change of government. During his stay in north-east Wales he is said to have established a monastery, which he ultimately leaves in the care of St. Asaph, one of his monks, who later becomes the patron of the Diocese which bears his name. It is interesting to note that eminent Welsh scholars like Sir John Edward Lloyd and Sir Ifor Williams appear to accept Jocelyn's story,[3] while

(1) Graham, T. H. B. and Collingwood, W. G., *Patron Saints of the Diocese of Carlisle. Cumberland & Westmorland Antiquarian and Archaeological Soc.*, 1925.

(2) Chadwick, N. K., *Celtic Britain.* London, 1963, pp. 147 and 230.

(3) Williams, Sir Ifor, *Wales and the North.* Cumberland and Westmorland Historical & Archaeological Trans. New Series Ll 1951 p. 87, and Lloyd, Sir John, *History of Wales,* Vol. I, p. 167. A strong case for the Jocelyn story from sources independent of Jocelyn himself is also made by Simpson in his latest edition of *St. Columba* (1963).

Jackson after examining the literary and historical evidence is convinced that the whole story of Kentigern going southwards "smells strongly of the twelfth century".[1] It may well have something to do, he argues, with the establishment of the See of St. Asaph at this time. A bishopric of St. Asaph was mooted as early as 1125 with the proposal that it should be subject to York and not to Canterbury. It was not actually established within the Canterbury framework until 1143. The probability is that the St. Asaph story was embodied into the *Life* of St. Kentigern by Jocelyn himself, who at Furness may have been in touch with North Wales. After further consideration of the matter, and citing the recent work of the Rev. S. M. Harris,[2] Jackson concluded that "Jocelyn's tale of Kentigern in Wales is bogus from start to finish".[3] This would appear to dispose of the matter finally and completely, but we can not overlook the fact that in north-eastern Wales we are still well within the limits of the wide corridor reaching from the Welsh Border to Hadrian's Wall—a zone wherein northern and southern cultures overlap. We remember that the technique of building and firing timber-laced walls so characteristic of the vitrified forts of the Grampian province had migrated southwards in the Iron Age, using either the land, or the sea route, to this very area in north-east Wales with which these stories of the great northern saint are associated. We have already cited enough archaeological and cultural evidence to make it clear that the vitrified forts are no isolated example of such a general trend.[4] The historical geographer and student of early cultures is, therefore, bound to be extremely interested in stories associated with St. Kentigern's sojourn in north-eastern Wales—'bogus' though they may be.

We cannot, however, leave the matter there, for there is available in a document, which can be dated to about 1256, a story that a monastery was founded by Kentigern at St. Asaph

(1) Jackson, K. H., op. cit. p. 315.
(2) Harris, S. M., *Journ. Hist. Society of the Church in Wales,* Vol. VI, pp. 5-24 (1956)
(3) Jackson, K. H., *op. cit.,* p. 315, Note 3.
(4) See also Bowen, E. G., *Archaeoleg a'n Llenyddiaeth Gynnar,* Llên Cymru, Cyf. 8, Rhif. 3a4, 1965, especially pp. 163-7.

and that it received benefactions in the form of lands and privileges granted to the saint by Malgunus of Deganwy in North Wales, following upon the settlement of an original dispute between them.[1] This is an important piece of evidence as it seems to bear witness to the existence of a story at St. Asaph which is not wholly derived from Jocelyn. It may well constitute independent evidence of the existence of the Kentigern legend at St. Asaph. The conclusion now generally accepted is that the relationship of Kentigern with St. Asaph seems to derive ultimately from St. Asaph itself and can scarcely have been invented entirely by Jocelyn, as it contains more knowledge of Welsh matters than he is likely to have possessed. The significance of this conclusion to our thesis is obvious. Another way of looking at the problem would be to follow up the clue given by the proposal to place the new See under York rather than under Canterbury. There is nothing exceptional here, because lands tributary to the north Wales coastal plain look naturally towards Yorkshire and the north of England generally rather than to the south of England. Professor Grimes maintains that this is the key-note of North Wales' cultural associations throughout prehistory.[2] Having sought attachments with the North it is thoroughly in keeping with medieval ecclesiastical politics that those who supported the idea should put it about that the monastery and bishopric were originally established by one of the greater saints of the northern British Church over which York certainly claimed supremacy.[3] Whichever way we look at the matter, we must accept cultural associations with northern Britain as axiomatic. In this way the legend of St. Kentigern at St. Asaph is what the geographer, interested in cultural distributions, would normally expect.

The final aspect of this study of the distribution of Kentigern dedications can easily be dismissed. Those that occur on the eastern side of Scotland, north of the Forth-Clyde isthmus, are best explained as derived from the 12th century revival of his cult resulting in dedications to him carried northward by the

(1) See Jackson, K. H., *op. cit.*, p. 217.
(2) Grimes, W. F., *Guide to the Collection illustrating the Prehistory of Wales*, Cardiff, 1939, p. 110.
(3) Jackson, K. H., *op. cit.*, p. 315, Note 3 and p. 318, Note 2.

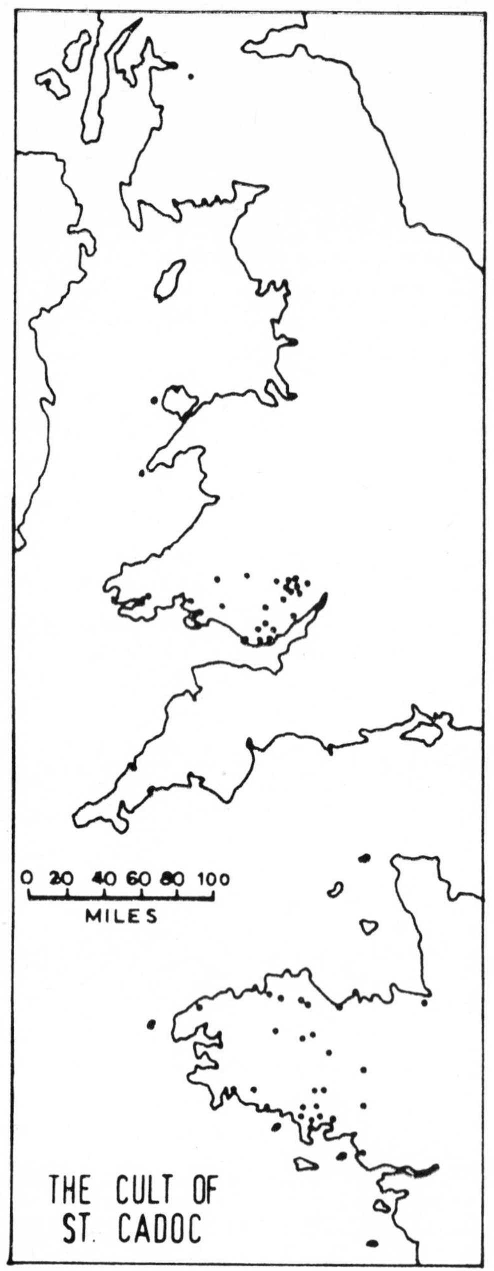

Fig. 20

zeal and enthusiasm of David I.—the first king of all Scotland. David himself had been Earl of Cumbria and might have had a special regard for Kentigern, so it was only to be expected that he should figure alongside of St. Ninian among the many southern influences which the new king introduced to the North. Like the dedications to St. Ninian in these parts, those to St. Kentigern are arranged along the same strip of country as that followed by Agricola's road, for the very sound reason that geographical considerations make it the one natural line of penetration towards the North.

(ii)

We can now seek a parallel distribution to that of St. Kentigern based this time on the southern end of the Outer Province of Britain. The cult of St. Cadoc of Llancarfan is clearly indicated here. After the patron saint, Cadoc is probably the best known of the Welsh saints. If we had no other evidence whatsoever it would be clear from Fig. 20, showing the overall distribution of his dedications, that the cult of St. Cadoc emanated from South-east Wales. The churches bearing his name form two marked clusters in this area, firstly around Llangattock-nigh-Usk in the ancient territory of Gwent (of which he is traditionally said to have been a native), and secondly, in the eastern part of the Vale of Glamorgan, focussing around his most important foundation Llancarfan (Nant Carban). Outlying dedications occur at such places as Gelligaer in northern Glamorgan, and Caerleon in southern Monmouthshire—both in a distinctly 'Roman' context. Others are found along the former Roman road leading up the Usk valley to Brecon and beyond, via Llanymddyfri, to the Tywi valley. To the southwards there are clear traces of his cult along the coast road into the southern parts of the Gower peninsula and thence westward to just north of Cydweli, and even beyond to Llawhaden in eastern Pembrokeshire.

When we turn to examine the historical evidence for the existence of St. Cadoc and the events said to be connected with his life we find ourselves in a position similar to that associated with St. Kentigern. A full and detailed *Life* of St. Cadoc appears in the most important of all the existing collections of

Lives of the Welsh saints written in Britain, now known as the Cotton MSS. Vespasian Axiv. The author is Lifris or Lifricus, son of Bishop Herwald, who was the chief bishop in South-eastern Wales from about 1056 to 1104. It would appear that this collection of saintly *Lives* was probably compiled at Brecon Priory about the year 1100, but the selection of the saints whose *Lives* are included in this manuscript, and the nature of the other contents was, no doubt, strongly influenced by the interests of the Norman Priory of Gloucester. The reasons, of course, were that the Norman conqueror of Glamorgan in the eleventh century had presented the Celtic monastery of Llancarfan to Gloucester Priory, so this community naturally acquired a great interest in the famous school that had trained so many saints in South-east Wales. It is generally accepted, therefore, that before Vespasian Axiv was compiled, some facts concerning certain Welsh saints had been collected at Gloucester.[(1)] Lifris, possibly writing at Brecon, as we have seen, was engaged upon exactly the same task as the author of the Herbertian *Life* of St. Kentigern at Glasgow. His aim was to bring the former Celtic church of South-east Wales into line with Norman practice and produce up-to-date versions of the legends of the local saints. Lifris, like Caradoc of Llancarfan (who wrote a second *Life* of Cadoc some years later) may be placed in exactly the same category as Jocelyn of Furness and the author of the Herbertian *Life* of St. Kentigern, in that they were all professional hagiographers, each with a standardized technique, and each with a similar aim. From the point of view of the orthodox historian their work is equally worthless. It should be remembered, however, that like the *Lives* of St. Kentigern, the *Lives* of St. Cadoc (although very late compositions), nevertheless, embody earlier traditions. Lifris' *Life* of St. Cadoc, in particular, has preserved interesting references to secular and local traditions. One of these concerns his parentage in South Wales, which, if we exclude the historically absurd (but culturally significant) claims that his father (a princeling of Gwent) was the descendant of a long and distin-

(1) Doble, G. H., *St. Cadoc in Cornwall and Brittany,* Cornish Saints Series, No. 40, Truro (1937), p. 5.

guished line of Roman emperors going back to Augustus, has an air of authenticity about it, and stands out in sharp contrast to what is said about the ancestry of the majority of saints—Kentigern included. Outside his own *Lives* there are references to St. Cadoc in the very early (8th century) *Life* of St. Samson of Dol and in the Breton *Life* of St. Gildas, which can be dated before the Norse raids on Brittany in the 10th century and thus antedate by many centuries the Welsh versions. It has been shown elsewhere[(1)] that St. Cadoc, like St. Illtud and St. Dyfrig, was renowned for his scholarship and that South-eastern Wales was the home of an early group of saints famed for their knowledge, their wisdom and their piety.

The map (Fig. 20) shows the expansion of the cult of Cadoc across Cornwall to the Vannetais in Brittany. The traces of his cult in Cornwall are associated with one of the well-known transpeninsular routes leading from Harlyn Bay in the Padstow area across to the estuary of the Fal on the south coast. Near the shores of Harlyn Bay are the ruins of what was once a very important chapel dedicated to St. Cadoc. The building of this chapel is described in Lifris' *Life*. Close to it was his holy well—one of the most famous in Cornwall. It is mentioned twice in the *Life* of the saint and also referred to three centuries later in the *Itinerary* of William of Worcester. At the other end of the route in the parish of St. Just in Roseland near the waters of the Fal is another holy well now called Venton-gassick, but Fenton-Cadoc in 1230.[(2)] Adjoining Padstow parish in the north is the parish of Mawgan with its church dedicated to St. Mawgan. Canon Doble has shown how the traditions incorporated in the *Life* of St. Cadoc and the dedications to both saints in the topography of Cornwall and Brittany point to a close connection between them. Along this same trans-peninsular route across Cornwall there are churches carrying the name of St. Petroc and, in consequence, he too, is introduced into the *Life* of the saint as Cadoc's uncle. It is worth noting in passing that this, and much other evidence, suggests once again

(1) Bowen, E. G., *The Settlements of the Celtic Saints in Wales,* University of Wales Press, Cardiff, 1954, pp. 44-5.

(2) Doble, G. H., *op. cit.,* p. 14.

that the dedications are older than the *Lives* of the saints and that geographical proximity of dedications is enough to suggest to the professional hagiographer, and possibly to local tradition, that there must have been some connection between these persons, although, of course, there is no evidence from the dedications themselves that these individuals were, in fact, contemporaries.

In Brittany, Fig. 20 indicates a concentration of dedications in the Vannetais—the territory of the ancient diocese of Vannes, with a trace of Cadoc dedications across the peninsula from the area of the Lannion peninsula to that of Vannes. There can be little doubt that the importance of the cult of St. Cadoc in the Vannetais has emanated from the Ile Cado—an island in the Sea of Etel on which there is a famous chapel dedicated to the saint. The island is connected by a causeway with the village of St. Cado on the mainland. We should not, however, accept at its face value Lifris' story of St. Cadoc establishing this monastery in the Sea of Etel in the sixth century, for, as Doble has shown,[1] it seems most likely that the island site was originally occupied by a local Breton hermit whose name bore some likeness to that of Cadoc, but of whom nothing whatsoever was known in Brittany in the 12th century. This is strongly suggested by the fact that charters relating to the Priory on the Ile Cado which precede in date the *Life of St. Cadoc*, refer to the local saint as Catvodus and not Cadocus. The day on which Catvodus was honoured in the church calendar is also different from that on which Cadoc is honoured in Britain. It is, therefore, very likely that the saint honoured on the Ile Cado was really a local Breton saint, afterwards identified with the famous British saint whose name was so similar. The further propagation of the cult of St. Cadoc in the Vannetais in the 12th century might well have followed the publication of Lifris' *Life* and the amalgamation of the two saints. Here we have an interesting example of how a saint's cult spread, absorbing the cult of another saint six hundred years after the individuals themselves were supposed to have lived. We should not, however, assume that there was

(1) Doble, G. H., *op. cit.*, (1937), p. 18.

no cult of the Welsh St. Cadoc in Brittany (as distinct from the Breton hermit St. Catvodus) before the 12th century. The evidence from the neighbourhood of Pleucadeuc near Redon in the east of the Vannetais is particularly interesting in this respect. The church of Pleucadeuc belonged to the Abbey of Redon and among the charters of the latter is one dated 837 signed at Pleucadeuc, *in plebe Catoci,* with one of the witnesses described as *Guas Cadoc*—the servant of Cadoc. Three matters are worthy of note. First of all, most scholars assume that Breton parishes with the prefix Plou—are associated with the earliest period of Celtic Christianization; secondly, that the saint's name is spelt *Catoc* which is an earlier form than *Catow* from which the many St. Cados and St. Cadous of Brittany are derived; and lastly, that in this neighbourhood there are place-names and parish names linking the saint with Maugan, Hernin, Petroc and others, as in Wales and Cornwall. Whatever may have been the origins of the cult in different parts of Brittany it is agreed that the identification of Catvod with Cadoc was generally accepted everywhere in Brittany after the 12th century and the present traditions of the Ile Cado and of other places dedicated to St. Cado or Cadou in Brittany all represent the saint as being the Abbot of Llancarfan. What is significant from the point of view put forward in this work is that we have here, Brittany (and particularly the Vannetais which had been the homeland of the Veneti), Cornwall, and the lowlands of south-eastern Wales united again within the same cultural stimulus. In the Iron Age the stimulus seems to have emanated from western Brittany; in the Age of the Saints the stimulus came from South Wales—but the culture area remains the same. We shall have more to say of this area later. We can now examine the traces of Cadoc's cult spreading northwards from its core in south-eastern Wales into that extensive corridor which we have had occasion to mention so many times before. Kentigern's cult, we remember, spread southwards into this area while Cadoc's cult spread northwards into the same region, whether by land or sea or partly by land and partly by sea, we do not know. Many have thought that the presence of Cadoc in Strathclyde is as 'bogus' as the presence of Kentigern in

North Wales, yet all the archaeological evidence we possess suggests that this corridor was a well established feature of the cultural geography of these islands for many centuries before the Age of the Saints, and if these individuals did not contact the farthest ends of the corridor during their lifetime, their posthumous cults certainly did. Cadoc has a church dedicated to him at Cambusland on the Clyde, very much in the territory of St. Kentigern. The story as given by Lifris of the establishment of this cell is especially interesting for its incorporation of a legend of a Pictish robber chieftain—Cau of Pictavia, whose collar-bone the saint accidentally digs up when excavating the foundations of his cell.[(1)] Cau is well-known as the centre of a whole cycle of sagas and folklore, but he is named in the *Life* of St. Cadoc as the father of St. Gildas, and, in turn, the 12th century *Life* of St. Gildas de Rhuys, written in Brittany, claims that Cau came from Strathclyde and was father of Gildas the saint. He is said to have been the father, too, of Engreas and Allectus and of a daughter Peteova. The Breton *Life* of Gildas which is much older than Lifris' *Life* of St. Cadoc tells how these children of Cau withdrew 'to a remote part' where each founded an oratory. It is at least a striking coincidence that in the commote of Twrcelyn in north-eastern Anglesey (which would very definitely be on the sea-route linking North Wales with Strathclyde by way of Morecambe Bay) the name Llangadoc is found. No church or ruins are to be seen at present—the name alone survives, but less than three miles away are Llaneugrad and Llanallgo—the oratories of Engreas and Allectus. It may, of course, be that these brothers and sisters of Gildas are completely fictitious persons, brought into family relationship with his father Cau by the accident of the close proximity of churches bearing these names in Anglesey, and the presence in the vicinity also of one of St. Cadoc's cells. Whatever the facts may be, there does seem to be a close relationship between the topographical and the hagiological evidence in the *Lives* of the saints, and the inference is once more that the topographical evidence is the older. Doble[(2)], who was a very careful and

(1) Chadwick, N. K., *op. cit.*, p. 114.

(2) Doble, G. H., *op. cit.*, 1937 pp. 7-8.

scholarly worker in these fields, was prepared to take the association of Cadoc with the Strathclyde area a step further by drawing attention to the presence of many churches in the Scottish lowlands dedicated to St. Machan (whom he equates with St. Maugan), a saint who has churches, as we have already seen, close to those of St. Cadoc in both Cornwall and Brittany.

(iii)

We have examined in some detail the dedication distribution patterns of two important saints associated with the northern and southern portions of the Outer Province of Britain. We can now turn to consider some sub-areas in the North. The key to the Christianization of the area north of the Antonine Wall is clearly the missionary activity of the Columban Church based on Iona. St. Columba was following in the wake of his fellow-countrymen—the Scotti or Irish, who in the closing years of the fifth century had moved across the seas and settled in the territory known as Dalradia, an area roughly co-terminus with the present county of Argyll. Tradition has it that the immigrants were the Sons of Erc, whose ancestral home was in north-eastern Ireland. They were certainly no brigands or marauders seeking Imperial spoil. They settled beyond the limits of the Roman world, and although the archaeological evidence for this 'invasion' is slight, the Dalradians, as we have already noted, introduced a new culture into western Scotland—a culture whose religious and linguistic aspects were to spread far and wide in that country, and beyond, in the centuries that followed. Some of St. Columba's followers seem to have confined their activities strictly to the Dalradian culture area, for there appears to be little evidence of their cult beyond Argyll. The cult of St. Chattan is a case in point. As an historical personage we know absolutely nothing about him, he might even be an entirely fictitious person. There is uncertainty concerning the precise period in which he lived, and his very name takes on a variety of forms: Chatan, Cathan, Kaddan and Cathandus. He is said to have belonged to a family whose home was in northern Ireland and he is mentioned in the *Martyrology of Gorman* as 'Cathan the abstinent, stern warrior'. Leaving Ireland, he crossed the sea to Bute along with his sister Ertha, who afterwards became the mother of St. Blane. The aspect of his cult that interests us particularly is its geographical pattern as shown on Fig. 21 and the clear

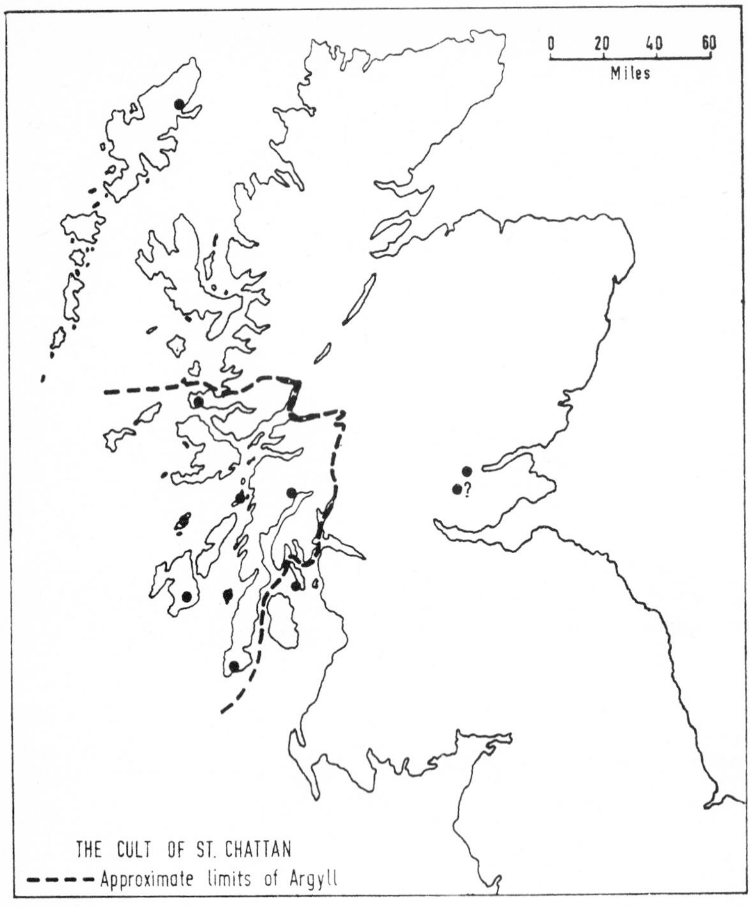

Fig. 21

indication it gives of the Dalradian culture area. The outlying dedications near Stornoway in Lewis and at Aberuthven in Perthshire (with documentary evidence in this case reaching back to the year 1200), indicate the limited spread of his cult along the natural routeways both by land and sea. Other Columban saints, such as Maelrubha, appear to have arrived

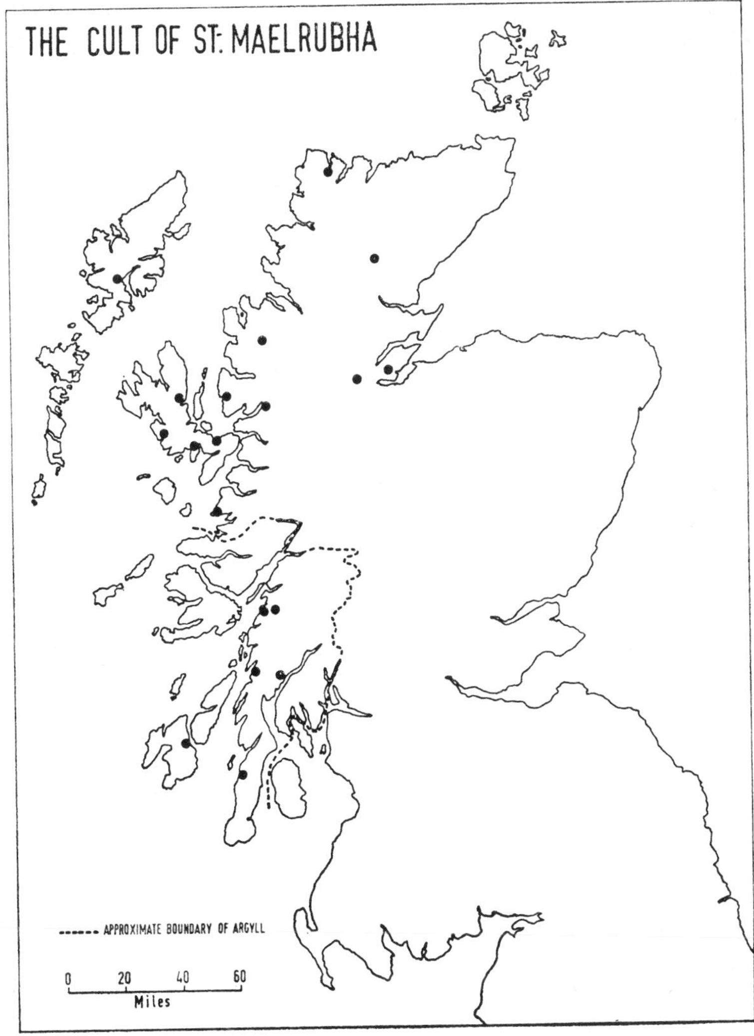

Fig. 22

from northern Ireland and entered Dalradia, but subsequently their cult spread northwards along the seaways and into the territory lying beyond the Great Glen (Fig. 22). In this case we have a clear indication of the re-emergence of the Broch culture area in the Age of the Saints. As was the case with St. Chattan, we know little about Maelrubha historically, the name appears in a variety of forms, but there seems to be no doubt about his Irish associations. He is said to be a descendant of Niall of the Nine Hostages, King of Ireland and through his mother belonged to the kindred of St. Congal of Bangor in Down, in which monastery he was apparently trained. He crossed to Scotland and worked in Argyll. There is little doubt about the permanence of his influence in the North. He is said to have established a settlement at Applecross in Ross and Cromarty which became the centre of his cult throughout a wide area. Thomas Pennant travelling in these parts in the mid-eighteenth century says that he was "regarded as the patron of all the coast from Applecross to Loch Brain".[(1)] While St. Maelrubha is obviously a saint of the 'Broch' area, he does not appear to have dedications in Caithness nor in the Northern Isles where the Broch culture was so clearly marked. This need not detract from the major argument here presented for, if necessary, it can be clearly demonstrated (in spite of some attempts to reason to the contrary from late dedications) that the whole of this region was originally Christianized from Dalradia and not by St. Ninian and his followers from Whithorn.[(2)] If it were necessary to stress yet again that we are concerned not only with the survival of prehistoric culture areas in the Age of the Saints but also with the continuity of tradition in the areas themselves, then we are provided with much interesting material in the case of St. Maelrubha. The well known pre-Christian rite of the sacrificial bull seems to have got linked up with St. Maelrubha and there are several instances of bulls being sacrificed to the saint in the remote North-West in order to secure the alleviation of some mischance. It is on record that as late as 1678 Hector Mackenzie in Mella of Garloch and certain of his relatives were accused before the Presbytery of Dingwall of sacrificing a bull on Innis Marle to St. Maelrubha

(1) Pennant, Thomas, *Tour in Scotland in* 1769 (1771), p. 293.

(2) Wainwright, F. T., *The Northern Isles,* Edinburgh, 1962, p. 103.

for the recovery of the health of his wife.[1]

The most important activity associated with the Dalradian saints was the way in which they Christianized the original vitrified-fort area. This region, as we have seen, had re-emerged politically at this time as the land of the Picts. St. Columba's famous mission to King Brude, near Inverness, was the beginning of the conversion, while later on his work was taken up by many others. As a result of this ecclesiastical penetration of Pictish territory based on Iona, the Goidelic speech of the Scots of Argyll had probably made some definite penetration of the area, before the Union of the Kingdoms under Kenneth McAlpine at the end of the 9th century. It must not be forgotten that in pre-Roman times the territory of Argyll was itself within the vitrified-fort area. The distribution of dedications to St. Moluag reflects the pattern of the vitrified-fort area in Celtic Christian times. His background is similar to that of SS. Chattan and Maelrubha. His Irish name was Lughaih and one tradition reveals that he was a disciple of St. Brendan of Clonfert, and another that he was trained by St. Congal of Bangor. He is said to have crossed over to Lismore in Argyll, the area which later became the centre of his cult in Dalradia. There is clear evidence of his fame spreading northwards by the sea-lanes into Skye and the Hebrides, but the most unmistakable penetration is by way of the Great Glen into the Inverness area, the core of Pictish power in the eastern portion of Scotland between the Forth and the Moray Firth (Fig. 23).

In this brief survey of Scotland our method of approach makes no claim to add in any way to our knowledge of SS. Chattan, Maelrubha or Moluag as persons in the historical sense, nor, indeed, are we able to throw more light on the times in which they are supposed to have lived. All we can claim to have added is that by a study of the surviving dedications to these individuals we can detect in an ecclesiastical context the re-emergence of the culture areas of Scotland, north of the central valley, very much as we think they were in late pre-

(1) Mackinley, W., *Ancient Church Dedications in Scotland,* Vol. II, Edinburgh, 1914, p. 176.

historic times. We cannot date any of these dedications precisely, but it would appear to be certain that they all belong to the period between the landing of St. Columba on Iona in 563 and the expulsion of the Columban clergy from Pictland by

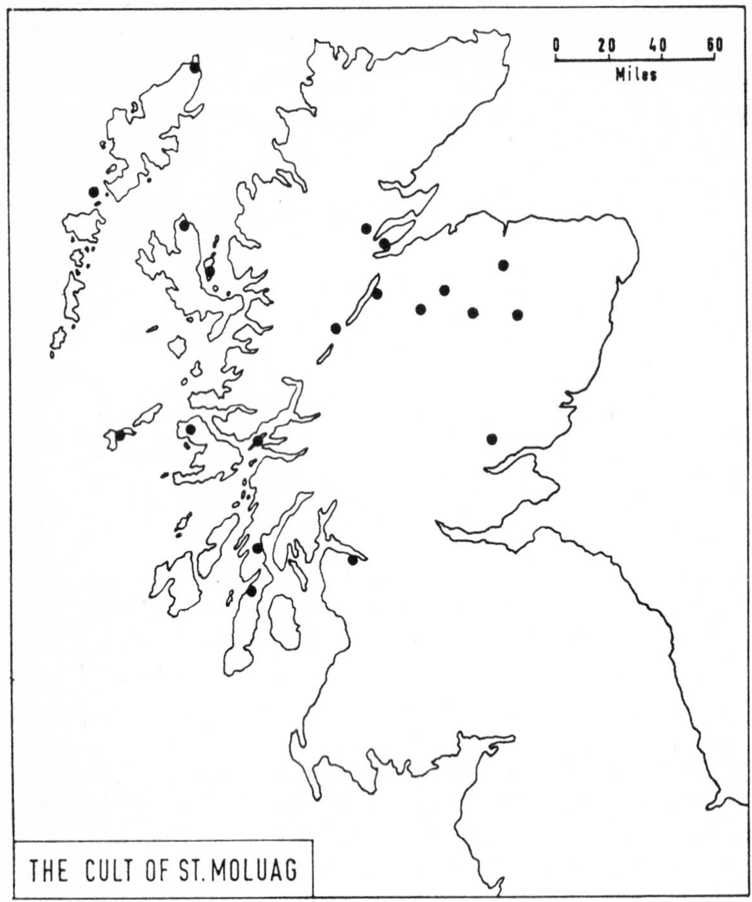

Fig. 23

Nechtan IV in the early years of the 8th century. Such a dating must certainly be assigned to the spread of the cult of St. Moluag.

We can now turn to a consideration of some of the sub-areas

in the South. First of all, there is the clearly established culture area of South-west Wales. The Irish settlement in these parts would appear to have been very similar to that made by the Dalradic Scotti in the north, except that in South-west Wales we have confirmation of this settlement as indicated by the presence of the Ogham inscribed stones. In the Age of the Saints the distribution of churches dedicated to St. Brynach are a clear reflection of this cultural sub-province (Fig. 24). Significantly, Brynach is known in Welsh hagiology as *Brynach*

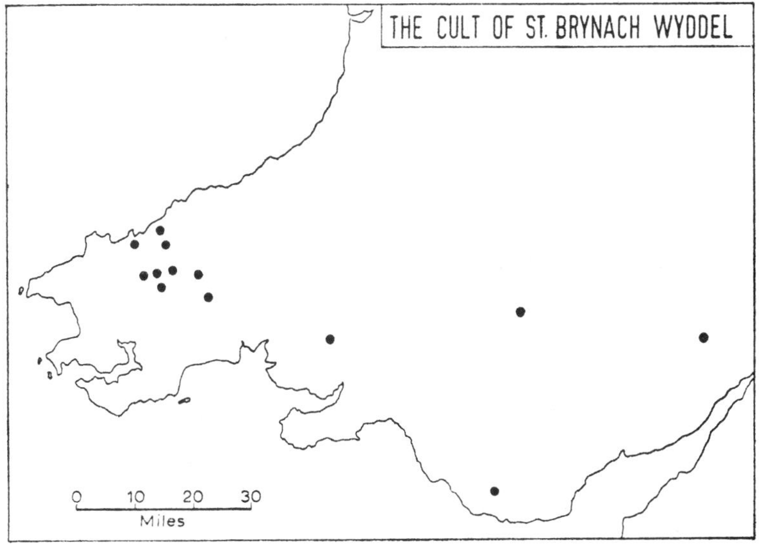

Fig. 24

Wyddel (Brynach the Irishman), but his *Life* appears alongside those of Cadoc and Illtud and other famous Welsh saints in the well-known MSS. Vespasian Axiv. In this *Life* Brynach is closely associated with Brychan—the half-Irish, semi-legendary king of Brycheiniog in whose territory, as we have seen, lies an important outlier of Ogham and Early Christian inscribed stones (Fig. 11). Here, too, are churches dedicated to St. Brynach. It may well be that neither Brynach nor Brychan ever existed as real persons. Indeed, some claim that Brychan is derived from Brycheiniog and not *vice versa*,[1] but this makes little difference to the cultural argument. In view of the close association between Brynach and the territory of the Ogham stones in South Wales it would be most fitting if the names of either Brynach or Brychan were recorded in Ogham on memorial stones, but, unfortunately, there is no evidence for this. It is, however, interesting to note that at St. Brynach's most important church at Nevern in north Pembrokeshire there are three Ogham stones. While by no means all Ogham inscribed stones are found in or near the precincts of Celtic churches in Wales (and even those that are, may have been removed there for safety by antiquarians in relatively recent times) we should not overlook the fact that there are several instances in Ireland of Ogham stones being set up near the oratory or monastic cell of a Celtic saint, as, for example, at St. Monchan's cell near Dingle in Co. Kerry.[2] If the Nevern stones have been associated with the precincts of the church from the earliest times (and there is no evidence to the contrary) then, culturally, the association is of the greatest significance.

The South-eastern Wales sub-area in prehistoric times consisted basically of the Vales of Glamorgan and Gwent. This was the area, as distinct from the mountain country that lay beyond, that received cultures from across the Severn Sea, or by landward penetration from Lowland Britain. From across the Severn channel came the multiple rampart forts of Iron Age B (Fig. 7) which, on the Welsh side, are found precisely in this area. From the point of view of the physical geographer this sub-area may be designated the *Bro* or the *Vale,* as distinct from the *Blaenau* or the *Uplands* that lay beyond. It has been shown elsewhere that in the Age of the Saints the *Bro* contained the vast majority of the dedications to such well-known saints as Dubricius, Cadoc and Illtud,[3] while interspersed among them are dedications to other saints representing cultural overspills from across the sea similar to those noted in Iron Age times.

(1) Jarrett, M. G., "*Excavations at Llys Brychan, Llangadog* 1961." Carmarthen Antiquary 1962, Vol. IV, pp. 2-8.

(2) Macalister, R. A. S., *Corpus Inscriptionum Insularum Celticarum,* Dublin 1945-49, No. 170.

(3) Bowen, E. G., *op. cit.*, p. 38, Fig. 8b.

Fig. 25 shows the known dedications to two selected saints. Those bearing the name of St. Cynog—one of the reputed sons of Brychan Brycheiniog—indicate clearly an upland association. This would be natural for any cult emanating from central Brecknockshire. In many ways the background evidence at our disposal would suggest that it represents a cultural overspill from the south-western sub-area, rather than anything specifically characteristic of the South-eastern province proper. For the latter we have to look at another dedication pattern—that of St. Dochau, also known as Dogwyn and Cyngar. The *Life* of St Cyngar is a very late one and is an unsatisfactory document of negligible historical value. In its present form it was probably written by John of Tynemouth, although it is not included in the Cottonian collection, Tiberius E 1. It is, however, printed in Capgrave's *Nova Legenda Angliae.*[1] St. Dochau is said to derive from a famous West country family and his monastery at Docco (now, St. Kew, alongside the Padstow-Fowey transpeninsular route in Cornwall) is considered by all scholars to be a very early and important Celtic sanctuary. Another famous settlement of his was at Congresbury in Somerset, so called from his other name Cyngar. If we follow Wade-Evans' interpretation of the topographical evidence[2] his chief centre in South-east Wales was at Llandough-juxta-Cardiff, and although not so important as some of the other famous monasteries in south-east Glamorgan (such as Llanilltud Fawr and Llancarfan) it, nevertheless, received much prominence in the early Middle Ages. The names of many of its abbots appear as witnesses in the Cartulary of Llancarfan, and especially in the famous *Liber Landavensis.* Wade-Evans shows that its daughter establishments, clearly associated with the founder saint, include Llandough, near Cowbridge; Llanddyfrwyr, which once existed at Tredunnock in Monmouthshire, and Bishopston in the same county. To these must be added a monastic cell at Cardiff, closely associated with the original Llandough. The overall pattern formed by these settlements is to be seen on Fig. 25. It bears a striking resemblance

(1) Baring-Gould, S. and Fisher, J., *Lives of the British Saints II,* 1908, p. 249.

(2) Wade-Evans, A. W. *Welsh Christian Origins,* Oxford, 1934, pp. 125-6.

to that formed by the multivallate forts of the Iron Age, whose immediate links, like those of St. Dochau, were with the South-west Peninsula. We must now turn to the sub-regions in the Age of the Saints in the Peninsula itself.

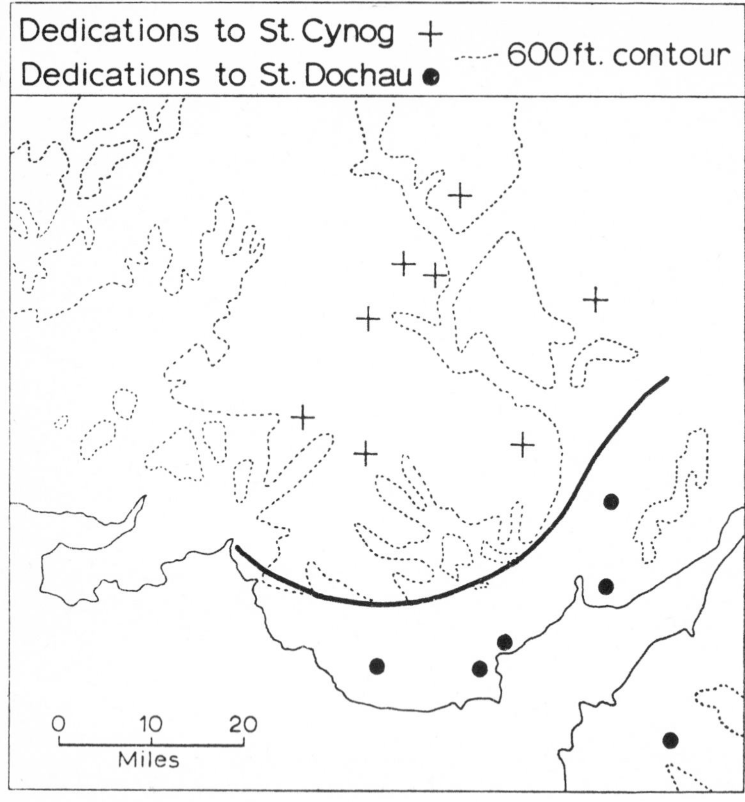

Fig. 25

Dedications to SS. Cynog and Dochau in S. E. Wales.

All the evidence from prehistoric times points to this peninsula being in the closest touch with Ireland and South Wales, on the one hand, and with Brittany on the other. In the Age of the Saints it formed a transit zone with a clearly marked sub-division. In the east was an extensive area including Somerset, Devon and eastern Cornwall, receiving saints from

South Wales that lay immediately opposite. Further west was a very much smaller area including the Scilly Isles and the extreme western portions of Cornwall, used for the most part by the "outer-sea" voyagers. The larger eastern area contains many Ogham inscribed stones, derived, as we have seen, from South Wales across the Severn Sea. In exactly the same areas as the Ogham stones occur we have numerous churches dedicated to Celtic saints with South Wales associations, among whom

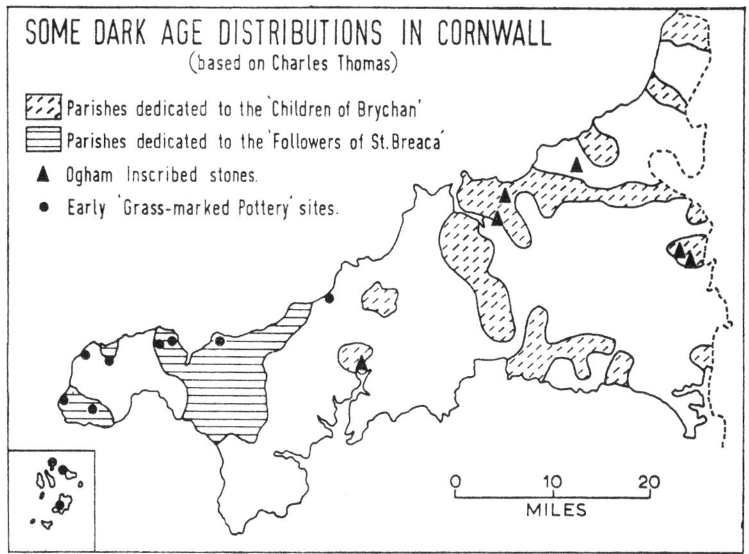

Fig. 26

the reputed Children of Brychan are clearly in evidence.(1) (See Fig. 26). Likewise, churches and chapels dedicated to Welsh saints from the lowland areas of Morganwg and Gwent (such as Dubricius and Cadoc) are found in these parts, including many others like St. Petroc whose associations appear to be with West Wales. The westernmost area of Cornwall has already been shown to be the area with the maximum Irish influence, comparable with South-West Wales and Dalradia.

(1) Thomas, Charles, "*Cornwall in the Dark Ages*" *Archaeology in Cornwall* 1933-58. Twenty-fifth Anniversary Number, *Proc. West Cornwall Field Club*, Vol. 2, No. 2, 1957-58, pp. 64-5.

Charles Thomas has shown that in the Dark Ages, while the major eastern area contained most of the South Wales-derived Ogham inscribed stones, the extreme south-western sub-region lying beyond the Perran Porth—Falmouth line was distinguished by archaeological sites yielding a characteristic 'grass marked pottery' comparable to the 'souterrain ware' of north-eastern Ireland, with which it is thought to be contemporary. It was in this area that Irish saints mainly settled. They are well represented by a group known collectively as the Followers of St. Breaca. These saints are all inter-connected through their *Lives,* which were lost at the Reformation, but are known to us from Breton sources, and from notes made by John Leland in the 16th century. In his *Itinerary* he quotes from the *Life of St. Breaca* which he found in Breage church in Cornwall. From this and other sources we gather that St. Breaca was born 'in parts of Leinster and Ulster', which is a point worthy of note in view of the corresponding archaeological evidence.[1] The party was obviously an important one, for we read that *'Breaca venit in Cornubiam comitata multis sanctis, inter quos Sinninus, qui Romae cum Patricio fuit, Maruanus monachus, Germochus rex, Elwen, Crewenna, Helena".* Thomas has shown clearly the correspondence between the area in which there are dedications to these Irish travellers and the early 'grass marked pottery' sites of roughly contemporary date. (Fig. 26). While the map makes a striking picture and vividly highlights the central theme of this book—namely the survival of prehistoric culture areas into the Age of the Saints—we must emphasize yet again that the greatest caution is necessary in approaching the hagiological material. Doble, for example, has shown that the equating of St. Sennan, the patron of the westernmost church in Cornwall, with St. Senan of Inis Cathy, (whose hermitage was on an island in the estuary of the Shannon), and who is included among the reputed followers of St. Breaca, is, in itself, extremely dangerous. St. Sennan of Cornwall in all available records is represented as a local female saint completely un-connected with the well-known male voyager—St. Senan of Inis Cathy. Nevertheless, details and

(1) Thomas, Charles, *op. cit.,* 1957-58 p. 67.

hagiological problems aside, the overall picture reconstructed from what has survived into the present-day landscape, indicates that in the Age of the Saints there existed in the South-west Peninsula two clearly marked cultural provinces, much in the same way as we presume there did throughout the long prehistoric ages that preceded the coming of Christianity into these Western lands.

CHAPTER V

IRELAND

FROM previous chapters it has been seen that Ireland lay very much in the path of the seaways, and from the beginning of the third millennium B.C. it seemed to be the goal of the many wayfarers in search of new lands for settlement and trade. In particular, emphasis must be placed on the intense activity that centred around the island in the last years of the Roman occupation of Britain, as it is to this period that the beginnings of Christianity in Ireland are to be assigned. In addition, it has been shown that from the earliest times two major cultural provinces developed behind the more important landing places, one in the north-east, receiving its cultures from Strathclyde, Galloway and the surrounding lands; and the other in the south and south-east, culturally associated with Northern Spain and Western France on the one hand, and with South-west Britain (more particularly, South-west Wales) on the other. It will be the aim of this chapter to show how both provinces are reflected again in the Age of the Saints and to evaluate their respective achievements in what is often termed the Golden Age of the Emerald Isle. Before doing so it is necessary to look more closely at the physical bases of the provinces concerned and also at the nature of the evidence which has survived concerning this period in place-names and other elements in the topography of modern Ireland.

The broad upland masses so characteristic of Wales and Scotland are not repeated across the water, for the Irish mountains are broken into many fragments and lie scattered around the coasts. They fall, however, into four major divisions which are broadly distinguished by age and structure; those of the north in Ulster; those in Connacht in the west; those of Munster in the south-west, and those of Leinster in the south-east. These broken masses encircle the Central Lowland where thin, dry, gravel or limestone soils have, from the earliest times offered a firmer foothold than the mountain land for settlement. The origins of this drift cover are to be sought in the glaciations of Pleistocene times. There were two main phases of glaciation—the older phase now generally referred to as the Eastern General, and a later phase, known as the Midland General, with a subsidiary glaciation centred in the mountains of Kerry and west Cork in the south-west. The older ice-sheet covered almost the whole of the island and much of the present sea-bed; while the later Midland General ice-sheet reached down to a line running from the mouth of the Shannon via Newcastle, Charlesville, Cahir to the Leinster chain, which it surrounded and penetrated. This moraine marks the southern limit of the drift lands and is a significant line in the historical geography of Ireland. We shall have occasion to refer to it later. The drift itself consists of drumlins and eskers—the former made up of more formidable ridges than the latter, and their distribution is useful in marking off very clearly the area in northern Ireland that appears most frequently to carry the intrusive cultures from across the North Channel, as distinct from the esker drift lands of the Midland plain which carry the intrusive elements penetrating westwards from the Meath coastlands (see Fig. 27).

We have seen that in the Celtic lands generally the most obvious evidence of the Age of the Saints surviving in the present landscape is the large number of churches still retaining the names of their presumed Celtic founders and very frequently it follows that the little settlement that has gathered around the church is known as the settlement of the saint in question. In Ireland, as in other parts of the Celtic world, dedications, as such, do not occur before the coming of the Normans, and early churches and monasteries were known by the name of the saint associated with them in one of three principal ways: possibly as reputed founder of the church itself, or as founder of the monastic family to which the church belonged, or, thirdly, because the saint's relics were housed in the church in question. On the other hand, a church or monastery may be known simply by a topographical name, or by some reputed incident in the life of the saint. Kildare (cill-dara—'the church of the oak') is thus named—the reference being to a certain favourite oak of St. Brigit. The most interesting feature in Ireland is the very large number of churches and monasteries that fall into

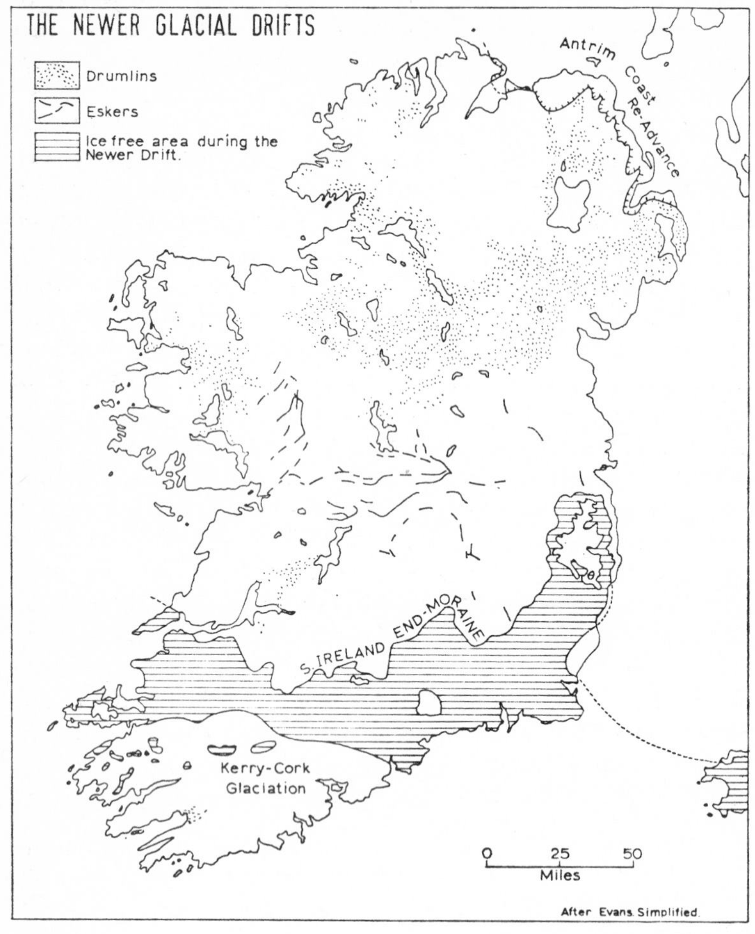

Fig. 27

the latter group, so that the saint's name does not form part of the present place-name as it does so frequently in Wales, Scotland, Cornwall and Brittany. It is true that we have Kilkenny and Kilronan and many other examples besides, but it is curious that when we examine an ancient list of Irish churches such names are few and far between. Likewise, if a study is made of a section of the Irish countryside it is difficult to discover much in the present place-name evidence concerning the patron saints of the churches of the locality. This is such an important feature of the Irish landscape and so vital for the development of this study that it is worthwhile instancing two examples of this rather special Irish feature before proceeding. One example is taken from a medieval ecclesiastical Taxation Roll for the Dioceses of Down, Connor and Dromore, and the other from a recent study of the exclusively rural diocese of Killaloe, which straddles the lower Shannon in the south-west. The Medieval Taxation was concerned with a law imposed on all churches by the Pope in support of the Crusades, and the return for the dioceses of Down, Connor and Dromore can be dated to 1306/7.[(1)] Over ninety per cent of the churches listed here have topographical names. For example, in the Deanery of Clondermod we have a reference to "the church of Miloc". This is not a reference to a church of an obscure Celtic saint, for the name derives from the Irish word 'miliuc' which occurs in several place-names in Ireland.[(2)] The word has clearly a topographical reference. P. W. Joyce says that 'Miliuc' is used for low marshy ground, or land bordering a lake or river,[(3)] so that 'the church of Miloc' as given in 1306/7 may mean little more than "the church by the river". Likewise, there are several references in the list to places called 'the church of the Desert' (Díseart or Dísert, in Irish) which, nevertheless, give us no indication whatsoever of the names of the saints who had first occupied these secluded retreats.

(1) Reeves, William, *Ecclesiastical Antiquities of Down, Connor and Dromore, Consisting of a Taxation of those dioceses, compiled in the year MCCCVI, with notes and illustrations.* Dublin, 1847.

(2) Royal Irish Academy, *Contributions to a Dictionary of the Irish Language*. Dublin, 1942-1966, and Myles Dillon, *Catalogue of Irish Mss. in the British Museum, Vol. III* by Robin Fowler. Revised by Myles Dillon, London, 1953.

(3) Joyce, P. W., *The Origin and History of Irish Names of Places,* 3 vols., London, 1910-13.

The recent detailed study of the Diocese of Killaloe[1] has shown that the authors have been able, in most cases, to list the names of the founder-saints associated with ancient sites and parish churches in the diocese, which have their origin in the Monastic Age, yet, the interesting feature is that it is most difficult to see the relationship (if any) between the names of the saints and the modern place-names. In many cases the old names have become completely Anglicised, or abbreviated, so that it is impossible on the face of things to see, for instance, any suggestion that Dromcliffe is connected with St. Connell, or Lorrha with St. Ruadan. All this is very different from place names like Llandeilo, Llanbadarn, Llanfrynach and Llangadog in Wales. Furthermore, in this context, it seems easy to explain the name Killaloe itself by relating it to the ancient name Cell-da-lua and so to St. Molua (allowing for the founder's hypocoristic prefix Mo—so often given to a Celtic saint), yet as D. A. Binchy has pointed out this name might equally well be derived from an Old Irish form Cell-dá-Lua meaning 'the church of the two waters', and so we revert to a topographical name once more. A study of the Irish Ordnance Survey's *Manuscript Memoirs* 1834-38, which contain such valuable topographical detail written by John O'Donovan[2] yields much the same evidence regarding the presence of Celtic saint names in the Irish landscape of the early nineteenth century, including those names mentioned by O'Donovan but not recorded on the early maps. It would appear, therefore, in the absence of any known list of Celtic 'dedications' in Ireland and the special nature of the place-name evidence as found in the present topography, that it is easier to work with distribution maps based on a series of well-known prefixes associated with Celtic church sites such as Kil,—Kill—Domhnach—Teampall—Díseart—, than to attempt to plot, as can be so easily done in Wales, Scotland, Cornwall and Brittany the churches bearing the name of a particular saint. We will depart from this procedure only in very special cases where sufficient evidence is available concern-

(1) Gleeson, D. F. and Gwynn, A., *A History of the Diocese of Killaloe,* Vol. I, Dublin, 1962.

(2) Ordnance Survey *Manuscript Memoirs* 1834-38 in Royal Irish Academy.

ing an individual saint, or a family of saints, to make a worthwhile distribution. The many philological and historical criticisms that can be levied against the use of the prefixes for our particular purpose will be discussed as occasion arises.

In order to appreciate the part played by the various cultural provinces in the evolution of Christian Ireland it is necessary at the outset to attempt to disentangle the Patrick legend. No serious historian can now accept the traditional view, that the history of Irish Christianity begins with the coming of Saint Patrick, or that the whole of the country had been converted by the time of his death. As is well known, there exists a copious literature on the saint, both ancient and modern. His biographers have been many and his legend magnified into a national epic. He has been split into a dual and even a triple personality, and much has been argued, and more guessed, from the vast store of hagiological literature that has gathered around the patron saint. Modern scholars are, however, greatly indebted to Binchy for his masterly analysis of the whole situation in the second volume of *Studia Hibernica* in an exhaustive article entitled *'Patrick and his Biographers: Ancient and Modern'*.[1] Binchy deals severely with most of what has been said in the past by famous commentators from Bury through to O'Rahilly, Esposito, Carney, Shaw, Bieler, Grosjean, John Ryan and Aubrey Gwynn, and attempts to outline the entire picture anew in the light of modern scholarship. His brilliant analysis of the situation makes it clear that little more can be said about the Patrick legend for a very long time to come. Nothing can be added in this chapter except the presentation of some distributional studies which clearly endorse what Binchy has said regarding the foundations of early Christian Ireland. Briefly, what appears to emerge is that considerable areas in the east and south of Ireland were apparently Christianized by British missionaries at an early date. Some knowledge of the existence of these Christians in Ireland seems to have reached Gaul and penetrated naturally to Rome—a fact which lies behind the famous action of Pope Celestine in sending

(1) Binchy, D. A., *Patrick and his Biographers: Ancient and Modern. Studia Hibernica.* Vol. 2, 1962, pp. 7-173.

a bishop (most likely, Palladius) *'ad Scottos in Christum credentes.'* Palladius' work was confined to the south-east of Ireland. Entirely independent of this we have the work of the historical Patrick. The few facts we know about him have to be gleaned from this own writings such as the *Confessio* and the *Epistola ad Coroticum.* They can be reduced to a few simple statements: that he was born in Britain, the son of a minor official who was also a deacon; that he was captured by Irish raiders and shipped to Ireland as a slave. He remained there for six years and finally escaped on a ship manned by a crew of pagans. The call to return to Ireland as a missionary continued to haunt his thoughts and visions, and after many years he returned to them and preached the Gospel. In this task he suffered great hardships and was exposed to criticisms and ridicule of all kinds, even by his own countrymen. Nevertheless, he continued and made many converts, penetrating into areas where no Christian missionary had ever set foot before. He tells us, too, that he was a Bishop and that he was determined to stay with his flock to the end . The main centre of his missionary activities lay in the north-east and he would appear to be the founder of Armagh, possessing, like many other saints in the Celtic lands a local and limited cult in these parts. There is nothing whatsoever in his own writings to suggest that he had ever been in Gaul, and it is much more likely that the ship in which he escaped sailed to Britain rather than to Gaul. After pointing out that there are extremely few references to Patrick in early Irish Christian literature before the eighth century—nothing about him in the great Penitentials composed by Finnian, Cummaine Fota and others, nothing in Cogitosus' *Life of St. Brigit,* or even in the writings of St. Columbanus, that great Irish patriot who mentions other Irish saints in his many letters to the Popes—Binchy shows that the origins of the great legend about St. Patrick are to be sought in the writings of Tírechán and Muirchú in the *Book of Armagh* and its derivatives, where the echoes of the historical mission of Palladius and the British Patrick were fused. The works of the latter as founder of Armagh were expanded and embellished, and a national hero—the founder of Christian Ireland was born.

As Binchy puts it "....I think it is all but certain that in the glorified Patrick of the Book of Armagh we have an amalgam of two saints....the great Apostle who founded Armagh and wrote the *Confessio,* on the one hand, and another missionary bishop, most probably Palladius who (whether or not he was also surnamed Patricius) had been responsible for the evangelization of the Midlands and Leinster. The first stage in the evolution of the Patrick legend, later destined to assume the proportions of a 'national epic', was a combination of the *acta* of Patrick and Palladius, which resulted in the virtual disappearance of the latter from Irish tradition except for a vague but obstinate memory of an 'older' Patrick."(1) As his legend assumed nation-wide importance, churches were dedicated to him all over the island, and it would be absurd to claim that because by the eighth or ninth century a number of churches, wishing to be associated with his labours, as expounded by Armagh, were named after Patrick, that anything concerning his real work and movements during his lifetime can now be gleaned from a study of their location. We shall be on safer ground if we retrace our steps and prepare distribution maps more in keeping with Binchy's major contentions. We can then discuss their significance and the resultant patterns can be compared with those of other distributions based on archaeological material of an earlier age.

Binchy lays great stress on the fact that the first series of Latin loan-words in Irish had already been borrowed before the mission of Palladius in 431. The religious vocabulary of this series, with the aid of certain old native words, was just sufficient to provide the necessary amount of Christian terminology in the initial stages. The list contained such urgently required words as *cruimther* (priest), *Cresen* (Christian) and *domhnach* (from Lat. *dominicum*) for church. Significantly, there is no word for bishop, no early Irish equivalent for *Episcopus.* Thus, the first stratum of Christian loan-words was established in the Irish language before the first bishop (Palladius) arrived(2). They were unquestionably introduced into the east and south-

(1) Binchy, D. A., *op. cit.,* 1962 pp. 167-8.

(2) Binchy, D. A., *op. cit.,* 1962 pp. 165-6.

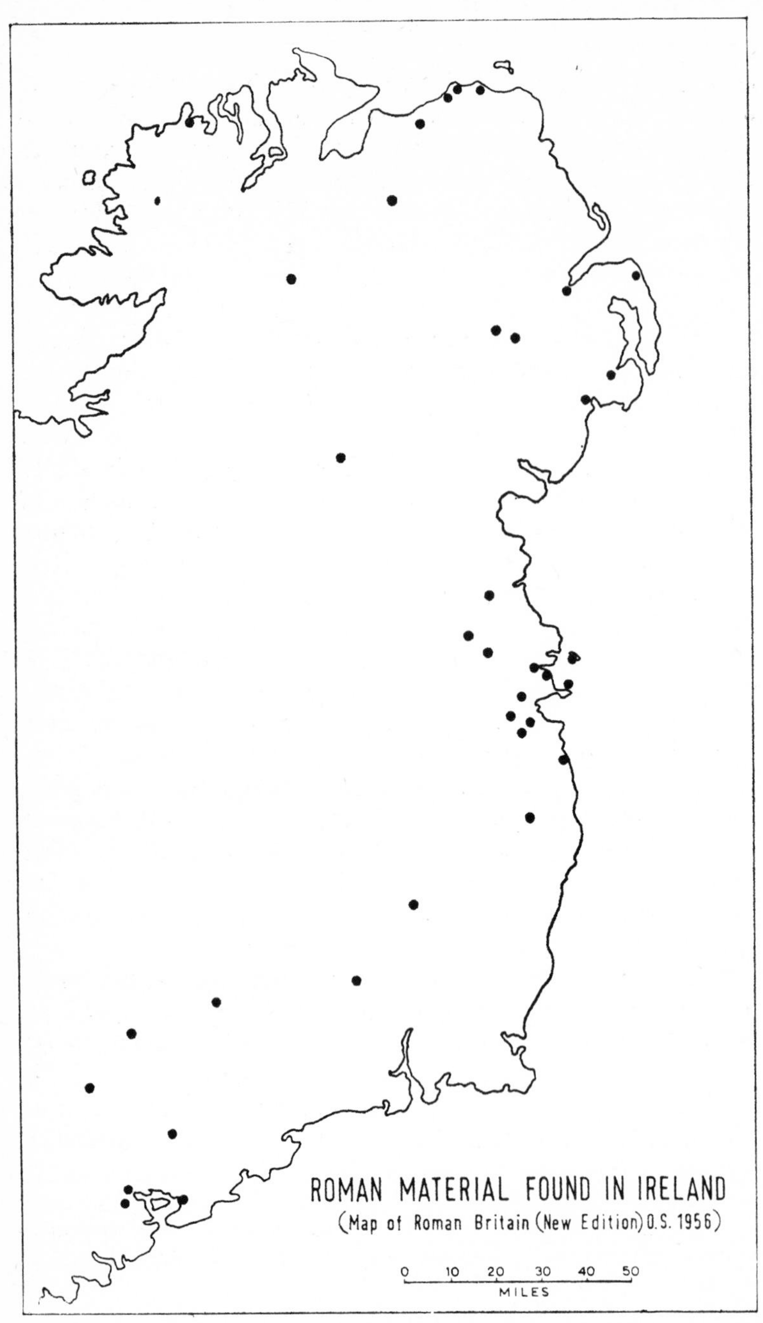
ROMAN MATERIAL FOUND IN IRELAND
(Map of Roman Britain (New Edition) O.S. 1956)
0 10 20 30 40 50
MILES

Fig. 28

east of the island by British Christians. Behind this picture we have the indisputable archaeological evidence for long continued contacts between Roman Britain and the east and south of Ireland. Fig. 28 is based on the third edition of the Ordnance Survey Map of Roman Britain which indicates, in addition, places where Roman material has been found in Ireland.(1) The finds represent the outcome of raids made by the Irish on Britain and Gaul and are the result also of some degree of trading. Equally significant is the fact that the objects found cover a great chronological range from those datable to the first century A.D. to pottery of Roman style which may be as late as the seventh century. This obviously covers the period during which contacts with early Christianity in Britain would be possible. There is, therefore, no question that trade and pillage contacts did exist and that pre-Palladian Christianity could easily have penetrated Ireland in the same way. It is worthwhile noting from the map that there is a tendency for the Roman material to occur in the north-east of the country; in the hinterland of Dublin; and again in the hinterland of Cork Harbour. It would be reasonable to interpret such a distribution by assuming that the great harbours of the south coast received Roman imports and influences direct from the Continent, while the harbours of the east coast received theirs from Britain. We shall have occasion to return to the importance of the links between the southern Irish harbours and the Continent in the immediate post-Roman period later, but the case for contacts between the east coast and Roman and post-Roman Britain is clearly established.

It is in this context that the historical geographer must consider the mission of Palladius and his associates in 431. Most students would agree that the initiation of this first official mission to Ireland is associated with a meeting between British bishops and Germanus during the latter's mission to Britain in 429. Germanus recommended Palladius, who was a deacon in his church at Auxerre, and who might even have accompanied

(1) The Irish evidence is based on S. P. O'Rìordáin's paper *"Roman Material in Ireland."* Proc. Roy. Irish Academy, Vol. 51 (1947) with additions by by Jope, E. M.

him on this famous mission to Britain. There is an ancient tradition mixed up with much spurious historical material that

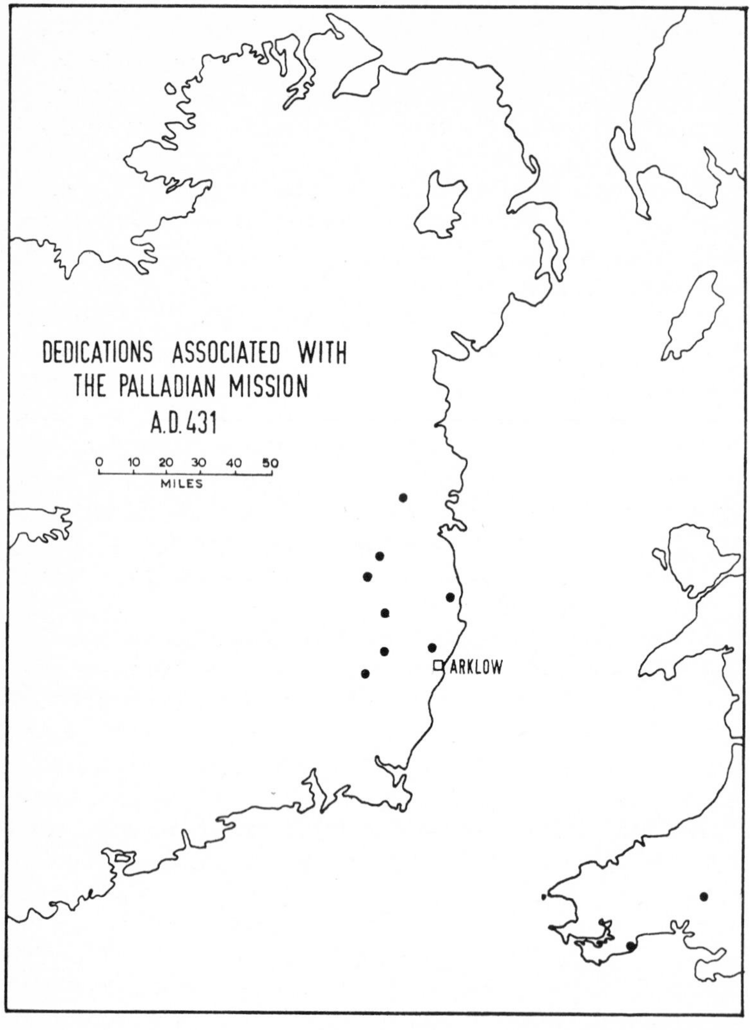

Fig. 29

Palladius landed near Arklow in Wicklow (Fig. 29). This may well be the case, for this region was in the closest contact with

Western Britain and since he came to work with those 'already believing in Christ', he might well have found some centres of British Christianity in the south-eastern area. He is, indeed, said to have founded three churches in Wicklow, now difficult to locate precisely, but one is significantly a *domhnach,* one a *ceall* and the third is known as Teach Romhanach.[1] Whether the other members of the mission, the auxiliary Gaulish bishops (Secundinus, Auxilius and Iserninus) arrived at the same time we do not know, but what is significant for the present argument is that they, too, have left their names associated with churches in the Midlands and the South-East. Binchy, in attempting to prove the fallacious nature of the later legend which made Secundinus the first bishop of Armagh, lays great stress on the location of the ancient church which bears his name at Dunehaughlin in County Meath. He obviously accepts this church as a fifth century foundation. "Even if we discount", he says, "all that is narrated of him (Secundinus) in the Patrician documents as legendary, his name and memory are still preserved in the place-name Dunehaughlin (Domhnach Sechnaill, or the Church of Sechnall)....and this evidence of an ancient cult, as the Bollandists have taught us, furnishes the most reliable information about the region in which we should locate the saint's principal activities".[2] In like manner Auxilius is associated with Killashee near Naas in Kildare, and Iserninus with Clonmore in County Carlow, and probably with Aghade and Kilcullen as well; the former in County Carlow, and the latter in County Kildare (Fig. 29). The Midlands and the South-East are, therefore, clearly indicated as the venue of this mission. The geographical implications of this location are important. Not only would we expect to find early Christian communities derived from Britain in these parts, but also it would appear that the Palladian mission very likely arrived in this part of Ireland from Gaul by way of South-west Wales, following the ancient sea-routes, partly by land across the peninsulas, and partly by the short sea-crossings. If they had come direct from

(1) McAirt, Sean, *The churches founded by Saint Patrick* Chap. V, *St. Patrick.* Thomas Davies Lectures (Ed. John Ryan). Published *Radio Eiréann* Dublin, 1958, p. 80.

(2) Binchy, D. A., *op. cit.,* 1962 p. 162.

Gaul by sea they would most likely have landed in the southern harbours rather than penetrated inland from the south-east coast as the distribution map suggests. Whether this is a valid assumption or not, there is interesting evidence to suggest that members of this mission had real contacts with south-west Wales, which we can but assume were made, while either the individuals in person, or their immediate followers, were moving along the ancient routes to south-eastern Ireland that passed this way. There is a church dedicated to Auxilius at St. Issells, near Tenby, in southern Pembrokeshire—a very significant landing place for the transpeninsular route, and more important still is the often overlooked Llanhernin (bearing the name of St. Iserninus) in the parish of Llanegwad in the mid-Tywi valley in Carmarthenshire. O. G. S. Crawford maintained that this was the oldest dedication in Wales,[(1)] situated alongside the well-established ancient routeway that linked southern Breconshire and beyond, by way of Llanymddyfri and the mid-Tywi valley to western Carmarthenshire, and thence beneath Mynydd Presely to Porth Mawr near St. David's in western Pembrokeshire. There is abundant archaeological evidence, as indicated by the Ogham inscribed stones (presumably contemporary with the age of Palladius), to say nothing of the many references in proto-historical literature of the use of this routeway between south-eastern Ireland and the south-eastern borderlands of Wales. The presumed movements of the Brychan family should be recalled in this connection, a matter to which further reference will be made later.

We can now turn to the Northern Province—the province in which the British Patrick laboured. His own writings help us very little in geographical matters. He tells us nothing about the years of his mission in Ireland, and gives us no information about his activities in the period between his escape from slavery and his return to the island as a missionary. We do not know from which part of Britain he embarked on his labours, or the districts in Ireland in which he preached. By inference we assume that his original home was in the Dum-

(1) Crawford, O. G. S., *Western Seaways* in *"Custom is King."* Essays presented to R. R. Marett, London, 1936, p. 190.

barton area, possibly somewhere in the Romanized districts south of the Antonine wall. It may well be that after his sojourn in Britain, following upon his escape, that it was from this—his home area—that he most likely left for Ireland once more. If such an assumption is correct, he would be following the most ancient route taken by man into Ireland, that from South-western Scotland to the Antrim-Down shores. Here was an area untouched by Palladius and his associates. They had worked, as we have seen, mainly in Leinster, the Midlands and parts of Connacht and Munster, an area more extensive than Muirchu and Tirechán, and the framers of the Patrick legend were prepared to admit. Yet, the whole of the North and most of Connacht—our Northern Province—were still untouched by the new faith. It would seem that Patrick established his centre at Armagh, although he may not have been Bishop of Armagh—these early missionary-bishops had wide spheres of influence. They moved from place to place and their pastoral work was not restricted to any territorial diocese.[(1)] Anyway, it is clear that Tirechán in the seventh century found the cult of St. Partick already well established at Armagh, and associated at this early date with elaborate liturgical practices linked to his feast day. No-one has been able to delimit the *patria* or *parochia* of this local saint—the real St. Patrick—before the propagandists of Armagh at a later date, not only combined his activities with those of Palladius and his associates further south, but raised the name of this composite personage on high as witnessed by the Book of Armagh. In this way his name was carried to places he had never visited and venerated among people to whom he had never preached. To attempt, therefore, to delimit Patrick's *parochia* by plotting all the ancient churches bearing his name in Ireland would be like attempting to plot all the Churchill Avenues and Churchill Ways in Britain, as an indication of how extensively the famous Prime Minister had visited his beleaguered people during the Second World War.

Sean MacAirt in an article, written on orthodox lines, concerning the churches said by Muirchú and Tírechán to

(1) Grosjean, P., *Analecta Bollandiana,* 62, p. 56.

have been established by Patrick in his missionary journeys makes a valuable suggestion in passing. He points out that

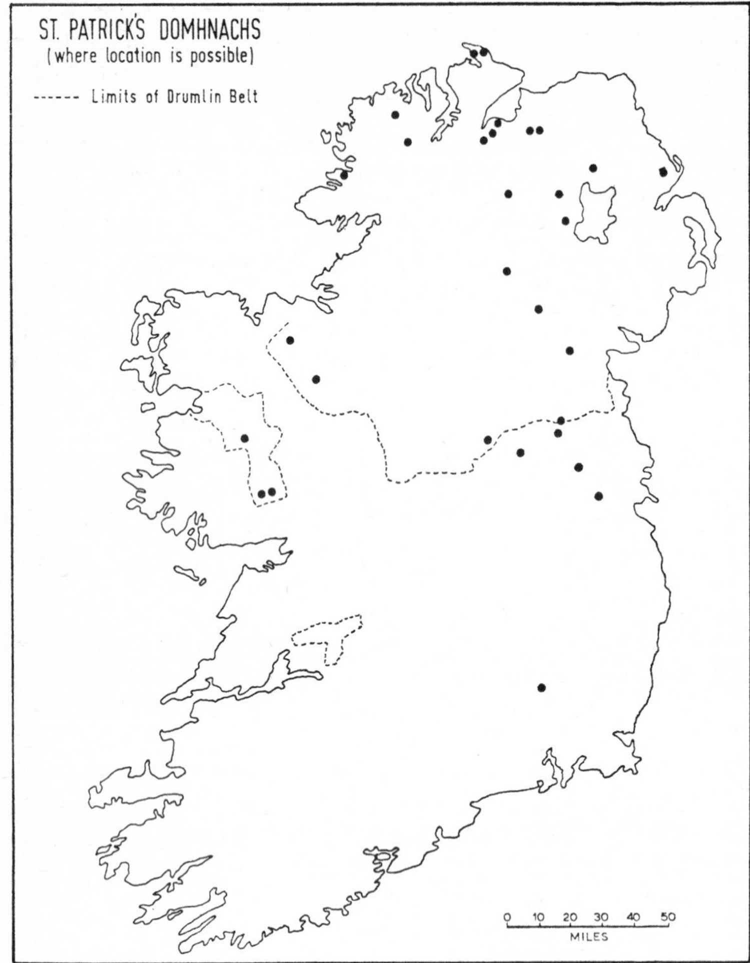

Fig. 30

there is considerable evidence for thinking that early churches incorporating the name *domhnach* were simply regional parish churches, non-monastic in character.[1] We have already noted

(1) MacAirt, Sean, *op. cit.*, 1958 p. 79.

that *domhnach* is a very early Christian loanword borrowed from British Latin during the period of the Occupation when the British Church was organised on diocesan lines, complete, where it existed, with Bishops, dioceses and possibly some regional 'parish' churches. The British Church was certainly non-monastic in character at this time.[1] This was the Christian environment in which Patrick was brought up and this is the type of church organization which he carried over to Ireland with him. When, therefore, we have a church called Domhnach Patraic it might represent a church with which Patrick had close associations during his missionary activities, before his name was blazoned far and wide in the interests of Armagh. If we can accept (with Binchy) Domhnach Sechnaill, it may be equally worthwhile plotting, after careful scrutiny, the Domhnach Patraics listed in Hogan's *Onomasticon* and re-checked by reference to O'Donovan's Ordnance Survey lists. The result is shown on Fig. 30. Whichever way we view the evidence on which this map is based it certainly reflects the North-eastern province, rather than anything in the Midlands or the South. A large number of sites appear to lie within easy access of the coast and most lie north-east of a line drawn from Sligo to Dublin. Such a pattern is clearly consonant with a culture that has impinged on the north-eastern quadrant of the island from the sea, and is exactly what we would expect to have resulted from the labours of the British Patrick. It is significant in this context that if we plotted all the known ancient *domhnachs* in Ireland, in addition to those carrying the name of Patrick, the vast majority would be found either in the North-east or in the hinterland of Dublin, or in other areas clearly associated with cultural overspills from Britain into Ireland in the late Roman period.

The earliest organization of the Irish Church as introduced by Patrick and his predecessors was based, as we know, on the Roman towns scattered throughout Western Europe. The towns were the seats of the Bishops and from them their dioceses were administered. Such an urbanized organization naturally

(1) Three British Bishops with territorial Sees attended the Council of Arles in 314 A.D.

proved unsuitable for the tribal society which then existed in Ireland, Wales and Scotland. Here there was no urban tradition—clusters of farmsteads alone covered the countryside. So the Roman diocesan system was replaced by the Celtic pattern in which the diocese gave way to a federation of monastic communities each with its *parochia* under the jurisdiction of the heir of the founder-saint of the chief monastery.[1] As early as the end of the fifth century Armagh had re-organized itself on monastic lines. We have already shown in a previous chapter how the monastic idea emanating from the Desert Fathers in Egypt spread throughout the Western Church in the second half of the fourth century. The Church in Gaul was particularly affected, and with ever increasing pressure from barbarian incursions, Gaulish Christian refugees, using the western sea routes carried the monastic ideal with them into Britain and undoubtedly into Ireland as well. It is obvious that the impact of these new ideas was first felt in the southern Irish Province which lay in the direct path of the sea routes. We must now seek what evidence is available to support this contention.

If we are correct in assuming that the Eastern form of the ascetic life reached Southern Ireland along the sea routes, the question arises as to where it first took root on Irish soil and where was its chief centre of diffusion. Mrs. Nora Chadwick has given much thought to this question recently[2] and has been able to show that literary material was entering the Munster coastlands at this time from Mediterranean countries as far afield as North Africa and Spain. Special reference is made to the island of Dair-inis at the mouth of the river Blackwater in Munster, on which was located a very early monastery where the *Collectio Canonum Hibernensis* was drawn up—this being one of the earliest literary works of the Irish Church.[3] The work has close associations with Brittany which proves that the well established Breton-South Ireland sea-route was functioning

(1) Binchy, D. A., *op. cit.* 1962, p. 169 and Chadwick, N. K., *op. cit.*, 1963 p. 77

(2) Chadwick, N. K., *op. cit.*, 1963 pp. 111-18.

(3) Kenney, J. F., *Sources for the Early History of Ireland,* New York, 1929. p. 248 and note 273.

fully at this time. Likewise, this Blackwater monastery and the important confederation of Munster monasteries of which it was the centre were also in the closest touch with other aspects of Western Mediterranean culture. Père Grosjean has recently been able to show that the Irish *De Mirabilibus*, commonly known as the Pseudo-Augustine was almost certainly written at Lismore, and Mrs. Chadwick points out(1) that the author of the Pseudo-Augustine with his references to Carthage and Eusebius was evidently a partaker in the literary triflings in Gaul at this period and later, when the names of great authors were assumed as a kind of *nom-de-plume* without the slightest intention to deceive. Another aspect of the direct contact of Ireland with the Continent in the early stages of Western eremiticism is shown by the popularity of the cult of St. Martin of Tours in the island at an early date. The evidence for this is overwhelming.(2) If we bear in mind the nature and significance of the western sea-routes, it is reasonable to assume that it is from Ireland, rather than from the little Kentish group, that all the early dedications to St. Martin in Western Britain are almost certainly derived. This alone can explain his associations with Whithorn, southern Herefordshire,(3) and possibly Somerset. The prestige of the saint in Ireland can be gauged by the fact that his *Life* by Sulpicius Severus was included in the Book of Armagh. It is considered by experts to be a very early version of the *Life* which possibly reached Ireland from Gaul before 460 A.D. Here is the saint who is credited with the introduction of monasticism into the West, so we would naturally expect the influence of his cult on early Christianity in Ireland to have been considerable. The southern monasteries could not have escaped its impact. Later on, literary work at Lismore, Ardmore and other centres in this region stimulated the great ascetic communities of North Munster and Leinster such as Clonferta-Molua, Mendrochet, Tamlaght, Roscré, Clonenogh (the monastery of St. Fintan), and Terryglass in the west. Ultimately the

(1) Chadwick, N. K., *op. cit.*, 1963 p. 113.

(2) Grosjean, P., *Gloria postuma St. Martini Turonensis apud Scottos et Britannos*. Ann. Boll. LV (1937) pp. 300-345.

(3) Rix M.M., *The cult of St. Martin in Wales*, Hereford Diocesan Messenger, October, 1957.

monastic idea spread northward and came into contact with the churches established by the Palladian missionaries and by St. Patrick. If, as we have suggested, the cult of St Martin with its monastic ideal had gained some adherents in Ireland, hostility towards the more conservative form of episcopacy represented by St. Patrick might well have aroused a sharp difference in ecclesiastical quarters similar to that of which Sulpicius Severus complains of in Gaul. As the cult of St. Patrick was elevated at Armagh so did the cult of St. Martin recede in Ireland.

Before leaving the contacts between Southern Ireland, the Continent and the Mediterranean world at this time, a special point should be made of the confirmatory evidence now being derived from archaeological sources. As long ago as 1934 A. W. Clapham[(1)] showed that certain art motives, such as the marigold design, probably reached Ireland by the same sea-routes from the south. The marigold pattern may be looked upon as the most characteristic feature of Visigothic art. It occurs all over Spain, and at Lisbon, and occasional examples are found in France from Poitiers southwards. More recently J. N. Hillygarth has persued the matter further and linked the evidence with Galician influences in the spread of monastic ideas into Ireland.[(2)] To all this must be added evidence which we have already considered, concerning the imported Dark Age pottery discussed by Ralegh Radford (see Chap. 1—and Fig. 3). It is significant that pottery of this type occurs in Ireland at Ballycatteen, Garranes and Garryduff (all in the hinterland of Cork harbour), Ballinderry in the western mid-lands near the Shannon, Lagore and Nendrum—more to the north and east. We have had occasion earlier in this chapter to note the concentration of Roman material in the hinterland of Cork Harbour, which was clearly as important a southern entry as that of the Blackwater and the Barrow in Munster. In the

(1) Clapham, A. W., *The origins of Hiberno-Saxon Art, Antiquity* VIII, 1934, pp. 43-57.

(2) Hillygarth, J. N., *Visigothic Spain and Early Christian Ireland.* Proc. Roy. Irish Acad. 62, 1962, pp. 190-1.

early centuries of the Christian era there lived in the neighbourhood of Garranes and Garryduff (sites where sherds of this Mediterranean pottery have been found—some with Christian symbols marked on them) an Irish people known as the Corcu Loirgdge for whom their genealogists claimed that they were the first in all Ireland to receive Christianity.[1] Who knows but that their claim might not be fully justified? Another distinguished archaeologist (Leslie Alcock) maintains that this imported pottery can be dated much earlier than Ralegh Radford suggests. Alcock would place it around about 450 A.D. This would then imply direct contact by sea between Southern Ireland and the Eastern Mediterranean (especially if the glass fragments at Garryduff in Co. Cork are Egyptian in origin) so that the basic eremitical ideas in Celtic Christianity in Ireland could have been derived directly from their source in Egypt, without reference to Gallo-Roman links of any kind. On the contrary, the concept of the sea-routes here presented, with their many branches and intensive activity, offered ample opportunity for the spread of eremitical and other ideas into both Britain and Ireland by a vast variety of routes in early Christian times. We shall have to return to this matter later.

Whatever its origins and by whatever routes the incoming monasticism reached early Christian Ireland it ultimately fused with the traditional Roman Christianity associated with the Patrick-Palladian complex. In order to understand how this fusion was made possible we must digress somewhat to examine in greater detail the nature and administrative structure of the great Irish monasteries that grew up upon these foundations. No real distinction should be drawn between the larger monasteries and their saintly founders (who according to the Irish Catalogus belonged to the Second Order of Saints) and the Anchorites who were classed as belonging to the Third Order. It can be shown that both belong to the same monastic movement. The Anchorites were clearly associated with the larger monasteries which developed as the monastic idea spread. We know, for example, from later records that the older monks, in-

(1) O'Riordáin, S. P., *Roman Material in Ireland.* Proc. Roy. Irish Acad., Vol. 51, C3, 1947, p. 39.

cluding abbots and bishops would frequently retire to join the hermit monks. These withdrawals would extend over considerable periods, and were in no sense courtesy or routine visits. The important point is, therefore, that the solitaries are an integral part of the earliest Celtic monastic pattern and are neither a "later development nor a reform."[1] Sometimes the sites that the holy men occupied developed into tiny churches or oratories which continued to bear their names—others, in due course, developed into some of the greatest monasteries in the land. At other times, the original tiny church decayed and all that now remains in the countryside are the stark ruins of a lonely and austere settlement. Frequently everything has vanished. The prefix cill–ceall–or kill–kil–was frequently associated with settlements of this type, and place-names with these prefixes tend to cover the map of Ireland. On the whole, a distribution map would indicate their predominantly southerly location and represent a cartographical confirmation of what has already been discussed. Nevertheless, there are several difficulties involved in preparing such a map, the chief of which being that the prefix kil(l)—might sometimes mean a forest and, of course, many of the names are likely to be of recent origin. It would appear, therefore, more satisfactory to select some other prefix of a more specialized kind, such as *Díseart, Teampall, Uaimh* (spelunca), or *inis* (insula) to indicate broadly those parts of Ireland where eremitical influences were most strongly felt. With the assistance of modern scholars in this field, particularly Dr. Liam de Paor and Dr. Gearoid MacNiocaill, I have selected *Díseart* (Dísert) and *Teampall* as the most satisfactory indices to use, in spite of the fact that the latter, in particular, may well contain a number of rather later examples. The former prefix, however, is an obvious link with the East, quite independently of Gaul. It is derived from *desertum,* the original home of the hermits in Egypt, Syria and Palestine, and its use in Celtic lands is clearly linked with its original connotation. The resultant distribution is shown on Fig. 31. The map speaks for itself and indicates clearly that this is an intrusive element, which although it has spread generally over the whole of

(1) Chadwick, N. K., *op. cit.*, 1963 p. 117.

Ireland is clearly a dominant feature of the South. In order to give the distribution a clearer definition Mr. R. Neville Hadcock (who was so closely associated with the preparation of the

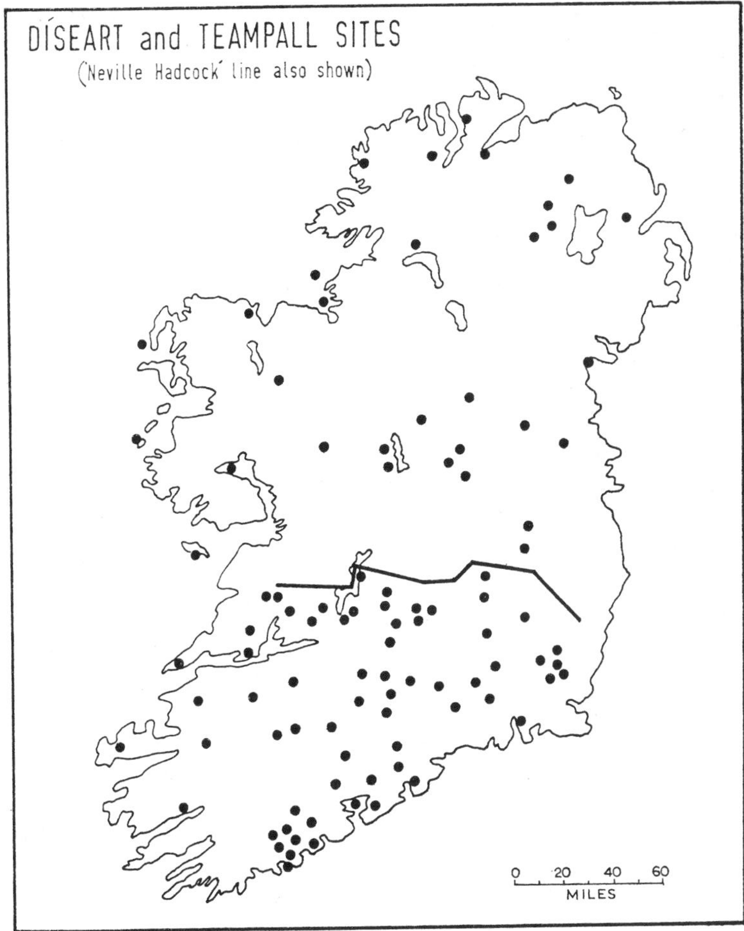

Fig. 31

Ordnance Survey map of Monastic Ireland),[1] has suggested to me that it would be worthwhile inserting a line running from

(1) Léarscáilíocht Éireann, Map of Monastic Ireland. Ordnance Survey, Phoenix Park, Dublin, 1959, and Second Edit., 1964.

Aghowle, Morne, Clonenagh, Agaboe, Monainche, Terryglas to Inishcaltra on the map, as this line appears to him to mark the southern limit of the great monastic houses established by St. Finnian of Clonard and his followers in the Central Plain in the 6th and 7th centuries. This line, following as it does the southern margins of the Great Central Plain, and approximately the great end-moraine of the Midland glaciation (see Fig. 27), is quite spectacular, and gives some indication of the distinction that might exist between the Ireland that was tributary to the great southern harbours, and first received monastic ideas, and the Ireland of the Midland Plain.

We cannot, however, leave the question of the introduction of monasticism into Southern Ireland without reference to the influences that came from sources other than Gaul, Galicia and the Mediterranean. These entered south-eastern Ireland by way of the much used Pembrokeshire-Wicklow crossing. Indeed, most textbooks maintain that the part played by Welsh saints like Cadoc and David was all important in this context. Whatever the details may have been, no-one can deny the very close cultural relations between the two countries at this time. We have already had occasion to note this in the case of the Ogham inscribed stones and the possibility of the Palladian mission reaching Ireland by this route. In a previous chapter dealing with Cornwall we drew attention to the argument of Charles Thomas, who emphasized the close connection between Cornwall, South Wales and Southern Ireland at this time as indicated not only by the Ogham inscribed stones, but by the presence of church dedications in the South-west peninsula to the famous Children of Brychan from South Wales.(1) Thomas did not indicate the influence of this famous family of Welsh saints in Ireland, but in view of the great importance of this group of saints in the hagiology of the Dark Ages it would be interesting to map what we can of their location in that country. Such a distribution might well show the influence of the 'Welsh' church in Ireland during this important formative period and, at the same time, show those areas where a second infusion of monastic ideas took place. The preparation of the map is

(1) See p. 109.

fraught with the usual difficulties. The list of the 'Children of Brychan' is probably far from complete and the legendary

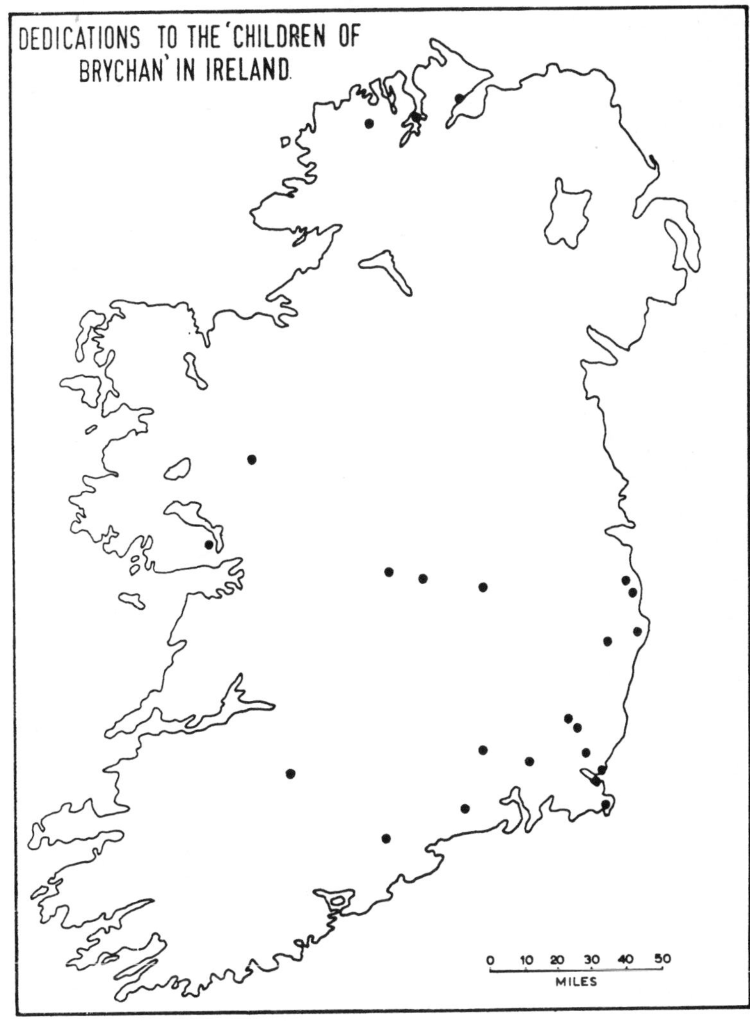

Fig. 32

associations considerable. The following saints are recorded in Irish hagiological literature as belonging to this family:

Mochonoc, Morgaroc, Cairpre, Molioc or Dalioc, Diradh, Dublan, Caenna, Carmine, Plane, Malach or MoElloc. The resultant distribution of sites said to be associated with their names is sufficiently clear to indicate a pattern in keeping with influences emanating from South-west Wales, and represents for the historical geographer a cartographical confirmation of an important historical contention that the Celtic Church in Wales (itself definitely monastic in character) played at least some part in the Christianization of Ireland (Fig. 32).

We have now surveyed the cartographical evidence for the incoming of Celtic monasticism into southern Ireland in addition to discussing the impact of the Palladian mission and the activities of the British Patrick in the north and north-east. It remains for us to study in more detail the subsequent story in central Ireland, where it would appear that these northern and southern influences met and fused to result in the establishment of the great Irish monastic houses of the 6th and 7th centuries. Traditionally, it is claimed that St. Finnian of Clonard was the pioneer of this Irish monasticism as we find it in the 6th and 7th centuries, and modern scholarship sees nothing improbable in this.[1] St. Finnian of Clonard (died 540 (A.V.) or 552 (A.I.)) with his contemporary Enda of Aran are said to have been the first of the Irish saints to recognize the opportunities which monasticism offered of combining the discipline of the religious life with good learning. Here we see one of the more important elements in the cultural fusion. The rigid discipline of the religious life was tied up in the Celtic Church with the asceticism that had come along the sea-ways from the Eastern Mediterranean. The early solitaries, in particular, were like many of the early Christians, suspicious of ancient learning, as it was so closely associated with the pagan world. This withdrawal from learning was not, however, a feature of the Western Church in Italy and Gaul—these churches were organized on a territoral rather than on a monastic basis, and they were the successors of Rome in so many ways. It has been pointed out elsewhere that a venera-

(1) Hughes, Kathleen, *The Cult of St. Finnian. Irish Hist. Studies,* Vol. IX, 1954-55, p. 26.

tion of classical learning was associated with such saints as Dubricius, Cadoc and Illtud in south-eastern Wales, when a cultural fusion of a type similar to that now described in the southern Central Plain of Ireland developed in that area.[1] Likewise, the British Patrick, whatever else we know of him, could write Latin and knew that his writing was grammatically poor and defective. Thus, in the great Irish monasteries the strict discipline of the religious life was joined to the cultivation of good learning, and it is both as a Holy Man and as a Master of Irish saints that St. Finnian is remembered. "Thereafter", we are told "the saints of Ireland came to Finnian from every point to learn wisdom by him, so that there were three thousand saints along with him, and from them, as the learned know, he chose twelve high bishops of Ireland. And the learned and the writings declare that no one of those three thousand went from him without a crozier, or a gospel, or some well-known sign: and around those reliquaries they built their churches and their monasteries afterwards".[2] Although there is no completely reliable evidence earlier than the 9th century for this scholarly reputation of Clonard, all the traditions agree that a pioneer school did develop here and this is intrinsically probable. Clonard was also extremely well placed geographically to command students from all parts of Ireland and, indeed, from overseas, as the Meath coastlands were well-known landing places for voyagers using the sea-ways. Moreover, the monastery was situated in one of the most fertile portions of the great plain and could, even in these primitive times, support quite a considerable community (see Fig. 33).

Another aspect of the culture fusion between the two versions of early Christianity entering Ireland that seems to have occurred in these larger monasteries was of an administrative nature. We have already noted how the territoral bishopric system was entirely unsuited for the Irish pastoral, non-urban, society. The monastic system whereby each great monastery

(1) Bowen, E. G., *The Settlements of the Celtic Saints in Wales,* Cardiff, 1954, pp. 44-45.

(2) Stokes, Whitley (Ed.), *The Lives of the Saints* from the *Book of Lismore,* Oxford, 1890, 2640 ff.

was independent and exercising control over a number of scattered daughter houses was a very much more suitable

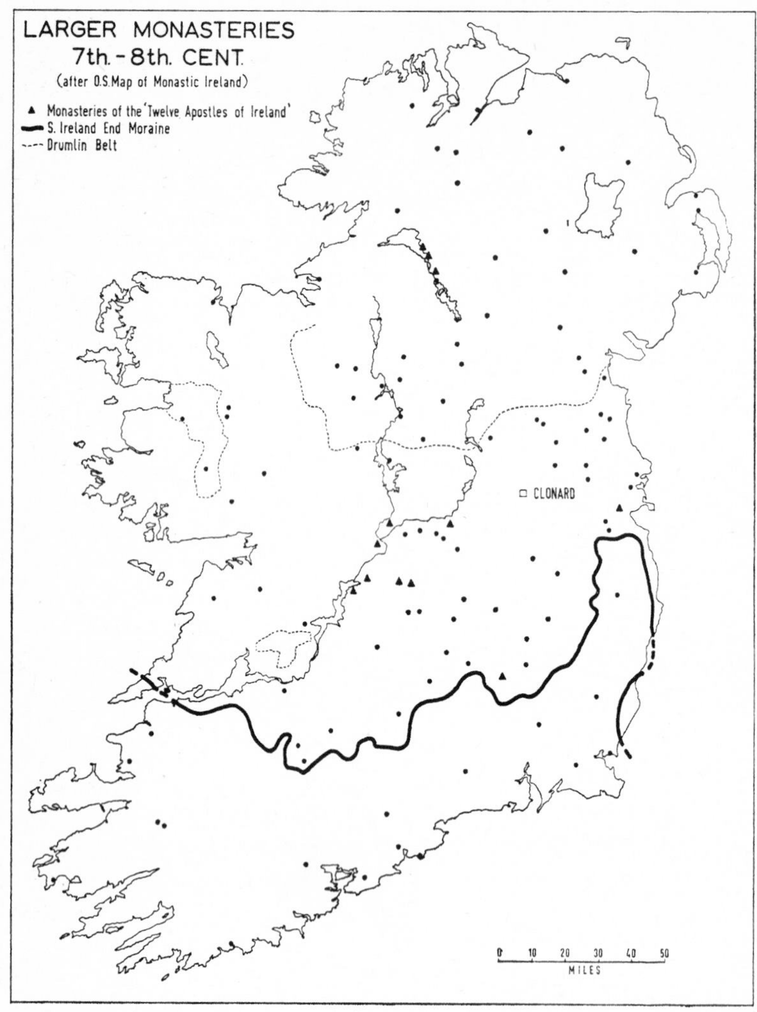

Fig. 33

system. An abbot presided over each monastic house and dealt with all the day-to-day problems and often went into retreat to one of the daughter houses, or to some solitary place.

Yet the bishops integrated with this system. They, too, coming from another tradition made their principal dwellings in the monasteries along with the abbots. The bishop had no authority in the economy or organization of the monastery and reserved his attentions for the ritualistic side, dealing with such matters as ordination, confirmation and consecration.[(1)] Sometimes the bishops, too, went outside to the daughter houses, and also to preach and instruct the people. Another aspect of the fusion shows itself on the technical side. These great monasteries were noted not only for their learning and their piety, but also for their great artistic achievements, especially the art of illuminating manuscripts. An entry in the Annals of Ulster proves that at least one individual managed to combine all these functions, for in the year 830 is recorded the obit of one Cormac mac Suibhne, Abbot of Clonard, 'scriba et episcopus'.[(2)] In order to look at this matter distributionally, which is the main function of this work, it might be worth reverting to a further consideration of the traditional Twelve Apostles of Ireland who are said to have received their training under Finnian, and then moved away from Clonard to establish their own houses. It is certain that many who are named in the traditional list were dead long before Finnian's day, or even unborn when he died, so that they can not claim to have been pupils of the great master. Nevertheless, the list is worthy of consideration for our purpose, for not only does it contain the names of some of the most venerated of Irish saints such as Ciaran of Clonmacnoise and the great Columcille, but it represents at least what later writers thought of the sphere of influence of St. Finnian, and his great school of learning at Clonard. The full list is as follows: Ciaran of Saigher, Ciaran of Clonmacnoise, Columcille, Brendan of Birr, Brendan of Clonfert, Colman of Tir da glas, Molaisse of Daiminis, Cainnech, Ruadan of Lothra, Mobi of Glas Noiden, Senel of Cluain Inis, and Nannid of Inis Maige Sam. The twelve religious houses concerned, together with Clonard are shown on Fig. 33, set amidst the pattern formed by the location of all the known monasteries

(1) Chadwick, N. K., *op. cit.*, 1963 pp. 77-78.

(2) *Annals of Ulster*, A.V.I. 326.

of the 6th and 7th centuries, based on the Ordnance Survey map of Monastic Ireland. The significance of the southern margin of the Central Plain as an important north-south contact zone is clearly brought out by the density of the distribution of the monasteries shown. The southern limit of the Midland glacial moraine has also been added to intensify the pattern. Before leaving this section it must not be assumed that the contact between the northern spreading monks carrying the monastic concept, and the people of the north and centre was always a peaceful one. It is well to remember that it was often hostile, as witnessed by the legends of the expulsion of St. Mochuta from Rahan. King Blathmac and his brother Díarmaid together with the chiefs of Meath requested Mochuta, together with his monks, to leave his monastery at Rahan and return southwards to his native territory in Munster. When he refused, he was forcibly ejected and finally made a new settlement at Ardmore where the political climate was more favourable.[(1)] Indeed, it can be argued that monastic affairs on the southern fringe of the Central Plain, and elsewhere in Ireland during the Celtic period, can most simply be explained as a reflection of the secular, and especially the political affairs of the region with which they were closely and dependently connected.[(2)] This general statement is true of the affairs of Clonard as well,[(3)] but it does not in any way invalidate the general argument put forward in this chapter.

No one who has studied the cultural life of Ireland throughout prehistoric times can overlook the fact that the island was no mere receiver of cultures by way of the sea-routes—she blended that which was received, and, in turn, re-diffused much of that which she had made her own. This extremely important point is put succinctly by Sir Cyril Fox—"Ireland was by no means a sleeping or merely receptive partner in the varied life of these islands in early days: she reveals an active creative life of her own based on the Mediterranean culture which she

(1) O'Hanlon, John, *Lives of the Irish Saints,* Vol. V, p. 254.

(2) de Paor, Liam, in personal correspondence with the author, September, 1963.

(3) Hughes, Kathleen, *op. cit.*, 1954-5, p. 16.

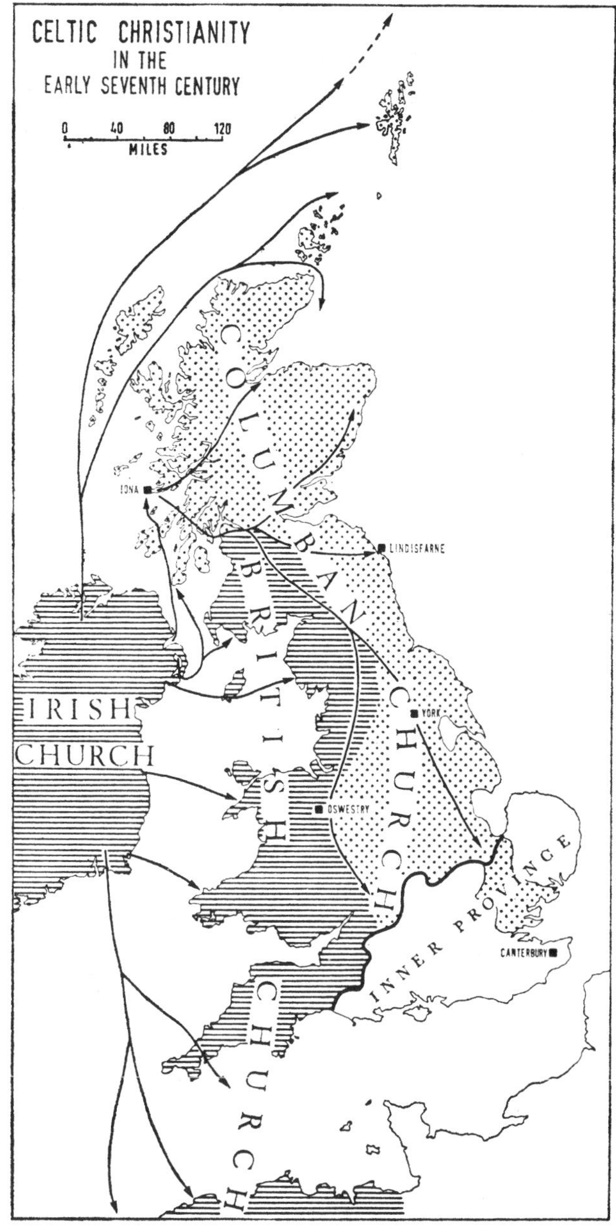

CELTIC CHRISTIANITY
IN THE
EARLY SEVENTH CENTURY
0 40 80 120
MILES
IONA
LINDISFARNE
YORK
OSWESTRY
CANTERBURY
IRISH CHURCH
COLUMBAN CHURCH
BRITISH CHURCH
INNER PROVINCE

Fig. 34

received by the Atlantic route in Neolithic and Early Bronze Age times and developed. This creative power...invigorated the Highland Zone of Britain, primarily the opposite coasts of the St. George's Channel and the Irish Sea, and South-western Scotland... Occasionally, the shores washed by the Irish Sea are universally affected as in the case of the Megalithic civilization."[1] It was exactly the same in the hey-day of Celtic Christianity in the early seventh century (see Fig. 34). One of the movements associated with Celtic Christianity was destined to carry the Faith further into Britain than the Megalithic people carried theirs, three millennia before. St. Columba had crossed over to the Irish colonists in Western Scotland and established his famous monastery at Iona. Soon the whole of Scotland beyond Strathclyde was involved, following upon the saint's famous interview with King Brude Mac Maelchon near Inverness; while to the southwards the famous routeway linking Iona to the Clyde by way of the Crinan Water opened up progress not only towards the eastern Scottish lowlands, but particularly south-eastwards to Lindisfarne, where Irish Christian monuments and illuminated manuscripts were soon to appear on the Northumbrian coast. Meanwhile, religio-political factors were at work that tended to increase still further the influence of the Columban church. In 597 St. Augustine had landed in Kent and the Kentish king had been persuaded to Christianity. Further progress of Roman Christianity was, however, slow. Ethelbert's attempts to convert the king of East Anglia came to nothing and his success with his nephew, the king of Essex, turned out to be only temporary, as this territory reverted to paganism after Ethelbert's death. As we know, the marriage of a Kentish princess to King Edwin of Northumbria brought the southern Christianity northwards for a very brief period, but after Edwin's death in battle there was a widespread reversal to paganism in the north. Wessex seems to have received a missionary direct from Rome, independent of Canterbury, while Sussex and the Isle of Wight held stubbornly to their paganism. Following upon Edwin's

(1) Fox, Sir Cyril, *The Personality of Britain,* Fourth Edition, Cardiff, 1947, pp. 43-44.

death, the situation in Northumbria changed markedly. The sons of Edwin's predecessor and rival had taken refuge in Iona during his reign and had been converted to Christianity there. So when Oswald returned to the throne of Northumbria it was only natural that he should turn to Iona for Christian missionaries. When, later, Oswald himself and his successor Oswiu became overlords of much of the territories in the south, it was the church of Northumbria that brought about the conversion of all of the Midlands and the re-conversion of Essex.[(1)] The resulting overall situation when expressed geographically (see Fig. 34) brings out a further interesting and vital point for the historical geographer, indicating once more how the Celtic Christian period is such a surprising reflection of what we now know happened several times previously in prehistoric times. When Fox wrote of the cultural relationships between Ireland and Britain he not only emphasized that Ireland was no "sleeping or merely receptive partner", but that "whenever culture centred in Ireland (as distinct from Irish trade) expands, its force is spent in the Highland Zone and in the northern outliers of the Lowland Zone (East Yorkshire). It does not effectively reach across the mountain barriers to southern England."[(2)] In the case of Celtic Christianity this culture would appear to have transgressed even "the northern outliers of the Lowland Zone". If however, we revert to the tripartite cultural division of Britain into an Outer, Intermediate and Inner Province as discussed in Chapter II (a division we considered to be much more satisfactory than Fox's simpler dual arrangement), we see from Fig. 34 an almost perfect correlation between the southern limits of the penetration of the Columban church at the hands of Oswald and Oswiu and the outer limits of the Inner Province in southern England. It was here rather than on "the northern outliers of the Lowland Zone" that this Irish-based Christian culture spent its force.

We cannot close this chapter on Ireland as "a non-sleeping partner" of Britain in the Age of the Saints without reference to the fact that she was, indeed, so very active and wide awake

(1) Whitelock, D., *The Beginnings of English Society,* 1956, pp. 155-9

(2) Fox, Sir Cyril, *op. cit.*, 1947, p. 44.

at this time that her activities embraced lands far beyond her partner's shores. We have already seen how St. Brendan and his followers were carried northwards into the Arctic Seas to leave their books, bells and crosiers on Icelandic shores, and neither must we forget the well-known statement of Dicuil,[1] at the end of the 8th century, that there were "many other islands in the Ocean to the north of Britain" on which Irish hermits had lived for a hundred years. Likewise, away to the southwards Irish monks were encircling the British shores and penetrating the continent by the great arteries of the Garonne, the Loire, the Seine and the Somme. In this way, Irish émigrés in the seventh and eighth centuries visited many well-established monasteries on the Continent and set up new ones of their own. The list of continental monasteries with Irish associations is most impressive and includes such houses as Bordeaux, Narbonne, Nantes, Angers, Tours, Auxerre, Beze, Moutier, Bobbio, Junigris, Meoux, Jouarre, Rebais, Luxeuil, Lure, St. Ursainne, St. Gall, Sackingen, Constance, Salzburg, Leuconnais and Würzburg. (Fig. 35) One of the most distinguished of the Irish missionaries on the continent was St. Columbanus. He founded a monastery at Luxeuil and preached among the Burgundians and Franks and eventually crossed the Alps into Italy to found Bobbio, possibly the most famous and interesting monastery in the list. We know a great deal about St. Columbanus, but we do not know exactly the route by which he travelled to the continent. In spite of Dom Gougaud's views,[2] it is almost certain that he used the western crossing, as stable conditions were not likely to have been restored to the eastern end of the Channel much before St. Augustine's landing in 597,—a decade or so after Columbanus's visit. In any case, when Columbanus was under sentence of deportation to return to his native land, it was at Nantes that he found a ship sailing direct to Ireland.

This is the age of the greatest achievements of the Celtic Church and brightly did the Emerald Isle shine out in the darkness of contemporary Europe. We should not, however,

(1) Dicuil, *Liber de Mensura orbis Terrae,* VII, 17, Ed. Parthney, p. 44.

(2) Gougaud, Dom L., *Christianity in Celtic Lands,* 1932, p. 174.

consider this intensive activity based on Ireland as evidence of any great missionary zeal on her part in the modern sense of the term. The Saints were absorbed by a desire to 'go on

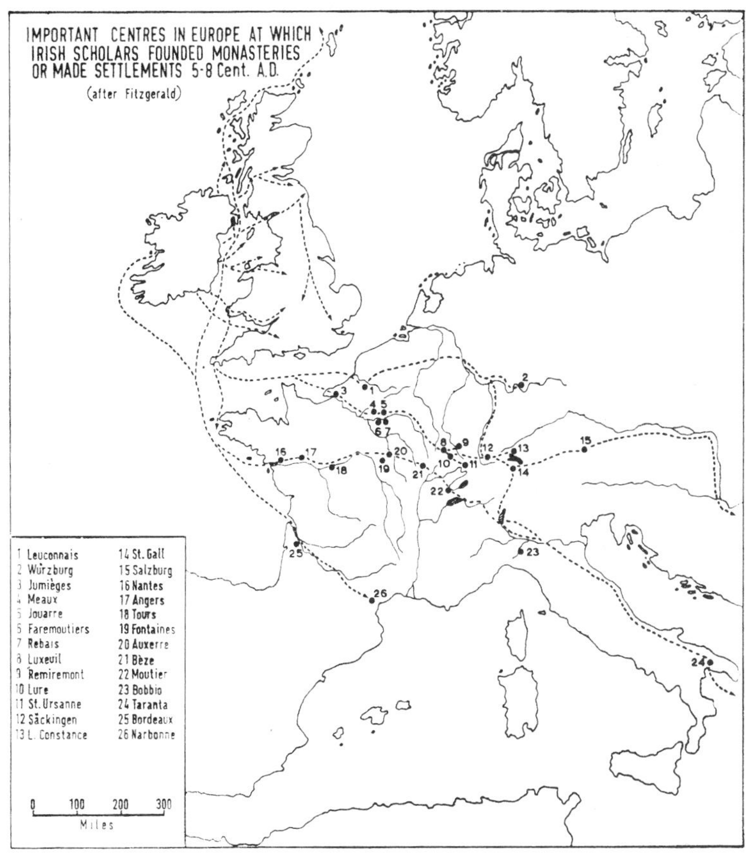

Fig. 35

pilgrimage,'—a sort of penance in itself, tied up with the monastic concept.(1) They voyaged at the mercy of the elements, with neither the sun by day, nor the stars by night to guide them. The real picture is vividly portrayed in the well-known

(1) Hughes, K., *"The changing theory and practice of Irish Pilgrimage," Journ. of Ecclesiastical History*, XI (1960) pp. 143 ff. and also Eleanor Duckett, *"The Wandering Saints,"* 1959, p. 26.

story of the three Irish 'peregrini' who appeared at the court of King Alfred. They had landed on the Cornish shores in their frail, skin-covered craft, drifting helplessly before the wind and tide for, as they told the king, they merely "wished to go into exile for the love of God; they cared not whither".

CHAPTER VI.

THE ISLE OF MAN

THE Isle of Man forms another sub-province of the Northern zone. Its insular character makes for clear regional delimitation, but its cultural associations in the Age of the Saints are particularly difficult to determine. Superficially, of course, one would have expected the reverse to be the case, for no fewer than twelve of the seventeen ancient parish churches of the Island are dedicated to Celtic saints, to say nothing of the saints associated with its numerous *Keeills*[1] and holy wells. The ruins of over two hundred *Keeills* have been recorded and there is a wealth of early crosses and inscriptions. Indeed, the Island shows a greater concentration of Early Christian remains than can be found in any other area of comparable size in the British Isles.[2] The difficulties arise from the fact that all the references to the Celtic saints are of late date and much doubt exists concerning the origin of the churches and the date of the *Keeills*. Dr. B. R. S. Megaw[3] in a recent study has argued that it is possible to disagree fundamentally with the orthodox view of the age of many of the *Keeills,* for there is little archaeological support for the belief that they were the oratories of the Celtic period in the fifth and sixth centuries down to the coming of the Norse. There is nothing to show that these ruins are older than the Viking settlement of the ninth century, and at least one *Keeill* cannot have been built before 900 A.D. since its walls contain a broken piece of monument erected by a Christian Norseman. Megaw concludes "One has a strong impression that most, if not all the *Keeills* we see today were erected after Irish, Scottish, or Manx

(1) The name applied in the Isle of Man to an early Christian oratory or tiny chapel.

(2) Chadwick, N. K., *The Age of the Saints in the Early Celtic Church,* Oxford, 1961, p. 70.

(3) Megaw, B. R. S., *The Norse heritage in the Isle of Man,* Chadwick Memorial Studies, 1950. *The Early Cultures of North-west Europe,* pp. 154-5.

monks had converted the Norse colonists. The alternative thesis that the *Keeills* of the Norse period were either old buildings which had survived the Viking conquest, or were reconstructed on the sites of pre-Norse chapels, and, therefore, of purely Celtic origin in all cases, cannot be proved or disproved without further excavation. It is a reasonable conclusion that many of the *Keeill* chapels, although inspired by Celtic usage were an integral part of the Manx-Viking culture.... Lest we have over emphasized this point we should admit that in selecting sites for their chapels the newly converted Norsemen must have chosen places venerated by the earlier inhabitants wherever they were found suitable. But there is no documentary evidence earlier than the 12th century concerning the age of many local dedications to Celtic Saints...". [1] This statement must apply equally to the parish churches in the Island as C. Marstrander[2] and others are of the opinion that the parish churches of today, were originally *Keeills* of the type just discussed. There is, therefore, little to go on that can be considered in any way as evidence contemporary with the Age of the Saints as far as dedications are concerned, throughout the Island.

We must, however, attempt an analysis of what we have. If we examine Marstrander's list of *Keeill* dedications and add to them the dedications of the seventeen parish churches, they can be considered as falling into four categories. In the first group are dedications to saints like Maughold, whose cult appears to be entirely local and confined to the Isle of Man.[3] Another group would include names like German, Carbery, Malew,

(1) An interesting comment on this statement is that the excavations of an important chapel on St. Ninian's Isle in the Shetlands in 1962, in which a valuable hoard of silver objects was found, indicated the presence of an earlier chapel beneath the Viking church, but, of course, there is nothing to show that the Celtic cell was dedicated to St. Ninian.

(2) Marstrander, C., *Norsk Tidskrift for Sprogundenskap* 8 (1937), pp. 287-442.

(3) A medieval scribe so confused the issue that many have claimed that the church at Lesmahagow in Ayrshire, formerly spelt Lesmahagn is dedicated to St. Maughold. Here, of course, what has happened is that the medieval scribe took Mahagn to be a form of Machutus—the name of a Celtic saint wrongly identified with St. Maughold. Lesmahagn means (St.) Mo-Flegu's enclosure, referring to St. Fechn the original founder of the site.

Marown, Santan, Braddan, Conchan, Lonan and others—names which can certainly be matched among the saints of Britain or Ireland. They represent common personal names in areas of common speech. Then come famous names such as Patrick, Brigit and Columba, saints whose fame was deliberately cultivated in later centuries. Churches and chapels may have been 'dedicated' to them (in the modern sense of the term), in the Isle of Man, between the 10th and 12th centuries. Finally, another group of dedications would include those to the Holy Trinity, St. Mary, St. Michael, St. John and St. Andrew all introduced under Roman church influence about the same time. Megaw[(1)] has shown that where we meet with patron saints with Celtic names, whose obscure reputations were presumably of little interest to reformers and others anxious to advance the reputation of their churches in a later age, it is fairly certain that we are "in the shadowy presence of the veritable founders of the Manx church". Such saints are included in the first of the above categories and, possibly, some occur in the second category also. The presence of Manx saints outside the Island is based on the assumption that when two saints, whose names resemble each other like the Manx Santan and the Irish Sanctan, have also identical feast days then they are almost certain to be one and the same person. We must, however, always allow for the possibility that the coincidence may very well be due to deliberate adjustment of the dates by churchmen in a later age, and that some of these Manx saints belong in fact to the local type.[(2)] The case of St. Maughold who is clearly in this category is worth persuing further, as what has been written recently about his associations is vital to the further development of our argument. The coastal parish, the parish church, and the holy well which bear his name are situated on the eastern side of the island in an area that was clearly of great significance from Megalithic times to the native Iron Age. A hill-fort of Iron Age date

(1) Megaw, B. R. S., *"Who was St. Conchan? A consideration of Manx Christian origins."* Journ. Manx Museum, VI, No. 79, 1962-3, p. 191.

(2) Megaw has proved conclusively that this was the case with St. Conchan., *op. cit.*, pp. 187-194.

overlooking a natural landing place is within a few hundred yards of the churchyard. We need pay little attention to the parish name as it is clear that parishes in the Isle of Man were not established much before the reign of King Olaf I, in the first half of the 12th century, as part of the general Romanization and the establishment of the first regular Manx diocese in 1135. Of greater significance is the parish church which bears his name. The earliest reference we have to this church is in Jocelyn's *Life of St. Patrick* written about 1185. The church is there called Kirk Maughold. This is now recognised as a special class of place name, a Norse adaptation of an older Celtic church name, which in this form can reasonably be ascribed to the Viking Age, possibly between 800 and 1100 A.D. Behind the Norse name may lie some original Celtic form such as Cill Maughold, in use not later than the 8th century and possibly as early as the 5th or 6th century.(1) In addition to the church itself, three *Keeills* and the site of a fourth are found within the precincts. In light of what has just been said about *Keeills* we must remember that these four need not all be of the early period. Cross slabs, no earlier than the 10th century, have been found in their walls but, nevertheless, these stone buildings may well be the successors of original wattle and daub structures. Of greater significance is the fact that the pattern of settlement here described, namely a Founder's church enclosed by a rampart accompanied by a number of smaller churches with various dedications, set up within the same enclosure is a well-known pattern for a Celtic monastery. Abundant evidence of this type of settlement exists at Clonmacnoise and at other sites in Ireland, while on the British side we have several early references to a similar arrangement.(2) The significant point in the present argument being that all the remains at St. Maughold look very much like the remains of a typical Celtic, pre-Norse monastery.

The archaeological evidence can help us still further. The parish of Maughold has yielded a richer harvest of archaeological finds of the Early Christian and Norse period than any

(1) Megaw, B. R. S., *ibid*, p. 188.

(2) See p. 198.

other parish in the Isle of Man. Here is abundant proof of the strength of the Christian tradition on this site before the Middle Ages. The parish of Maughold has produced a total of twenty-five pre-Norse cross slabs, of which twenty are associated with the churchyard and village. Here, therefore, is about one-third of the total Pre-Norse Christian slabs found in the Island, all at one centre, and that a centre where the layout is clearly reminiscent of an early Celtic monastery. The importance of St. Maughold's is still further enhanced by the fact that some of the cross slabs found there are, on epigraphical and other grounds, among the oldest early Christian inscribed stones found on the Island.

For the purpose of our general thesis we can now go a step further. If the Pre-Norse inscribed stones are, in this way, so closely bound up with the Celtic Church in the Island—it may be well worthwhile examining their overall distribution pattern. The majority of them were listed and mapped a long time ago in Kermode's great work on the Manx Crosses(1). Those that have since been recorded can easily be added. Fig. 36 shows the resultant pattern. Before proceeding, it is interesting to note that Kermode was in no way concerned with the overall pattern formed by these monuments. His geographical interests, so typical of his age, were purely locational, merely a desire to mark the exact site of the individual monuments and leave it at that. In order to have a map of sufficiently large scale for this purpose his magnificent volume shows the island on two separate sheets—a sheet for the northern and southern portions respectively. His maps naturally showed much material additional to the sites of the monuments with which we are now concerned.

The chief point to note, however, is that in spite of the very complex character of the monuments classified under such a general title as 'Pre-Norse', the overall distribution pattern shown on Fig. 36 is of the greatest interest to the historical geographer. It brings out the unmistakable 'south side' character of the distribution pattern, and we recollect the importance attached to the cultural dualism between 'Northside'

(1) Kermode, P. M. C., *Manx Crosses,* London, 1907.

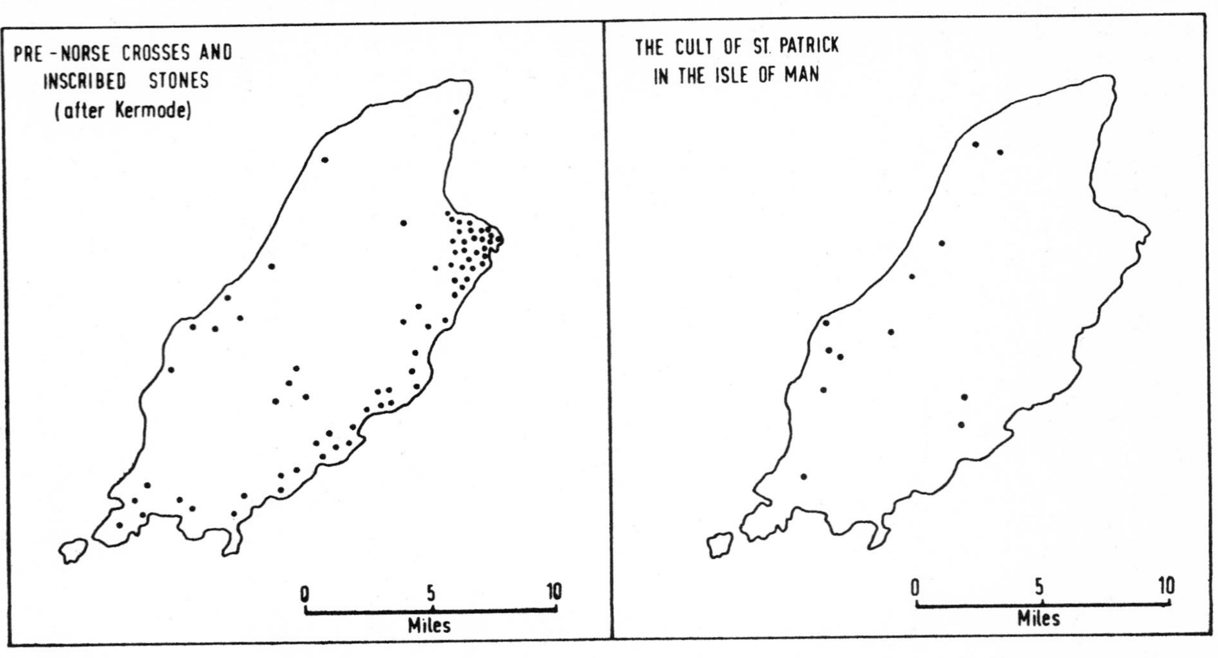
PRE-NORSE CROSSES AND
INSCRIBED STONES
(after Kermode)
0
5
10
Miles
THE CULT OF ST. PATRICK
IN THE ISLE OF MAN
0
5
10
Miles

Fig. 36

Fig. 37

and 'Southside' in the Island throughout prehistoric times. It would be well to stress also the 'southern' associations of much of the material represented by these slabs as well as their 'southside' distribution in general. One of the earliest of the inscribed cross-slabs at Maughold, bears the name IRNEIT or IRNEITUS in debased Roman characters, complete with hexefoil ornament, itself of Mediterranean origin, and a late form of the Chi-Rho monogram. Indeed, some Greek letters are used indicating that the carvers of these monuments were familiar with the Greek alphabet at this time, presumably towards the close of the 7th century. All these 'classical' and 'Roman' features suggest southern cultural origins either from Western Britain or even from Gaul. The parish of Maughold is also the home of the 'Crux Guriat' which formerly stood at a chapel about a mile from the church. This is of 9th century date and commemorates a Welsh chieftain, Gwriad, whose family were the rulers of Gwynedd. The family was originally of Northern stock and Gwriad's ancestors must have held land in the Isle of Man before passing on to North Wales. Gwriad himself would appear to have fled from North Wales before the year 825 and sought refuge in the former family home in Man. Whatever the details of the story may be the links are unmistakably with the north-south sea-route, and certainly not with Ireland.(1) We can now turn to the fuller confirmation of the southern origins of cultures on this side of the Island. The earliest of all inscriptions on this side is the Latin, sixth century, inscribed stone discovered when the present church was being built at Santan. It reads AVITI MONUMENTI—the monument of Avitus. The final I is cut horizontally, as is found frequently in Wales and half a dozen times in Cornwall and Devon. Other palaeographical details can be matched on South Wales inscriptions. The name Avitus does not occur elsewhere on the island, but again can be most nearly matched on a famous bilingual inscription of similar date at Eglwys Gymyn in south-western Carmarthenshire. The Avitus stone

(1) Chadwick, N. K., *Celtic Britain*, 1963, pp. 72 & 121. It is important to note that the view expressed here in no way conflicts with that outlined recently by Towill regarding St. Maughold (see page 73).

at Santan together with a bilingual stone of similar date found at Knock y Dooney, Andreas, belong to Nash-Williams' first group of Early Christian inscribed stones plotted on Fig. 10. We have already noted that they show unmistakably the influence of the chief sea-routes from the South carrying Gallo-Roman Christianity to the North. The 'southside' of Man would appear to have felt the major impact of cultures diffused in this way.

The 'Northside' of Man is the area where Irish influences are to be expected. The presence of Irish settlers in the island would appear to be only natural, their settlements being no different from other, and possibly greater, settlements of the Irish on the mainland, further north and south along the British coast. Jackson has shown that on linguistic grounds there is much evidence for a Brittonic population in Man in the Dark Ages, some of whom knew Latin, as well as the immigrant Gaelic people from Ireland. The presence of this Brittonic population is strongly attested by contemporary writers. Bede considered the island to be British and not Irish territory.[1] The only difference in the story of Man being that the Gaelic invaders and their culture were destined to overcome the Brittonic, while in other areas of Britain the Gaelic invaders were ultimately absorbed into the local population.[2]

When we come to look for the archaeological evidence for such a situation we find that it is slight indeed. Among Kermode's Pre-Norse inscribed stones and crosses are six Ogham inscriptions which can be looked upon as definite evidence of Irish influence in the Dark Ages. Their distribution is no reflection of the 'Northside' of the island. One of these stones is at Maughold and is extremely late in date, being associated with a Runic inscription of about 1200 A.D., while another in Andreas parish is a Latin-Ogham bi-lingual stone. The remaining four inscriptions in Ogham characters alone are in the parishes of Rushen and Arbory on the south side of the

(1) Bede, *Operae,* Book II, Chapter 3.

(2) Jackson, K. H., *Language and History in Early Britain,* Edinburgh, 1953, p. 173.

island. The presence of these four monoglot Ogham stones on the south side of the island suggests that the people they commemorate might have come from the south, possibly from some of the Irish colonies in north-west or south-west Wales, or even from southern Ireland itself. They might, indeed, very well have come from these areas and not directly across the water from North-eastern Ireland where Ogham inscriptions are few (see Fig. 8). It might well be, therefore, that the decisive factor in the Gaelicization of Man was associated with the spread of the cult of St. Patrick as shown on Fig. 37. When the Patrician cult appeared in the Island it seems to have emanated from North-eastern Ireland. The distribution of *Keeills* bearing St. Patrick's name (Fig. 37) suggests not only such an origin, but also reveals unmistakably a 'Northside' distribution, in sharp contrast to the 'Southside' patterns previously discussed. The formidable nature of the Patrician cult (when-ever it entered the Island) can be seen from the way in which it penetrated through the Greeba Gap between Peel and Douglas. However we explain the distribution pattern we have at least been able to establish the main point of the historical geographer's thesis, namely, the survival of two physical and cultural provinces in Man — the 'Southside' and the 'Northside.'

The choice of Patrician dedications to illustrate a 'Northside' distribution should obviously not be adopted without comment. In the first place, the Apostle of Ireland falls into our third category of saints whose names are perpetuated in the Island. They were distinguished leaders in their time and their fame, in consequence, might have been deliberately cultivated in later centuries. There is, in fact, abundant evidence for the revival of the cult of St. Patrick in many parts of northern and western Britain in the 12th century. It reached considerable proportions in Ireland itself at this period with the re-dedication of the church of the Holy Trinity at Down to St. Patrick as part of John de Courcy's political expedient, involving the spurious 'discovery' and translation of the bodies of St. Patrick, St. Columba and St. Brigid to this site. The propagation of the cult of St. Patrick in Man may well have belonged to this time and may even have emanated from this part of Ireland. The whole purpose may have been to endow what must have been contemporary reforms of the church, such as the institution of parishes and the establishment of the Diocese of Man on Roman lines, with the most honourable and ancient authority. MacQueen[(1)] thinks that much the same thing happened in Scotland, accounting for the widespread development of the cult of St. Ninian as late as the reign of King David I. There is, of course, not a shred of evidence to show that the Apostle of Ireland ever visited the Island in person, nor, indeed, for considering as in any way historical, the well-known story of his granting to St. German authority over Man, and enjoining him to build chapels, and otherwise to confirm the people of the island in the Faith. All this belongs to a later age and must be attributed to Jocelyn of Furness who wrote his *Life* of St. Patrick towards the close of the 12th century.

A detailed examination of this *Life* does, however, produce some interesting problems, in particular, the references to Pelagianism and to some early religious customs of the Celtic Church. These suggest that the author had access in the 12th century to very ancient sources of information. No one knows exactly what these sources were, but many workers, including Megaw, think that a proto-ballad, a legendary account of the early Manx Bishops, which ultimately formed the basis of the *Traditionary Ballad,* was available to Jocelyn when he wrote his *Life* of St. Patrick. Some would go even further and suggest that such a document was most likely written in response to a request by Jocelyn himself for Manx material for his *Vita*[(2)]. Recently R. C. Shaw[(3)] has attempted to take the matter further. After showing that the mission of the British Patrick was opposed to the semi-Pelagian heresy which lasted for several generations in Northern Ireland (as

(1) MacQueen, J., *St. Nynia. A study based on literary and linguistic evidence.* Edinburgh and London, 1961, pp. 84-5.

(2) Megaw, B. R. S., *op. cit.*, p. 190.

(3) Shaw, R. C., *Prolegomena to a Re-appraisal of Early Christianity in Man relative to the Irish Sea Province,* Proc. Isle of Man Nat. Hist. & Ant. Soc., Vol. VII, No. 1, pp. 7-9.

proved by the letter of Pope John A.D. 640)[1], he finds it significant that Jocelyn (who had been a monk of Grey Abbey, Co. Down and later Abbot of Rushen) should make reference to St. Patrick and the Isle of Man within the context of Pelagianism in his *Vita* written at the close of the 12th century. Shaw maintains that this point of view, together with other matters, demonstrates the early provenance of Jocelyn's exemplar, and that if he was commissioned to invent a *Life* of Patrick with special reference to his anti-Pelagian policy (a schism long since forgotten by this time), and the monks disregarded his account, then there is little reason to believe that there was any political factor involved, certainly none to justify a mass of dedications to St. Patrick in Man at this time, unless ancient tradition for the same had survived, which would have been of direct significance to the Manx people, being of primary origin associated with the saint's work. It is highly improbable, Shaw argues, that after an interval of four centuries or more, either the people themselves or their rulers had the faintest knowledge of the Pelagian heresy, while as far as the medieval ecclesiastics were concerned there was no cogent reason to invent such a linkage between St. Patrick and Man. All this suggests to Shaw that Jocelyn's account must have been based on an early exemplar describing Patrick's anti-Pelagian campaigns and the foundation during his lifetime (as in North-eastern Ireland) of an early episcopal organization in Man[2]. Whether the cult of St. Patrick in Man is of ancient or medieval origin we are left in no doubt concerning the persistent tradition in the Island of a 'Northside' and a 'Southside' contribution to early Christianity. In the writings of the distinguished historian and geographer—William Camden at the close of the 16th century we read of the dualism we have emphasized in this chapter—"The Manxmen," he says, "own St. Patrick for their apostle and hold him in great veneration. Next to him they honour the memory of S. Maughold, one of their bishops,

(1) Bede, *Hist. Eccl. II* p. 19 and Shaw R. C. *Post Roman Carlisle and the Kingdoms of the North-west;* Preston, 1964, p. 17.

(2) Shaw, R. C. *ibid.* p. 9.

whose feast they never fail to celebrate twice a year."[1]

One further matter remains for consideration. In an earlier chapter great emphasis was placed on the central position of the Isle of Man in the North Irish Sea basin, and we should now discuss the great variety of ethnic and cultural influences which, in consequence, have approached the Island from all directions. We have already stressed the Christian cultures impinging from the south and west between the fifth and the twelfth centuries. Equally clearly are the influences emanating from the North and East. Even if we ignore the possible influences of the Ninianic church[2], there are *Keeills* dedicated to St. Columba and St. Adamnan in such northern parishes as Andreas, and Lezayre, of whatever date is immaterial to our argument. From the eastern side there is both archaeological as well as dedication evidence. At Maughold church there is an 8th century cross slab inscribed in Runic characters with the unmistakable Saxon name Blakman. With the expansion of Northumbria at this time it would appear that Teutonic settlers were moving across the north of England and southern Scotland towards the western seas, and absorbing the culture of the native peoples. At this time the Celtic church of Galloway had passed under the control of Saxon bishops and there might well have been overspills into Man. It is equally well-known that the famous Calf of Man crucifix of the late 8th century, together with several other Manx crosses of this period, have designs and lettering which may have been influenced by similar ones from Northern England, indicating that there were some connections between Man and the Anglican kingdom of Northumbria at this time. This would help to explain the fact that Marstrander noted two *Keeills* dedicated to St. Cuthbert on the Island, one at Ballacubergh in Lezayre and the other at Keeille Rhogleragh in the same parish. The dedication of Christian churches in the Isle of Man, together with the study of the Island's early Christian monuments is thus a topic of

(1) Camden, W. *Britannia.* 1586. Gibson's Edition. 1695.

(2) St. Ninian's name survives at St. Trinian's in Marown parish in an area in which we know that the Priory of Whithorn held lands. (Kinvig, *History of the Isle of Man,* 2nd. Edit. 1950. p. 40).

absorbing interest, dependent upon the continuing activity along the sea-routes, and the geographical position of the island in relation to the larger units of the British Isles.

CHAPTER VII

BRITTANY

BRITTANY became a colony of Outer Britain in the Age of the Saints—indeed—it acquired the name of Lesser Britain. Many have thought that the process of colonization was occasioned by refugees escaping from the plagues and pestilences that appear to have ravaged Britain in the fifth and sixth centuries. Others have spoken of the growing pressure exerted by the Anglo-Saxon invaders, while, more recently, Mrs. Chadwick(1) has pointed out that while Anglo-Saxon pressure was increasing from the east, so, too, were the Irish infiltrations from the west, so that the Britons of Wales were thus caught between two pressures and emigration was forced upon them. We need, however, a broader view of the overall situation. The movement of British Celts into the Armorican peninsula and beyond must be recognized not as a matter of local refugees seeking safety, but as a fully-fledged movement of people seeking new homes, exactly in the same way as the Germanic peoples (including the Anglo-Saxons themselves) were doing throughout northern and central Europe at this time, when the power of the Roman Empire was passing away. The Irish movements of the third and fourth centuries A.D. into north-western and south-western Wales, together with their settlements in Cornwall and in Dalradia were but the beginnings of a movement of Celtic peoples within this major framework which later produced the colonization of Armorica. This possibly began about 450 A.D. and extended over several centuries. As is obvious, the extensive use of sea-ways was involved and it must not be forgotten that such great folk movements did not expend themselves in the colonization of Armorica alone, but passed on to the southwards reaching possibly into north-western Spain.

(1) Chadwick, N. K., (Editor) *Celt and Saxon: Studies in the early British Border*. Cambridge, 1963, p. 12.

Such folk movements left few traces behind them for the archaeologist. If we need a demonstration of a well-attested movement of people in early times, expanding without leaving behind it any archaeological evidence—we can find no better example than the incursion of British people into Brittany from the fifth to the seventh centuries A.D. The colonization itself is thoroughly well attested by history, by linguistic evidence and by place-name evidence and even by physical anthropology as Dr. P. R. Giot has recently argued[1]. Yet of this extensive movement there remains no archaeological evidence whatsoever. Dr. G. E. Daniel[2], when discussing the position, reminds us that when a situation of this kind occurs on the margins of the historic period, we can but query the validity of attempting to correlate linguistic and folk movements in prehistoric times with distributions based solely on archaeological evidence.

In the case of Brittany it would appear that British immigrants made settlements in forest clearings, and that their leaders were accompanied by ecclesiastics—the Saints (to whom they were often related). It was the Saints who negotiated settlement sites and other matters with the existing rulers, and also administered to the religious needs of the newcomers. They were not all of the *peregrini* class. It is reasonable to assume that the immigrants did not always settle without clashing with the inhabitants of the country, whom Giot thinks were more numerous than has frequently been assumed. Nevertheless, there is no suggestion that the Saints were engaged in any large scale missionary activity in the sense understood by this term today. Indeed, the Armoricans were for the most part members of the Roman Church in Gaul,[3] and the two facets of Christianity—Roman and Celtic-seem to have settled down besides each other quite amicably.[4]

(1) Giot, P. R., *Armoricains et Bretons: Étude anthropologique*, Rennes, 1955.
(2) Daniel, G. E., "Who are the Welsh?", *Proc. Brit. Acad.*, 1954, Vol. 40 p.160.
(3) See R. Couffon (1944) and P. Merlet (1950 & 1951) in *Mémoires de la Société d'Histoire et d'Archéologie de Bretagne.*
(4) Duine, F. M., *Memento des sources hagiographiques de l'histoire de Bretagne*. Première Partie. Les Fondateurs et les primitifs Ve–Xe siècle. Rennes, 1918.

Brittany itself had much to recommend it for the type of colonization that ensued. It was one of the prominent western peninsulas of Europe, built up of very old geological formations; shales and clayey schists on the lower ground, and hard sandstone or granite on the higher. If we take an overall view of the peninsula we find two main ridges running through the region. The northern one can be traced from the Alençon massif in the east to the Montagnes d'Arrée (1,283 ft.) in western Britanny. A southerly line of hills runs parallel to the south coast and can be followed structurally to the Gâtine hills of La Vendée, south of the Loire. These southern hills rarely reach more than 600 ft. above sea-level. The land falls gently to the coastal or interior lowlands on either side from these main ridges, except in western Brittany where the Montagnes Noires (1,069 ft.) interpose a third zone of upland (Fig. 38). Between these three ridges are two important depressions, the smaller of which lies between the Montagnes d'Arrée and the Montagnes Noires and centres around the small town of Chateaulin. It is drained by the river Aulne which flows into Brest harbour. The larger depression lies across the peninsula to the eastward consisting of the basins of the Rance and the Vilaine. In it stands Rennes. It should be stressed that all these uplands have many gaps through them, the southern line of hills especially being discontinuous, so that with the assistance of these gaps and the intermontane lowlands just described, the transpeninsular crossing of the country would be fairly simple. The most frequented ways would appear to be the Rance-Vilaine lowland in the east, the Gouet-Blavet crossing in the centre, and the St. Pol de Léon-Aulne depression-Pont Aven route in the west (Fig. 38).

Of equal importance in the relief of the country, from the point of view of the type of settlement pattern revealed by the distribution of monastic cells and churches, are those features which have resulted from the tectonic movements of Tertiary and post-Tertiary times. The great Tertiary movements that folded the Alpine area of Central Europe slightly uplifted the older mass of Brittany to the west and thereby rejuvenated the rivers. Near the river mouths deep, steep-sided gorges resulted

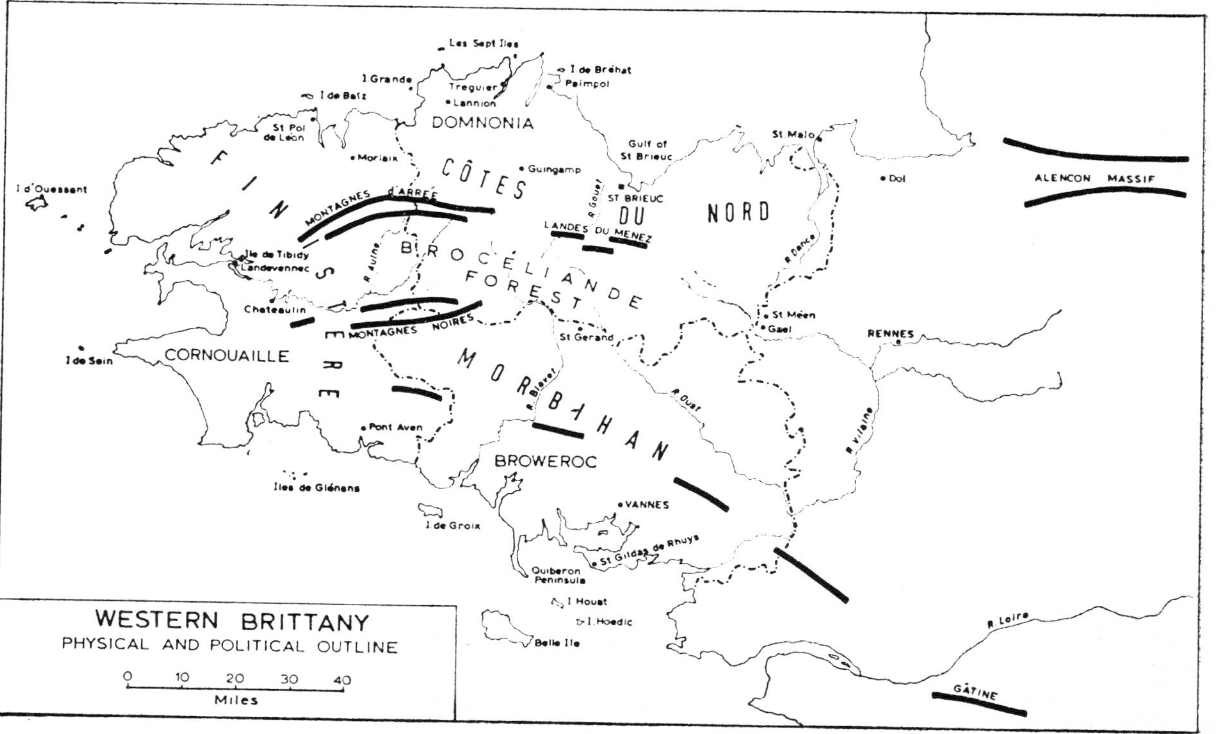
WESTERN BRITTANY
PHYSICAL AND POLITICAL OUTLINE
0 10 20 30 40
Miles
Les Sept Iles
I Grande
I de Batz
Treguier
Lannion
I de Bréhat
Paimpol
DOMNONIA
St Pol de Léon
Morlaix
I d'Ouessant
CÔTES
Guingamp
Gulf of St Brieuc
St Malo
Dol
ALENCON MASSIF
ST BRIEUC
R Gouet
DU
NORD
LANDES DU MENEZ
MONTAGNES D'ARRÉE
FINISTÈRE
R Aulne
BROCÉLIANDE
FOREST
R Rance
Ile de Tibidy
Landevennec
Chateaulin
MONTAGNES NOIRES
St Gerand
St Méen
Gael
RENNES
I de Sein
CORNOUAILLE
MORBIHAN
R Blavet
R Oust
R Vilaine
Pont Aven
BROWEROC
Iles de Glénans
VANNES
I de Groix
St Gildas de Rhuys
Quiberon Peninsula
I Houat
I. Hoedic
Belle Ile
R Loire
GÂTINE

Fig. 38

from the uplift, but before the process could reach far upstream a slight subsidence allowed the sea to penetrate these newly-made valleys. In this way was formed the typical ria coastline that characterizes the peninsula today. The whole coastline, and especially the south coast, presents, therefore, a ragged outline owing to the numerous inlets which penetrate far inland. They became the territory's natural means of access and penetration and were fully utilized in the Age of the Saints. Equally important is the fact that such submerged coastlines carry with them numerous peninsulas and islands. On the south coast is the spectacular Quiberon peninsula and Belle Île; the Ile de Groix, the Iles de Glénans; the Ile de Sein and the Ile d'Ouessant with several other smaller islands. Off the north coast are the Ile de Batz, Ile Grande and les Triagoz, les Sept Iles and Ile de Bréhat. Islands had a particular fascination as settlement sites for the Saints. It was on islands that they most often made their first landings. Indeed, J. Largillière[(1)] has suggested that it is a fixed rule that the saints of the *peregrini* class who settled in Brittany first tarried as hermits on the shore (most frequently an island site was selected, on which a chapel, bearing the saint's name is usually found), then they moved inland to minister to the colonists there. The physique of Brittany proved ideal for such a scheme (Fig. 38).

One further matter concerning the physical geography of the country is worthy of note, namely, that in the Age of the Saints it was densely wooded, except near the coast where the salt tang in the sea-winds checked the growth, and again on the tops of some of the higher ridges where trees were replaced by much gorse and bracken. The slopes of the ridges which formed the backbone of the peninsula were, however, densely forested—the whole forming the vast inland forest of Brocéliande. Thus, we have the traditional division of Brittany into the Armor—'the land of the sea'—a belt of some six to eight miles wide around its coastal margins, and the Arcoet—'the land of the forest'—in the interior. It is significant in this context that historical geographers today, throughout Western

(1) J. Largillière, *Les Saints et l'organisation chretienne primitive dans L'Armorique bretonne.* Rennes, 1925.

Europe, think of the great folk movements of the Germanic, Slavonic and Celtic peoples, which took place in the immediate post-Roman centuries, as a movement "into forest land." The movement of Celtic peoples into Brittany at this time was, therefore, no exception.

Our study of the pre-Roman culture areas showed that there would appear to have been sharp cultural contrasts between the Morbihan, on the one hand, and Finistère and Côtes du Nord, on the other, throughout prehistoric times, but that in the immediate pre-Roman period the extension of Venetic influence, based on sea-power, certainly reached up north-westwards from Le Morbihan to include the southern half of Finistère, so that the two major provinces in Late Iron Age times were Venetic Morbihan linked with southern Finistère, and a northern province involving northern Finistère and Côtes du Nord. It will be our aim to show the survival of these territories as cultural provinces into the Age of the Saints. Before doing so we must bear in mind that in Britain the south-western portions of Cornwall had become a true Venetic colony, in contrast to a veneer of Venetic influence, in the form of a south-western Iron Age B culture, which covered Devon, Somerset and Dorset, and much of the south-eastern borderlands of Wales.[(1)] At the same time, the south-western culture had spread by the outer sea-routes into the Irish Sea Province, and, in a modified form, had reached the northernmost regions of Britain. Stated, therefore, in the simplest possible terms we are concerned in the Age of the Saints with cultural movements traversing these same areas, but in the reverse direction, as it were. Those emanating from the south-eastern borderlands of Wales and the Welsh coastlands of the Severn Sea, as far west as Carmarthenshire, impinged, in the main, on the coasts of Côtes du Nord and northern Finistère, while those utilizing the 'outer' sea routes made contact with southern Finistère and Le Morbihan. It will be convenient to examine the 'inner', or more 'easterly', line of movement first of all.

The accepted modern view is that the founding saints of

(1) See pp.37-8.

northern Brittany were either Welshmen or saints coming from

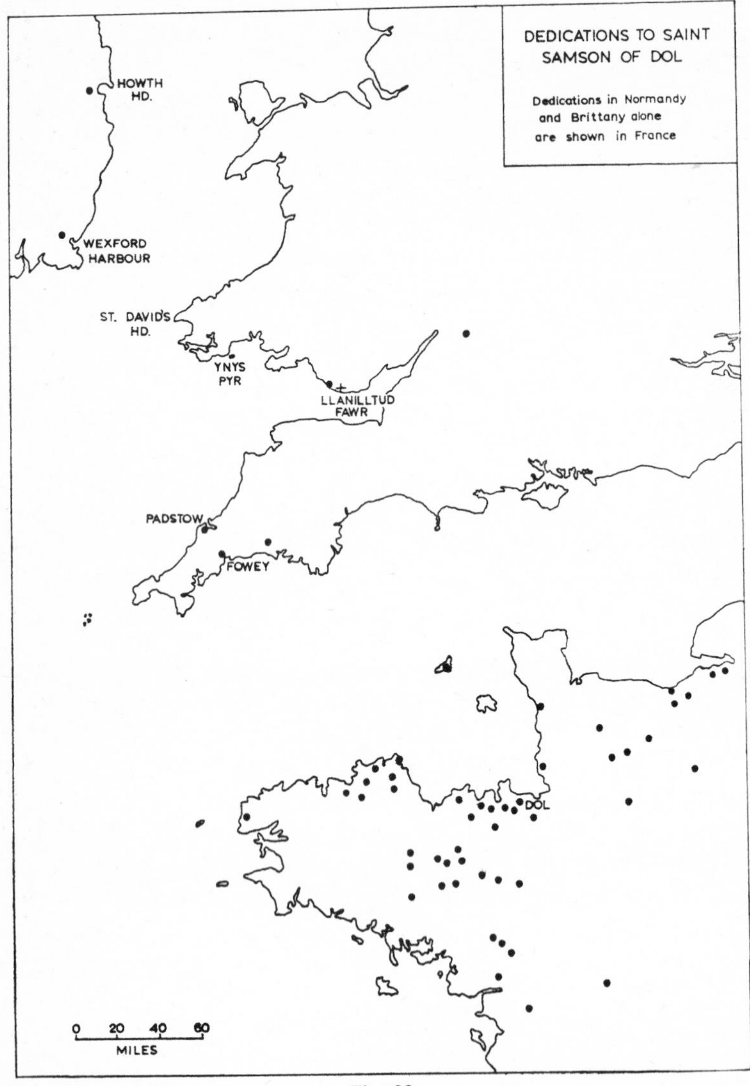

Fig. 39

a Welsh provenance. A very large number of these who have left their names in northern Brittany were trained by the great

St. Illtud in the Glamorgan monastery of Llanilltud Fawr—these would include St. Samson of Dol, St. Gildas de Rhuys and St. Paulinus, who has been identified with St. Pol de Léon. Another group with ultimate Welsh or Irish associations seem to have based themselves on the islands of the Bréhat group in the gulf of St. Malo before starting upon their ecclesiastical work in Brittany. St. Maudez (St. Mawes) clearly belongs to this group. Then, finally, a further contribution was made to the colonization of northern Brittany by the saints when numerous monks of lesser importance claiming descent from the famous Brychan Brycheiniog settled in the area. It is convenient to consider the contributions of these pioneers in turn.

St. Samson holds chief place among the founders of the Celtic Church in Brittany. His *Life*, which may be as early as 625, cannot be later than 850. It is the earliest, longest, and fullest of all those of the Celtic saints that have come down to us. The information that it contains is far less hagiological in character and has, in consequence, far greater historical significance.[(1)] Samson was not of royal birth and seems to have been a native of South-west Wales. He was taken as a youth to the school of 'Eltutus,' the head of a great monastery, which must have been at Llanilltud Fawr in south Glamorgan. We are told of a visit to this monastery by Bishop Dubricius who ordained the young Samson there. He became abbot of Piro (a monastery on Caldy Island, off Tenby, in Pembrokeshire), and is known to have visited Ireland, where, among other things, he purchased a cart or 'chariot' which he seems to have taken with him across the seas in later years. Like other Celtic saints, he withdraws 'to the desert' and lives the life of a hermit on the banks of the Severn. He returns to the monastery at Llanilltud Fawr and is elected bishop, but it is revealed to him that he must become a *'peregrinus'* and leave his native land and journey overseas. Some details taken from his early *Life* are worth recording as illustrative of the general conditions of his time. Apparently, before leaving Ireland he puts

(1) See Duine, F. M., *Questions d'hagiographie et vie de Saint Samson,* Paris, 1914, and also Doble, G. H., *St Mawes,* Cornish Saints Series, p. 5. For a modern translation of the *Life* of St. Samson see Taylor, T.. *The Life of St. Samson,* London, 1925.

his 'chariot', which carried his holy books, in a boat, and on arrival in south-west Wales the boat is placed in the 'chariot', and horses are hired to draw it across to the southern coast. When the time comes for him to leave Illtud's monastery the process is reversed and the chariot is placed in the boat for crossing to Cornwall. We have a vivid description of him using the famous transpeninsular route from Padstow to the Fowey (Fig. 39). On his way across the peninsula he notices a crowd of people on a hill-top nearby, gathered around a huge standing stone, obviously performing some religious ritual. He intervenes, and after a miraculous occurrence, proceeds with the aid of an iron instrument to cut the sign of the Cross on the pillar stone. Later, he continues on his journey, placing his chariot and books once again in a boat for the crossing to Brittany. Here we seem to have a genuine example of the actual use of the transpeninsular routes, and of that 'continuity of tradition' which characterised the cultural life of Outer Britain throughout prehistoric and later times.[1] Samson appears to have had some contact with the Channel Islands, as there is a church dedicated to him on the island of Guernsey. In Brittany he appears as the founder of Dol and several other monasteries and churches (Fig. 39). Above all, he was a born leader of men who took a very active part in Breton politics, becoming the successful champion of one Breton Count against another. We find him making several journeys to Paris using the same chariot as he had brought with him from Ireland. On one journey he meets with an accident in which one of the wheels of the chariot comes off! His *Life* brings him into contact at this period with Childebert, King of Paris (511-558). We find him signing the decrees of Church Councils held in Paris in 553 and 557 as 'Samson peccator episcopus.' The map, Fig. 39, of his churches and chapels in northern France presents a complicated picture.[2] The settlements in the lowlands behind the estuary of the Rance are unmistakable, and would appear in some way or other to be directly linked with Dol itself.

(1) Bowen, E. G., *The Travels of St. Samson of Dol, Aberystwyth Studies*, xiii, 1934, pp. 61-67.

(2) Based on Duine, F. M., *Saint Samson*, Rennes, 1909.

They may well represent some of Samson's original foundations. There is a secondary grouping to the southward associated with the basin of the Vilaine and with BroWeroch, occasioned, doubtless, by St. Samson's joint religious and political influence with the Welsh settlers there. A third group of dedications is found in the Lannion peninsula of Dumnonia, reflecting the saint's political contacts with the sixth century rulers of these parts.[1] Fourthly, we can observe the wide scattering of settlements in Normandy associated with the saint's activities in these parts and his journeys to the Frankish court in Paris. The overall picture (diffuse and powerful as the cult of St. Samson must have been during his lifetime and later) leaves little trace of him in southern Finistère and along the Morbihan coastlands—areas which, we shall observe later, were occupied mainly by immigrants who seem to have used the outer sea-ways, and not those associated with cults emanating from the inner Bristol Channel area. An interesting sideline on the colonization of Brittany can be deduced from the fact that northern Brittany is referred to as Dumnonia in the *Life* of St. Samson. We know that the Romans had inherited from the conquered tribes of north-western Gaul a system of geographical divisions and names, which survived until the break-up of the Empire, but during the Dark Ages several of these were swept away. The northern part of the Breton peninsula became known as Dumnonia, and the south-western part as Cornubia. This change of nomenclature is very largely the result of the migrations from Wales and south-west Britain which we have been considering, and it is clear that when the author of the *Life* of St. Samson wrote in the seventh century the change had already taken place.[2]

There is an important appendix, as it were, to the activities of St. Samson in Brittany which had a great deal to do with the spread of the Celtic saints. We have already referred to his skill as a political negotiator and his great influence over

(1) Some of this territory remained an *enclavé* of the Diocese of Dol until the French Revolution.

(2) Hencken, H. O'N., *Cornwall and Scilly*, The County Archaeologies, 1932, p. 219, and more recently Fahy, D., *When did Britons become Bretons?* Welsh Historical Review, Vol. 2, No. 2, 1964, pp. 111-124.

the Breton chieftains of his day. On one occasion St. Samson sent one of his deacons (and a close relative of his)—St. Méen-on an embassy to the king of BroWeroch (Bro Erech) in the forest lands of eastern Brittany. In order to reach the court of the king he had to pass through the forest of Brocéliande (Fig. 38). On his way he received hospitality from a local chieftain named Caduon, who had made a settlement there, and this he offered to the saint and his monks. In this way was founded the monastery of Gaël. Another monastery only two and a half miles north of Gaël is also believed to have been founded by St. Méen at the village of St. Méen-le-Grand, of which Gaël ultimately became a dependency. St. Méen-le-Grand grew rapidly into a famous abbey which has survived into modern times. Mrs. Chadwick[1] is convinced that St. Méen is "one of the most authentic of the Breton Saints." We know that his life-long friend and relative King Judicaël of Dumnonia ended his life in the great abbey of Gaël, while a charter of Louis the Pious in 816 speaks of the Abbey of Gaël as the 'house of the church of St. Méen and St. Judicaël which is in the place called Wadel' (i.e. Gaël). The significance of this episode from our point of view is not necessarily its well-authenticated historical foundation, but, more especially, the way in which it represents very clearly three important aspects of our general thesis. In the first place, here is a clear and unmistakable example of 'movement into forested land,' a point stressed at the beginning of this chapter, secondly, here we have the establishment of a very important settlement on the route from St. Malo to Bro Weroch which was to play an important part in the spread of Celtic Christianity into the Vannetais, and ultimately over most of the southern Morbihan and even into Ille et Vilaine. We shall see the influence of these transpeninsular routeways even more clearly when we come to discuss the settlements of the saints belonging to the family of St. Gildas de Rhuys. The third point of interest is that traditionally St. Méen is stated to be an immigrant from the king-

(1) Chadwick, N. K., *The Colonization of Brittany from Celtic Britain.* Sir John Rhŷs Memorial Lecture. *British Academy,* 1965. Proc. Brit. Acad. LI, p. 298.

dom of Erging (otherwise Archenfield) in the southern borderlands of Wales.[1] We have had occasion to refer to this very important area in the development of Celtic Christianity before, in connection with the cult of St. Dubricius, and there would appear to be mounting evidence to suggest that many early immigrants to Brittany, besides St. Méen, hailed from this Breconshire-Herefordshire-south Powysland countryside. This matter, too, is more profitably discussed in greater detail after we have examined the distribution of dedications to the family of St. Gildas de Rhuys.

We have a sound historical basis for the existence of St. Gildas. He was the author of the only literary effort of his age and country—the *De Excidio Britanniae.* This was not intended to be a history of Britain; in fact, it was an indictment written in the prophetic style and directed against five ruling princes in Britain, the most important of whom was Maelgwn Gwynedd. Since he is reported in the *Annales Cambriae* as dying of the yellow plague in 547, we can, therefore, date the *De Excidio* before that year. It would appear to have been written about 540 A.D. Gildas is also mentioned by the great Irish saint Columbanus in a letter to Pope Gregory about the year 600.[2] Two *Lives* of St. Gildas have come down to us, the first is a *Life* written by a monk of his monastery at Rhuys in southern Brittany in the ninth century based on earlier material. Scholars think this was begun about 880 A.D. with additional chapters added at a later date. The second *Life* is ascribed to Caradoc of Llancarfan in the twelfth century and is, in fact, but a figment of the imagination of the monks of Glastonbury, who desired to associate this famous Briton with the early history of their house. It is perfectly clear that the first *Life* is the more valuable from the student's point of view. According to the Rhuys *Life*, St. Gildas came from Arecluta on the banks of the Clyde and we have no reason whatsoever to doubt this. It is said that he was forced southwards by the inroads of the Picts and Scots and finally received his educa-

(1) De la Borderie, *Histoire de Bretagne,* Vol. I, p. 423, note 3.

(2) See article on Gildas in *Y Bywgraffiadur Cymreig hyd* 1940 by Sir Ifor Williams, p. 259.

tion at St. Illtud's great school, and that it was here that he

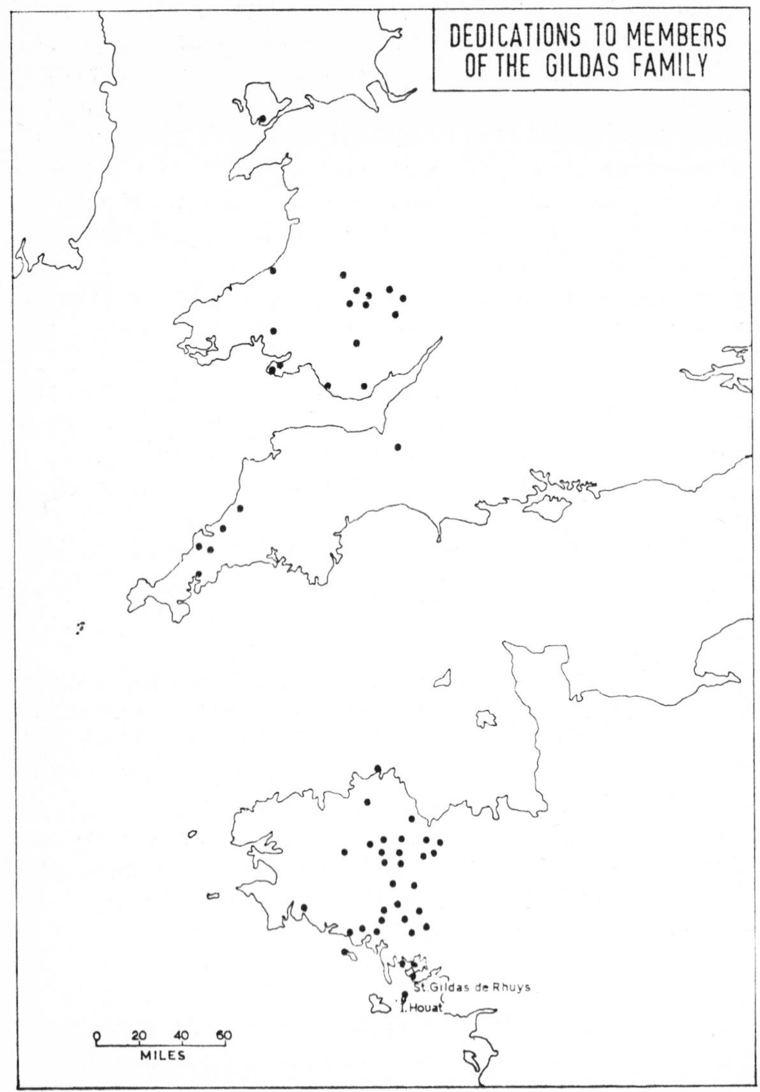

Fig. 40

came under the spell of monasticism. After this he migrated to Brittany and set up his chief monastery at Rhuys near

Vannes. It is said that he landed first of all on the island of Houat, on his return from a visit to Rome, and then crossed over to the mainland where he established his monastery. The journey to Rome, of course, must be considered as highly fictitious. In the year 919 owing to the raids of the Northmen the monks of Rhuys, taking with them the body of their founder, fled to Locminé, where they were joined by the monks of that community and, together, both retired to Berry, and remained at Déols until 1010, when Rhuys, and, after that, Locminé, were restored.

In Wales and Ireland there is little evidence of the religious influence exerted by St. Gildas as far as the foundation of monastic cells is concerned. No church, for example, is dedicated to him in Wales. If, on the other hand, we take into account the whole of the Gildas family (brothers, sisters, sons and grandsons) a fuller picture is obtained. In the *Life* by the Rhuys biographer only four brothers and a sister are named: Guillin, Maelog, Egreas, Allectus and sister Peteova or Peteona, but the Welsh genealogies (written long before the days of Caradog of Llancarfan) assure us that he had five sons: Cenydd, Gwynog, Nwython, Maidoc (or Aidan) and Dolgan. The first named having in addition two saintly sons—St. Ufely and St. Ffili, grandsons of Gildas.[(1)] Fig. 40 attempts to plot the known dedications to members of the whole family in the Celtic lands and the overall picture gives a very vivid impression of the 'eastern route,' important in the Iron Age, and now used in reverse. Particular attention should be directed first of all to the concentration of dedications in the southern part of the eastern borderlands of Wales, which in Roman and immediate pre-Roman times formed part of the territory of the Cornovii. The region was then heavily forested, with poor communications, yet the number of hill-forts, and their size, found in the area indicates a relatively large population. After the establishment of the XIX and XX legions at Viroconium (Wroxeter), the Cornovii, who inhabited the hill-forts, were, doubtless, settled on the plain under supervision, as was the Roman custom. Here they carried out a good deal of forest clearance. Towards

(1) Baring-Gould, S. and Fisher, J., *Lives of the British Saints,* III, pp. 103-4.

the end of the Roman occupation there are signs that this borderland became much disturbed. J. G. Collingwood and J. N. L. Myres[1] have noted that excavations at Viroconium reveal a story of failure and decay in the Romanization of these parts, beginning earlier than in the more civilized areas of the Province; while, more recently, H. N. Savory[2] has drawn attention to the fact that this failure in Romanization is reflected in the late policy of allowing the people of these parts to look after themselves against Irish and other raiders, and, as a corollary, we find the Romans making use of, and controlling the military talent thus renewed by enrolling a *Chors* I *Cornoviorum* for service on Hadrian's Wall.[3] This use of the Cornovii can be compared with the transference of the Votadini under Cunedda into north-west Wales in the last days of Roman Britain. Were these borderlands one of the areas from which people like the Cornovii (who had a long experience of settling in forest country) moved, with their chieftains and ecclesiastics, over to Brittany in relatively large numbers? We think that the answer is in the affirmative and would reiterate the fact that the evidence comes not only from the family of St. Gildas, but is found again associated with St. Méen. Likewise, the Bro Weroch territory in the hinterland of Vannes drew its earliest saints from the Powys, Gwrtheyrnion and Brycheiniog districts in Wales, that is from areas associated with the ancient domain of the Cornovii.[4]

It is time now to return to a consideration of some of the other important matters indicated on Fig. 40. It will be observed that the family of Gildas used the eastern crossings in Cornwall (not the Hayle-St. Michael's Mount crossing). This is followed by the unmistakable trace of their settlements across the Breton peninsula, utilizing the Gouet-Blavet valleys in their penetration to the Vannetais. It may well be that the Blavet valley, in particular, was a special region of influence of the

(1) Collingwood, J. G. and Myres, J. N. L., *Roman Britain and the English Settlements,* 1936, pp. 195-201.

(2) Savory, H. N. *Some Sub-Romano-British Brooches in South Wales* in *Dark Age Britain.* Studies presented to E. T. Leeds. London, 1956, pp. 56-7.

(3) See *Trans. Cumberland and Westmorland Ant. Soc.* XXIX, 1929, p. 200 n.

(4) Chadwick, N. K., *Celtic Britain,* London, 1963, p. 241.

Gildas family, and it is conceivable that his grandfather Geraint had been granted a domain there, for we find St. Géran with its sanctuary in the upper reaches of the valley, while his uncle Selyf, or Solomon, may well be the saint commemorated at Guern. We have, of course, no documentary evidence of any settlement being made in the Blavet before the days of Gildas, but it is a remarkable topographical coincidence that we should find the names of members of his family, both ancestors and descendants, in a cluster in this area. Whatever may be the precise detail it is obvious that all these religious settlements ultimately have a Welsh origin. Historians of the Celtic Church would consider, as we have already noted, any visit of a Celtic saint to Rome as spurious, so that it is far more likely that the island of Houat functioned as an indispensable adjunct to Gildas' great monastery at Rhuys —a barren island on which the abbot and the more devout of his followers could find solitude and an ideal retreat—than that he first landed there on a return journey from Rome. The Rhuys biographer says that he died on the island which is far more likely to be the case than that he first landed there.

As an example of a cultural spread from the more westerly parts of the inner Bristol Channel area by way of Cornwall, and impinging on north-western Brittany, we can cite the distribution of the churches and chapels ascribed to St. Paul Aurelian, the centre of whose cult would appear to be the cathedral city, always known as St. Pol de Léon, or, in Breton —Kastell Paol.[1] We are fortunate also, in this case, in possessing a *Life* of the saint that was written before the general destruction of the Breton monasteries by the Northmen in the 10th century. It would appear that about the year 960 one of the bishops of St. Pol withdrew to the famous Abbey of Fleury a few miles from Orleans. He brought with him, among other gifts, the body of St. Paul, which was received at Fleury with great honour, and, doubtless, at the same time a copy of the *Life* of St. Paul Aurelian which had been written in Brittany some eighty years before by a monk named Wrmonoc. This copy is now preserved in the public library at Orleans. It is in

(1) Duine, F. M., *Kroc'hennik: légende de Saint Paul de Léon.* Vannes, 1903.

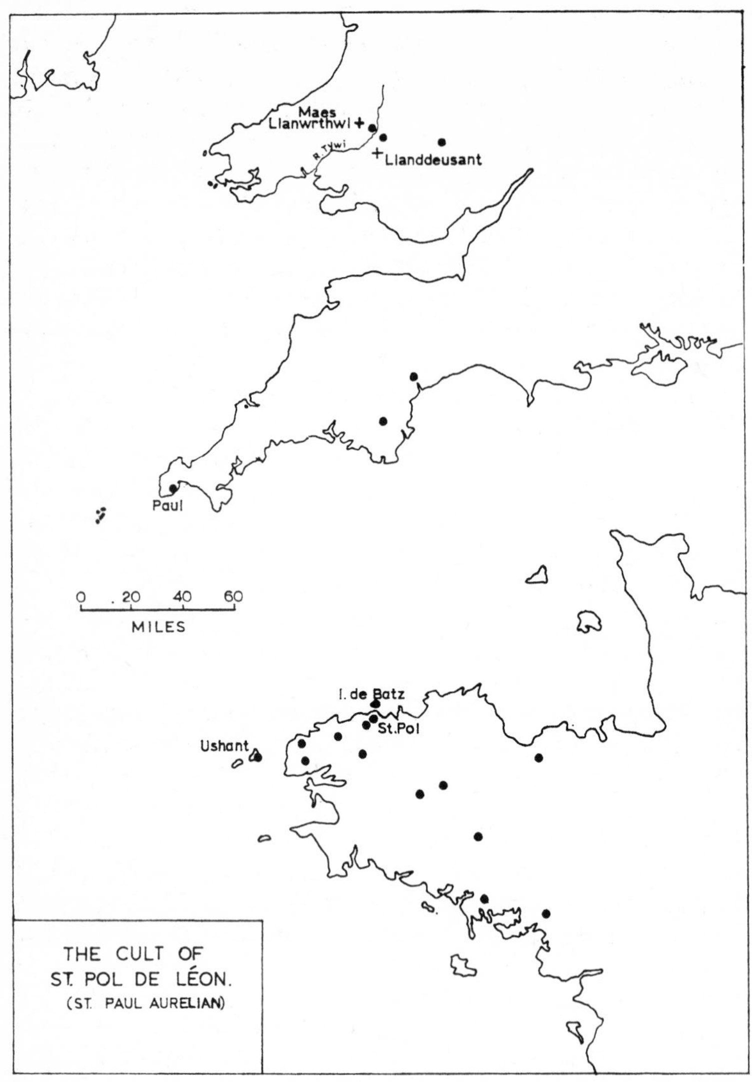

Fig. 41

the handwriting of the 10th century, but lacks some portions of the original which are to be found in another and later copy of the *Life* in the National Library in Paris. Wrmonoc divides his work into two books—the first describing Paul's life in his native Wales, and the second his work in Brittany. He has certainly written up the first book, using certain traditions brought over from Wales, and probably from Cornwall, too. He twice mentions *transmarini,* and it is on their authority that his evidence rests. He had heard of a Paul of Penychen, who was of noble birth and had a share of the domains of king Glwys called Penychen. This territory was located in what is now the county of Glamorgan. He had also heard of a famous saint of Carmarthenshire whose name was Paulinus and whose monastery was at Llanddeusant in that county (Fig. 41). He knows that the Breton Paul was also sometimes known as Paulinus and he cannot make up his mind as to which of the two-the Glamorgan Paul or the Carmarthenshire Paulinus is synonymous with the founder of St. Pol de Léon. Consequently, he attempts to amalgamate them, and in giving a list of Illtud's famous students alters Paulinus to Paul and states that this disciple is the hero of his story. So here we have the possibility of three persons; Paul of Penychen; a famous saint of Carmarthenshire called Paulinus, and the founder of St. Pol de Léon who was also frequently known as Paulinus. To what extent Wrmonoc is dealing with one person or several persons of the same name we shall never know, but there is little doubt that the region around Llanymddyfri in Carmarthenshire abounds in associations and church dedications to members of the family of a famous saint named Paulinus. These traditions and dedications are supported by the existence of a memorial stone found at Pant-y-Polion, Maes Llanwrthwl in the parish of Caio, north-west of Llanymddyfri which bears his name. There is nothing unreasonable, therefore, in accepting Wrmonoc's account of the traditions he found in Léon based on the evidence of *transmarini,* that this Paulinus took with him a party of twelve presbyters from Llanddeusant to the court of King Mark—'who is called Quonomorus'[1] in Cornwall, and afterwards accompanied

(1) This king (a prominent figure in Arthurian romances) is traditionally associated with Castle Dore in Cornwall, which is also the original site of an inscribed stone mentioning him and one of his sons by name *"Drustaus hic iacit Cunomori filius"* (see Hencken, H. O'N., *op. cit.,* pp. 228-9).

them to Brittany. As Doble points out the coincidences between Wrmonoc's statements and the information derived from Welsh and Cornish topography and archaeology is most striking and cannot be fortuitous. The Tywi valley in Carmarthenshire opens out on to the western Bristol Channel and must have played an important part in the evangelization of Brittany, and that these traditions were not forgotten there in the ninth century when Wrmonoc decided to identify St. Paul Aurelian with the founder of Llanddeusant, who, in turn, might have been Paul Penychen as well in his mind.[1] Léon lay directly across the channel from southern Cornwall and here we have the parish of Paul about two and a half miles south of Penzance. Fig. 41 shows that in Brittany the places called after him, or the churches and chapels bearing his name, are clearly concentrated in Léon, and are very sparsely found elsewhere, although there is some evidence of a transpeninsular connection with the Bro Weroch area. In the rest of France his cult is practically unknown, except in the valley of the Loire. One point in the distribution is, however, of very great interest to the historical geographer in that the Ile de Batz off the north coast is richer in traditions about the saint than any other place. In spite of Wrmonoc's narrative, it is likely that his little monastery on this island was founded by the saint before St. Pol de Léon itself. The Celtic saints were fond of island monasteries as is shown by the *Lives* of St. Budoc, St. Maudez, St. Gudwal and many others. It is noteworthy that Wrmonoc himself makes Paul's party land first of all on the island of Ushant. The significance of islands in the Age of the Saints lay in the fact that they provided natural landing places for travellers used to small ports and little shelter, while, as we have seen, they formed ideal retreats for those for whom the eremitical life was such an attraction.

We can now examine the rather different case of St. Maudez, whose *Life,* composed in the eleventh century, by a monk of Tréguier, claims that the saint was born in Ireland. He appears to have retired to the island of Enes-Modez (Ile Modez), in

(1) Doble, G. H., *The Saints of Cornwall,* Part I. Chatham 1960. *St. Paul Aurelian,* p. 36.

the Bréhat group in the Gulf of St. Brieuc and to have formed there a monastery of Celtic type with St. Budoc and St. Tudy, and possibly others, as his disciples. The distribution of his dedications in northern Brittany shows a spectacular cultural

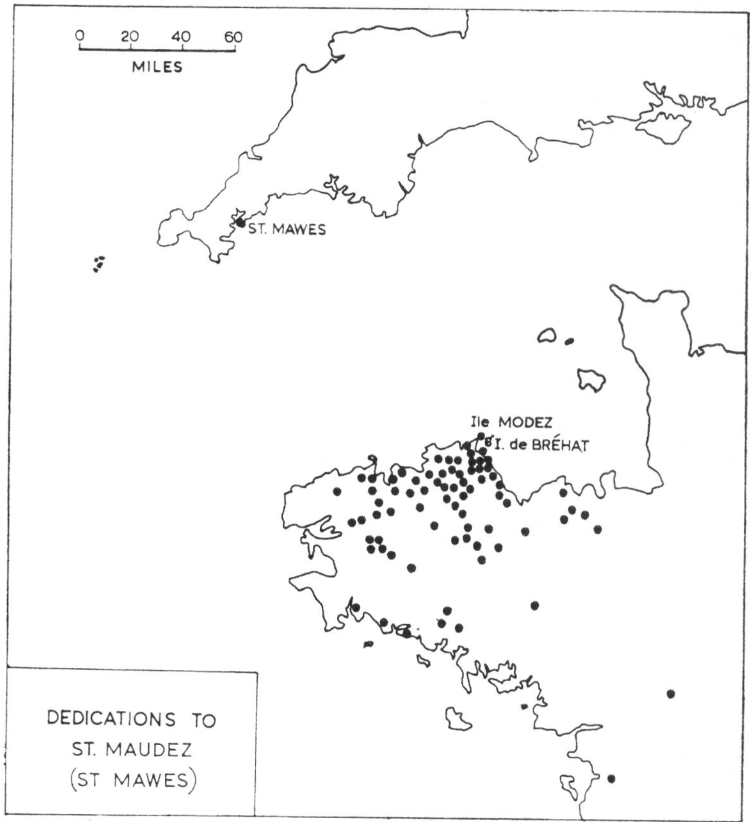

Fig. 42

pattern based on a dispersal from the Ile Modez.[1] It is particularly concentrated in the lowlands north of Guingamp forming the north-western peninsular area of Côtes du Nord, and in the lowlands around Morlaix in north-eastern Finistère (Fig. 42). There are altogether over sixty churches and chapels bearing

(1) Trépos, P., *Les Saints Bretons dans la Toponymie*, Rennes, 1955, p. 9.

the name of this saint in Brittany, and from this concentration on the north-eastern coastlands of western Brittany traces of his cult can be seen penetrating southwards along the Gouet-Blavet route in the east, and along the St. Pol de Léon-Pont Aven crossing in the west, where there are several dedications to him in the Aulne basin.

It should be noted, however, that there is only one place-name of the earliest type containing the name of St. Maudez, namely Lan Modez, but there is also Locmaudez in Plestin and one in Clohars-Carnoët. All the other places named after him (with the exception of Ile Modez) belong to a later period when churches and chapels owed their foundation not to their founders, but to the popularity of their cults, or, possibly, that the land nearby belonged to a particular monastery. When the monastery on the Ile Modez was destroyed by the North-men—the monks and their treasures became scattered, and the cult of St. Modez was carried far and wide into northern and central France. His cult is known in the Paris area, at Bourges and Orleans and in the dioceses of Chartres, Périgueux, Poitiers and Saintes. In spite of the popularity and widespread nature of his cult, we have very little documentary evidence for St. Maudez which is contemporary with his Age. Of the two *Lives* of the Saint, one, as we have seen, was written in the second half of the eleventh century, and the other is found in a fourteenth century manuscript formerly belonging to the Cathedral of Orleans. The later *Life* is only a literary re-arrangement of the earlier. Both *Lives* begin with his princely origins in Ireland, but, of course, we should be very careful in accepting such statements in late documents, for after the foundation and rapid growth of the great monasteries in Ireland it became the fashion for hagiographers to maintain that the saints of Cornwall and Brittany who came over the sea were of Irish extraction. Maudez's name is a British name[1] and he almost certainly came originally from Wales. A British Magudith would become Maudith in Old Welsh, and this would give a form Mause in Cornish, and Mause would be Anglicised into Mawes which is the present name of a small town on the

(1) Loth, J., *Les Noms des Saints bretons*, 1910, p. 89.

south coast of Cornwall, on the eastern side of Carrick Roads, just opposite Falmouth (Fig. 42). The latter town grew up within the parish of Budoc and it cannot be a mere coincidence that these two saints should be found side by side both on the south coast of Cornwall and on the north coast of Brittany, for in the Middle Ages there was a chapel dedicated to St. Budoc on the Ile Modez. We cannot but agree with Doble[(1)] that the conclusion to which all this evidence points would seem to be that Budoc and Maudez were monks and missionaries from Wales, or from some other part of Britain, who founded monasteries in Cornwall and Brittany and were in some way connected with Dol, as the territories from which their Breton cults would appear to have emanated remained administratively *enclavés* of the Diocese of Dol down to the French Revolution.

It is appropriate to close this aspect of our study by considering the distribution of dedications to the famous 'Children of Brychan' in Brittany. We have already seen that this semi-legendary family of saints appear to have come from the region of modern Breconshire. We have noted the traditional links of this family with southern Ireland and the presence of dedications to them there, as well as in central and eastern Cornwall and in Devon—a region which we found to be culturally distinct from the extreme south-western portions of that peninsula where 'outer seas' influences are found (see page 109). From central and eastern Cornwall and Devon members of this family, or missionaries carrying their cult, migrated to Brittany. Fig. 43 shows that the greatest number of dedications occur on the northern coastlands. Some, it is true, appear in Cornouaille, but the significance of this will emerge later.

In view of the evidence presented thus far it is not surprising that the whole of northern Brittany down to the period of the French Revolution remained divided into five bishoprics, those of Dol, St. Malo, St. Brieuc, Tréguier and St. Pol de Léon, all of which in turn were founded by monks from South Wales. It must be remembered, however, that the territorial bishoprics of later centuries were regional developments set up for conven-

(1) Doble, G. H., *ibid*, p. 192.

ience of administration on the Roman model, but their original nucleus in each case would appear to be an important settlement of one of the Welsh saints.

It is convenient to turn now to the 'outer' or 'coastwise' route. We recall the archaeological evidence for the spread of south-western Iron Age B culture up the Irish Sea coastlands in the pre-Roman era. We have now to show how this 'outer' sea-route was used, like the more 'inland' route, in reverse, in the Age of the Saints. The evidence is not quite so distinctive

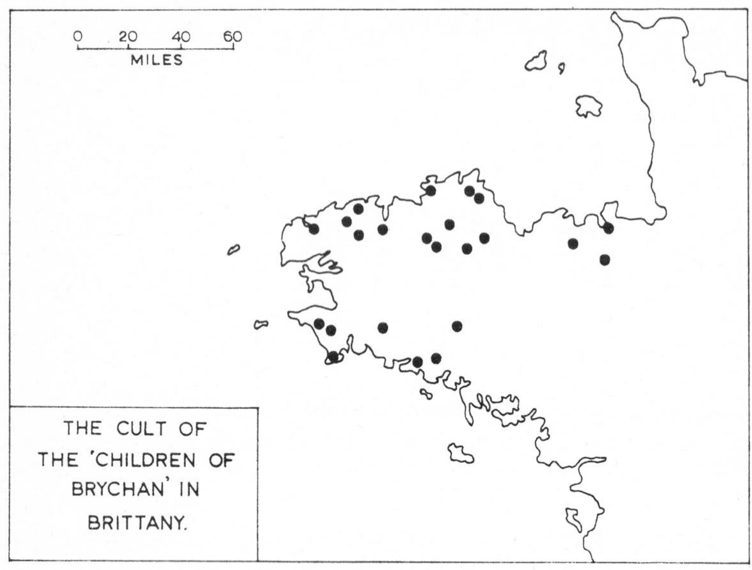

Fig. 43

in this case as both routes tended to overlap somewhat both in the South-west peninsula and in Brittany. This is one of the factors that helps to explain the somewhat confused distribution presented by the churches dedicated to the 'Children of Brychan' in Brittany, as already mentioned. Nevertheless, the use of the 'outer' sea lanes has left an unmistakable trace on dedication distribution patterns in the Celtic Lands. This fact has already been clearly demonstrated when discussing the 'Saints and the Seaways' in Chapter 3 (Fig. 15) with special reference to the churches bearing the names of SS. Petroc, Brioc and Carantoc. If we use Fig. 15 as a basis, and add to it dedications to SS. Nonna and Budoc (who are associated with a Welsh provenance); SS. Columb, Tudy, Day, Gudwal and Gwinear from a Cornish provenance, we have the interesting composite pattern shown on Fig. 44. A little more needs to be said about these saints before proceeding.

There are dedications to St. Nonna (everywhere in Wales regarded as the mother of St. David) in the outer margins of South Wales, particularly on the coast of Cardiganshire and Pembrokeshire. In Brittany St. Nonna is a male saint, possibly a companion rather than the mother of St. David.[1] In Wales there are several coastal sites involved. For example, a chapel on the edge of the cliffs, a little to the south of St. David's in Pembrokeshire, is dedicated to St. Nonna, while Llannerch Aeron and Llansanffraid (Llan-non) on the Cardigan Bay coast also carry the name of this saint. He or she appears again at Llan-non in Carmarthenshire and in Radnorshire, and still nearer the Bristol Channel coast at Ilston in Gower and at Eglwys Newydd about a mile from Margam abbey in Glamorgan. The parishes of Altaron and Pelynt in Cornwall, and Bradstone, just over the Devon border, indicate the presence of St. Nonna's cult in the South-west Peninsula. St. Budoc is well represented in Devon and Cornwall and again in Brittany. In the latter country he had a cell or monastery on the famous island of Lavré in the Bréhat group. This monastery is both interesting and important as it has been shown, as the result of archaeological work, to have been located within the ruins of a fourth century Roman villa. Mrs. Chadwick emphasizes its early origin and the importance of this group of islands as a nursery of many Breton saints.[2] Furthermore, traces of the cult of St. Budoc are to be found in the extreme coastal parts of South-western Pembrokeshire—the name appearing as St. Botolph's in the parish of Steynton, and close by is the site of an ancient chapel of St. Budoc on the banks of Hubberston Pill. Some doubt, however, may be cast on the antiquity of

(1) Doble, G. H., Cornish Saints Series. *St. Nonna,* p. 77.

(2) Chadwick, N. K., *Sir John Rhŷs Memorial Lecture,* op. cit., Map, p. 237.

the cult of St. Budoc in South Pembrokeshire. It may reach back to the Age of the Saints, but, on the other hand, the strong Anglo-French settlement of the area in the Middle Ages must not be overlooked. We can now pass on to consider other names in the list of saints mentioned above. St. Columb would appear to be associated with the Welsh party so strongly represented in the New Quay area of Cornwall. Close to settlements of Carantoc, Brioc and Petroc in this area we have St. Columb Major and St. Columb Minor, while Plougoulum occurs again in north-west Brittany. Saint Tudy is found some six miles south-west of Camelford in north-eastern Cornwall and he has several churches dedicated to him in southern Brittany. Saint Day, likewise, is patron of the parish of Gwennap, near Redruth, and has many dedications in southern Finistére. Moving still further westwards towards the ocean we can instance the examples of saints Gudwal and Gwinear. Saint Gudwal has a church about one and a half miles north-east of Penzance, while St. Gwinear's lies four miles south-east of Phillack in the Land's End peninsula. Both saints have chapels dedicated to them in southern Brittany, particularly in the Vannetais (see Fig. 44). Most scholars think that SS. Gudwal and Gwinear are Welsh saints, although they have left no memorials in Wales itself. Every effort has been made by place-name enthusiasts to find traces of their cult in the Principality. Attention, for example, has been drawn to the fact that in the parish of St. Dogmaels in the extreme north-west of Pembrokeshire, there is a place called Trewidwal[(1)] which many would wish to associate with St. Gudwal. Whatever view we take of the place-name evidence it is clear that the four 'Cornish' saints were as clearly associated as their Welsh colleagues with the 'outer' sea-lanes of Western Britain, and used them freely in their movements, including their crossing over to Brittany. Finally, there were saints like the Followers of St. Breaca (see page 110) said to have journeyed from Ireland, who clearly used the 'outer seaways.' There are dedications to the Followers

(1) Doble, G. H. *The Saints of Cornwall,* Part I—*St. Gudwal.* Chatham, 1960, p. 78, note 27.

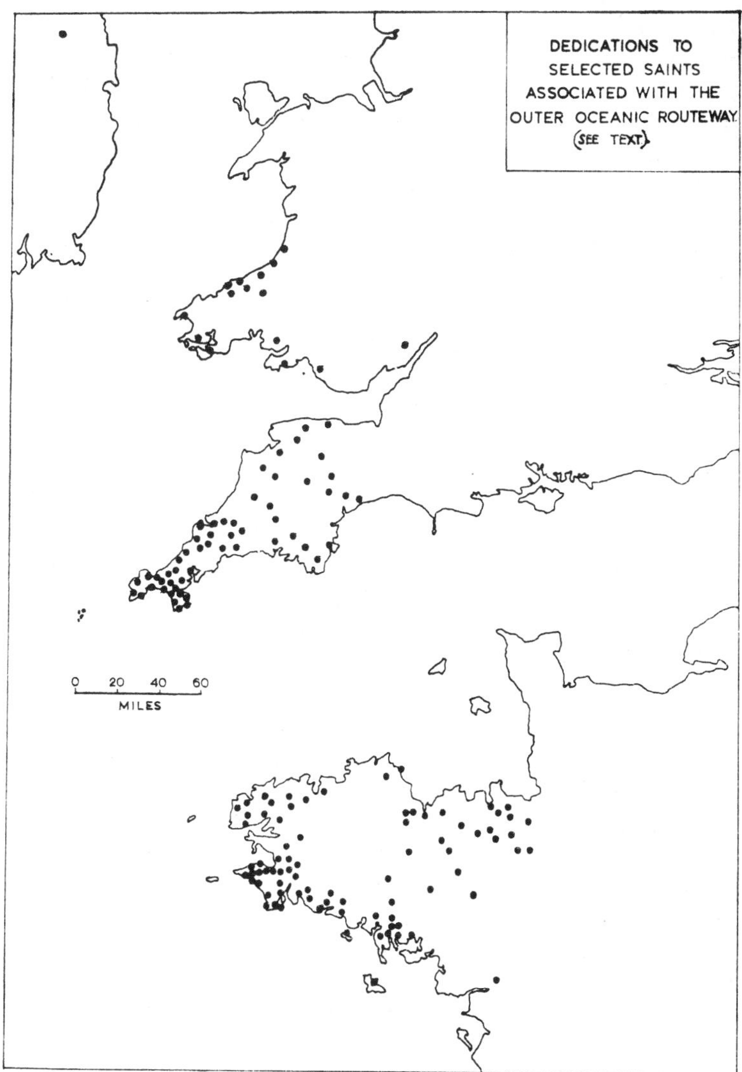

Fig. 44

of St. Breaca in Brittany as well as in Cornwall and Ireland, and so we should add their names to our list of Welsh and Cornish coastal *transmarini,* and indicate their settlements on

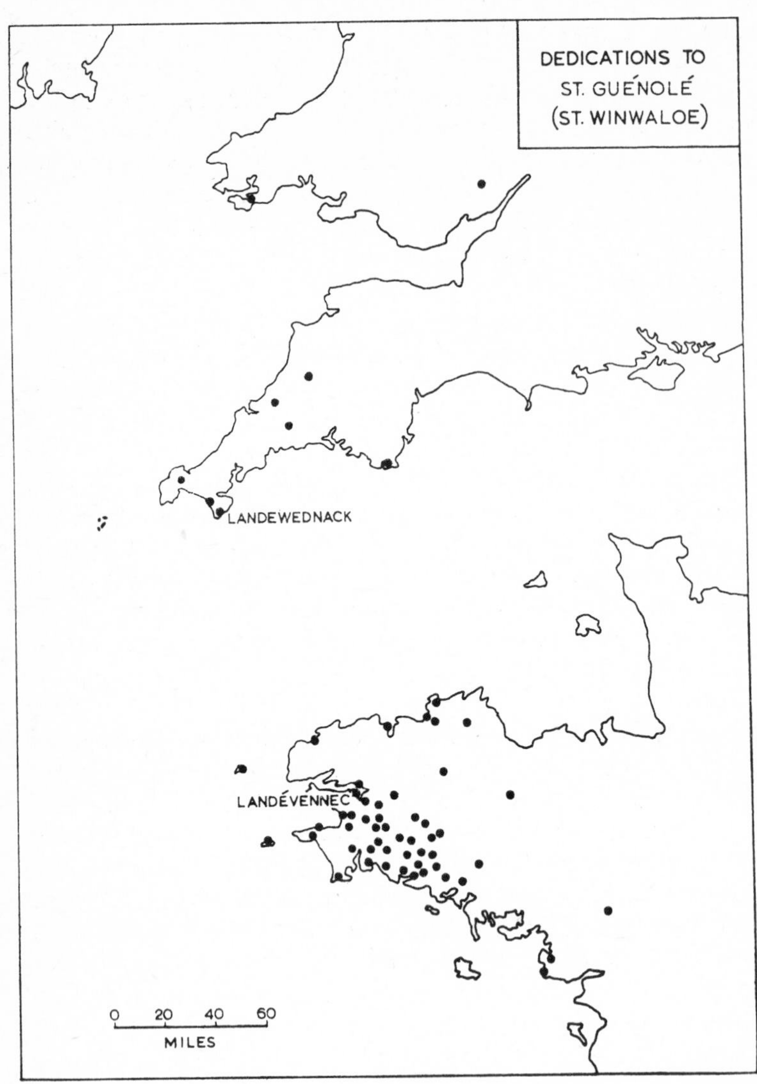

Fig. 45

Fig. 44. The map illustrates the important point that although there is evidence both in Cornwall and Brittany that the routes along which cultures seem to have spread from western France into Britain in Iron Age times tended to overlap somewhat, it is, nevertheless, clear that the 'outer' route was still in use in the Age of the Saints. Nowhere is this more clearly indicated than in Brittany by the concentration of dedications to saints using the 'outer' route in southern Finistére and along the Morbihan coast, as distinct from the north coast dedication distribution patterns associated with the saints who used the more 'inland' or 'easterly' crossings of the Severn Sea (Fig. 40 and Fig. 42).

Any doubts concerning the distinctiveness of these routes are dispelled when we consider the dedication distribution pattern of a well-known Breton saint like Winwaloe (Guénolé) (Fig. 45). All the evidence we possess indicates that St. Guénolé was Breton born, representing the second generation of immigrants. Place-name and literary evidence point to his parentage and early education having been associated with the Bréhat archipelago at the entrance to the Gulf of St. Brieuc, where St. Budoc is mentioned as his teacher. It is possible that his saga might be closely interwoven with that of the followers of St. Samson of Dol. In his *Life* written by Wrdisten, or Gourdisten, in the second half of the 9th century, we are told the usual story of how a vision appears before him beckoning him 'to move on,' and after putting aside his desire to visit Ireland, he sets out with eleven disciples on pilgrimage to some unknown destination. He finally reaches the coast of western Finistére, and sets up the great monastery of Landévennec, a community over which, later on, Wrdisten became abbot. In this way we have, at least, a record of the traditions concerning its origins preserved at a great monastery, written before the destruction of records by the Northmen in the tenth century. When eventually the Northmen burnt Landévennec in 914 the monks had to leave their home, but they took with them the body of St. Guénolé, his bell and other relics, including a copy of his *Life,* as written by Wrdisten. They made their way, first of all, to the Chateau du Loir between Le Mans and Tours. From here the Landévennec monks went on to Montreuil-sur-Mer, not far from Boulogne. The body of St. Guénolé was placed in the church of the abbey of St. Sauve in Montreuil. By the year 939 the Breton exiles were strong enough to amalgamate and push the Northmen out of Brittany, and the monastery of Landévennec was re-built. St. Guénolé's body however, was not brought back there and remained at Montreuil until the French Revolution, when it was destroyed. Meanwhile Montreuil became a new centre of the cult of St. Guénolé which then spread widely over northern France and even into lowland Britain itself. We are, however, concerned here with the cult of St. Guénolé in Brittany in the Age of the Saints and with the establishment of Landévennec. We can detect three major stages in the spread of his cult. First of all, there was an ancient tradition in the abbey that the first settlement of St. Guénolé was on the island of Tibidy in a nearby inlet of the sea. This illustrates once more the fondness of the Celtic saints for islands. Secondly, came the establishment of Landévennec and the gradual extension of its property accompanied by the erection of several churches and chapels dedicated to the founder saint. This extension is virtually the spread of the saint's cult from its established base. The resulting pattern in St. Guénolé's case is shown on Fig. 45, which, in turn, occupied much the same territory as that of the Venetic hill-forts in Iron Age times. The third stage in the spread of the cult of St. Guénolé followed the journeyings of his body and his relics until they found a permanent home at Montreuil. With this later post-Northmen spread we are not concerned. More important for our present thesis is the cult of St. Guénolé in South-western Britain, for in the southern part of the Lizard peninsula is a parish named Landewednack. In the year 1310 it was written Landéwennec. It is clearly the same name as Landévennec, and the church in both places is dedicated in honour of St. Winwaloe. Close by is Gunwalloe where the saint is likewise honoured. He is also patron of Tremaine in north Cornwall. Here we notice the spread of a south-western Breton cult into the extreme western portion of Cornwall. It could not, of course, have been the other way round, as Landewednack is a tiny unimportant place, sheltering in a hollow just above a little landing place called Church Cove—obviously chosen for its direct contact with the sea. Landévennec in Brittany, however, is magnificently situated, and became the principal religious centre of western Brittany with numerous sub-chapels and smaller monasteries under its jurisdiction, of which Landewednack in Cornwall might well have been one. Before the Reformation there were two other chapels in Cornwall dedicated to St. Winwaloe—one near Roscraddock, and another in the parish of St. Germans, while the church of Portlemouth at the mouth of the river Salcombe in the extreme south of Devon is also dedicated to him. These churches and chapels are located on sites much beloved by the Celtic saints and may well date from their time and be connected with the Breton monasteries, and even with Landévennec itself. It is thus worthwhile observing that cultures based on Cornouaille affect not only the extreme tip of the South-western peninsula, but spread into eastern Cornwall and Devon, possibly in a somewhat diluted form, as they did in prehistoric times. If we accept the views of Wade-Evans and Baring-Gould and Fisher(1) that Wonastow near Monmouth has St. Winwaloe as its patron, and that St. Twynnells in south-western Pembrokeshire (which was described as *Ecclesia S. Winnoci* in 1291) may have some connection with St. Winnol (as he was known in England) then, indeed, the pattern of a prehistoric Iron Age diffusion into south-western Britain is most faithfully reproduced in this later Age.

This study of the Breton evidence has shown once again the importance of the western sea-routes, and the great activity that must have been associated with them. We cannot, therefore, rule out the possibility that there were quite extensive movements of *peregrini* passing in both directions from peninsula to peninsula at this time. We need not necessarily agree with Doble(2) in this case, that a landing of Latavian(3) saints on the coasts of Wales in large numbers (as is said to have happened

(1) Wade-Evans, A. W., *Welsh Christian Origins,* Oxford, 1934, p. 163 and Baring-Gould and Fisher, J., *Lives of the British Saints,* Vol. IV, p. 36 but see also Doble, G. H., *St. Winwaloe, The Saints of Cornwall,* Part II, Oxford, 1962, p. 101.

(2) Doble, G. H., *Saint Patern,* Cornish Saints Series, No. 43, 1940, p. 17.

(3) *Latavia* is the Latinized form of the Welsh *Llydaw*, 'Brittany' in English.

when St. Cadfan[1] and his followers landed in the neighbourhood of Tywyn, and others moved up the Teifi, Ystwyth and Rheidol rivers, and affected the coastlands as far north as Bardsey) is as ridiculous to imagine as a return movement across the Atlantic, organised by eighteenth century English colonists in North America, to Christianize Britain at that time. We know that the analogy in this case would, anyway, be a false one, for such missionary enterprises were not the first concern of the Celtic saints—their urge was to go on pilgrimage "for the love of God, they cared not whither." In any case, if we accept survival of prehistoric culture regions into the post-Roman age in the west, as is the main theme of this work, then the *'Latavian' peregrini,* wherever they originated, seem to have moved much in the same way, and in much the same areas as their prehistoric predecessors had done.

(1) It is not without some significance in this context that the Welsh genealogies make St. Cadfan the half-brother of St. Winwaloe.

CHAPTER VIII

SETTLEMENTS

TWO types of ecclesiastical settlement appear to be associated with the Celtic Church. The more important, the monasteries in the stricter sense of the term, were usually large settlements. They began as small missionary stations but grew into more important centres, becoming the great schools of learning from which the saints set out. It was in this way that Clonmacnoise, Clonard, Lismore, Kildare, Bangor, Nendrum and many other great Irish monasteries arose; while in Wales we had Llancarfan and Llanilltud and others which developed in later centuries into the 'mother churches' of Wales, each with its *clas,* or community of canons, with an abbot at their head. Other settlements took the form of hermitages wherein individual monks or small communities sought a place of solitude where they could serve God and live frugally on the produce of their labour. References to idividuals 'seeking the desert' (eremum) on the headlands and islands of Wales, Ireland, Cornwall, Scotland and Brittany are common in the *Lives* of the saints. Such a community at Muirbulcmar in the 6th century is mentioned by Adamnan in his *Life of St. Columba* as *'locus anchoretarum'* while Giraldus refers to examples which survived until his own day, notably on the island of Priestholm (Ynys Lannog) off Anglesey.[1] It would be useful to consider in a little more detail selected examples of each type of settlement.

About seven miles along the western shores of Strangford Lough in Ulster is an island anciently known as Noendruim or Nendrum but now called Mahee Island. At the present time it is joined to the mainland by two causeways. The name Mahee is derived from Mochaoi, the reputed founder of a Celtic monastery on the island in the fifth century. Experts see

(1) Adamnan, *Vita Sancti Columbae* III, 23, and Giraldus Cambrensis, *Descripta Kambriae,* II, 7.

no reason to doubt that St. Mochaoi was connected with Nendrum and the frequency with which his name is coupled with the site strongly suggests that he was the founder. The site itself is on the landward side of the island, so that it faces the mainland—a situation strongly suggesting that the founder must have come over the seas and chosen such a base for future work—a land to evangelize before him and a great sea-lough behind him, through which he could maintain contact with his parent monastery and the outside world. Indeed, the most recent interpretation of the activities of St. Mochaoi relate him to the northern cultural province of the Irish Sea Basin, to Candida Casa rather than to Armagh as the initial source of his inspiration and base of his operations.(1) Such a view is, of course, completely in keeping with the general arguments set out in this book.

The site of Nendrum remained unidentified until 1845, although, of course, the name appeared in early manuscripts such as the 9th century Félire of Oengus, where it is coupled with the name of St. Mochaoi. It was the Irish scholar William Reeves, Bishop of Down, who identified Nendrum with the site on Mahee Island. He recognised straightaway the stump of a round tower, and a partial excavation revealed a church foundation nearby, as well as the fact that St. Mochaoi, had elected to place his original settlement within the innermost enclosure of an abandoned cashel, or fort, which had been defended by three concentric embankments. Reeves' report on his excavations in 1845 contains a plan of the monastery which differs but little from that now available after the extensive excavations of the whole site carried out by H. C. Lawlor between 1922 and 1924.(2) While we cannot now accept Lawlor's association of St. Mochaoi and Nendrum with St. Patrick, we can, however, use his carefully prepared plan of the monastery, derived from his excavations, as a representative picture of the lay-out of a large Celtic monastery in the Age of the Saints.

The essential features are shown on Fig. 46. Dominating

(1) Towill, E. G., *Saint Mochaoi and Nendrum,* Ulster Journ. of Archaeology, 3rd Series, Vol. 27, 1964, p. 103 ff.

(2) Lawlor, H. C., *The Monastery of Saint Mochaoi of Nendrum,* Belfast, 1925.

the lay-out are the concentric cashel walls built of dry stone walling and enclosing between them an area of over six acres.

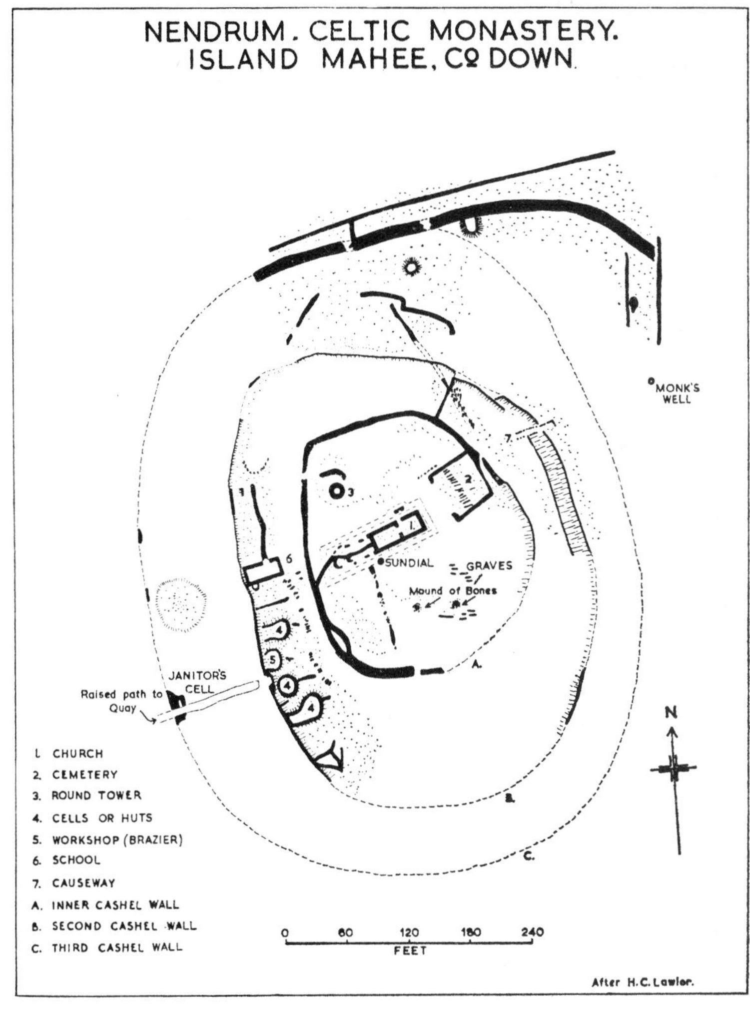

Fig. 46

Each wall had several gateways, one of the most important being the west gate of the third cashel leading to the quayside, with the foundations of the janitor's cell near the entrance.

This emphasizes once more the supreme importance of contact with the sea in the days of the Celtic saints. Then, in the centre of all is the church itself. The ruins now include a nave and chancel and they certainly represent the foundations of what was a late medieval building. Judging from examples elsewhere, this church is most certainly the successor of earlier buildings in wattle, wood and stone, and might even have contained the shrine of St. Mochaoi himself. Graves of the monks are found near the west end of the church and at some distance away to the southwards there are others. There are many more within a walled-in cemetery to the east of the church. Reeves found these graves together with skeletons in 1845, while, in addition, there were many Irish crosses and other carved stones. Slightly to the north-west of the church is the base of the Round Tower. Such towers, tall and slender, and often forty or fifty feet high, seem to have been a feature of most Irish monasteries, especially following upon the early raids of the Northmen from about 850 A.D. The Nendrum tower can be shown to have been built from stones collected from the cashel walls. These towers were the last refuge of the community in times of peril, and peril, indeed, there was—Nendrum itself being destroyed in a raid in 974. Between the inner and the second cashel wall was another very important building. It is rectangular in shape and orientated similarly to the church. This was the monastery school. We know from the *Life* of St. Finnian of Clonard that Nendrum was well-established as a place of learning by the end of the fifth century. It was in schools of this kind, often referred to as the *scriptoria,* that the Scriptures were copied and the magnificent Irish illuminated manuscripts were written. The plan does not show the other buildings, the guest house and the refectory, usually found in large monasteries of this type. The plan does, however, show numerous hut sites. Four of them were excavated in some detail, showing them to be circular or oval in form and very similar to those at Iona. From material found near these cells it was clear that they were workshops—one being the brazier's shop, indicating that the early Celtic monasteries were engaged in metal work as well as woodwork. Some of the more important monasteries produced excellent early jewellery and glass. Some of the workshops must also have made pottery, for near the base of the round tower was found some sherds of hand-made pottery. This was probably local work and may be quite early in date owing to the fact that it was not wheel-turned. More important, however, in the ceramic field is the recognition in recent years of the presence of imported Dark Age pottery at Nendrum. A few fragments of a rather coarse red ware with a rough surface have been found on the site. This is the same type of pottery as that recorded at Garranes and Garryduff in southern Ireland, and at Padstow, Castle Dore, and Tintagel and other sites in Britain.[(1)] Its significance in relation to the sea-routes of the Dark Ages has already been discussed and in this context it proves conclusively the trade links of Nendrum with southern France, and possibly with the Western Mediterranean as well. Along these trade routes wines and other luxuries entered the northern monasteries.

Many of the other features revealed by the excavations indicate various aspects of the day to day life of the monks. There are the domestic cells usually constructed of wickerwork. Most frequently two monks occupied a single cell so that one may make confession to the other as occasion arose. The plan shows also the paved pathways, or causeways, for moving around the large site in wet weather, and the all-important well on which the monastery's water supply depended. In addition, it had a pillar sundial, obviously the public clock, and most interesting of all, the saint's hand-bell which called the community to prayer at the appropriate hours, was also found. Finally, we should notice the large midden or rubbish heap, and the mounds of bones collected together—a detailed examination of these might be of the greatest interest to the archaeologist, providing further details of the food they ate and its possible sources.

To the student of historical geography these larger monastic settlements present a picture of a miniature town—complete with its arrangement of houses, administrative, domestic and

(1) Radford, C. A. R., *Imported Pottery found at Tintagel, Cornwall,* in *Dark Age Britain* (Ed. Harden), London, 1956, p. 64.

religious buildings, its industries and trade. Many of them, like Nendrum, were located in positions that were admirably suited to the conditions of their time. When these conditions changed many of the monasteries lost their *raison d'etre,* and decayed, leaving nothing whatsoever behind them, as was the case at Nendrum. Other large monasteries located on sites that continued to possess strategic and nodal advantages, or distinct prestige even under the changed circumstances, continued to gather population around them, and the settlement has survived in one form or another to this day. Some have become towns of appreciable size, as in the case of Armagh, and since, like Nendrum, it was originally located inside a former cashel "with triple concentric ramparts", geographers have seen their reflection in early plans of the settlement and even in the lay-out of the city today.(1)

At the other end of the settlement scale we have the isolated hermitages of the monks who left the larger establishments and sought the 'desert.' The eremitical aspect of Celtic monasteries has already been fully discussed, and was one of the special features commented upon by early workers in this field. H. Zimmer writing in the early years of the present century sums up the position as follows: 'Single individuals or groups of three, seven or twelve were seized with the desire of separating themselves from the large colonies of monks—for such the Irish monasteries were..and went to live in still greater seclusion from the world. At first they were satisfied with little isles in their native lakes and rivers, not far from the monasteries forming a *civitas.* Then they began to retire to the numerous islands off the Irish coast, and when these were no longer places of solitude, a voyage in frail boats was risked to search out some desert isle in the ocean.'(2) For illustrative purposes we can select the last example quoted by Zimmer and look at one of the most famous of all sites of Celtic eremiticism—the small community on Sceilg Mhichíl, eight miles out from the Kerry

(1) Price, J. T., *The Urban geography of Armagh.* Unpublished M.A. Thesis presented to the Department of Geography, Queen's University, Belfast, 1959.

(2) Zimmer, H., *The Celtic Church in Britain and Ireland* (Translation, Meyer), London, 1902.

coast, where a solitary rock holds on its summit a tiny group of monastic buildings seven hundred feet above the pounding waves of the open Atlantic. Here, surely, is a veritable "desert isle in the ocean." The date of the founding of this settlement is unknown, but it was certainly in existence in the ninth century when the 'dedication' to the now unknown hermit or hermits, who first founded the settlement, had already been replaced by that of the Archangel. It should be noted that the cult of St. Michael spread rapidly in the Celtic west following

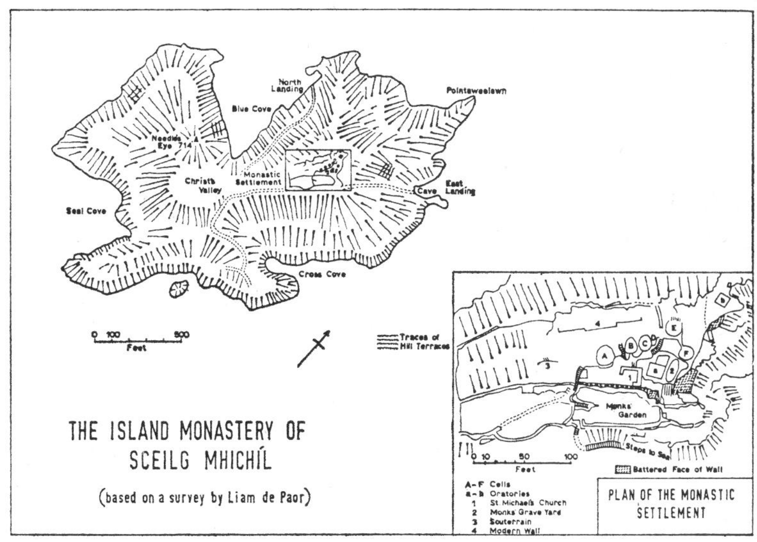

Fig. 47

upon the supposed apparition on Mont San Michel in Normandy in the year 710.[1] The dedication was frequently applied to sanctuaries in high places. The earliest buildings on Sceilg Mhichíl (there are also ruins of a later church) consist of six beehive cells and two little oratories (see Fig. 47). In addition, there is a small graveyard with rough slabs incised with crosses, and a main enclosure in which there are two tall slabs roughly shaped to the outline of a cross and carved in low relief with a simple cruciform pattern. We need not be worried

(1) Baring-Gould, S. and Fisher, J., *op. cit.*, Vol. iii, pp. 156 and 311.

by the fact that there are two oratories associated with such a small community. It was a frequent occurrence in these early hermitages for cells to be 'dedicated' to several saints within the same enclosure. At Hentland in the Welsh Border country we read of an oratory of St. Dubricius and another of St. Teilo occurring side by side in the same churchyard—*Heunlaun Debric et Laun Teliau in uno cimiterio.*[1] The original meaning of the Welsh *Llan,* the Irish and Scottish *cill,* the Manx *Keeill* and the Cornish *Lan* was precisely that of an enclosed cemetery containing a chapel or chapels of early Christian date. It is in this way, too, that we can explain such modern place names as Llanddeusant, Llantrisant and Llanpumsaint in Wales. What is more interesting at Sceilg Mhichíl is the construction of the cells and oratories in relation to the peculiar physical conditions of this remarkable site. The usual practice would appear to be that the oratories were constructed either of wickerwork or wattles, or that they were rectangular timber buildings thatched with brushwood or reeds—*more Scottorum*—"in the Irish fashion," according to Bede.[2] As H. G. Leask says these little churches have no architectural pretentions, they have only a special interest in that they were evolved, unlike those of Western Europe at the time, in almost entire independence of Roman traditions of building.[3] It is clear also that many of the first stone-built oratories preserved something of the form of their wooden prototypes. Recent excavations of an early Hiberno-Celtic monastic site at Ardwall Isle near Gatehouse of Fleet in Kirkcudbrightshire in southern Scotland have revealed the complete sequence.[4] The first stage revealed the postholes of a wooden church[5] containing several burials with a partly subterranean shrine which must have contained a wooden chest holding the bones of some holy

(1) Doble, G. H., *St. Dubricius,* Welsh Saints Series No. 2. Guildford, 1962, p. 15, quoting the original statement from the *Book of Llandav.*

(2) Bede, *Historia Ecclesiastica gentis Anglorum,* Book III, Chap. 25.

(3) Leask, H. G., *Irish Churches and Monastic Buildings,* Dundalk, 1955, p. 1.

(4) Thomas, C., *"Ardwall Isle: the excavations of an Early Christian site of Irish Type."* Trans. Dumf. and Galloway Nat. Hist. & Ant. Soc., 3rd Series, Vol. XLIII, 1966.

(5) Compare the excavations at Church Island, Co. Kerry (O'Kelly, M. J. *"Church Island near Valencia, Co. Kerry,"* P.R.I.A., 59, C2 (1958) p. 57 ff.)

person, presumably the saintly founder of the site. The second phase is another wooden chapel or oratory with further inhumations, but now containing a free standing stone shrine into which had been translated the skeletal remains of the individual previously interred in the rock-cut shrine of Phase I. Then, finally came the stone built chapel with altar and shrine possibly combined, the last resting place of the Sanctus who had occupied successively the rock-cut shrine of Phase I and the postulated free standing shrine of Phase II. Such stages of growth would have been impossible on Sceilg Mhichíl with neither wood nor thatch—so that the monks' cells and the two tiny oratories must have been built of unmortared masonry in the first instance. They were remarkably well constructed, being paved, and probably drained, and waterproof. Even on this extremely exposed site every care was taken to make the maximum use of the limited geographical facilities. Alternative landing places were available in the separate coves—Seal Cove, Blue Cove, Cross Cove and East Landing–according to the vagaries of the wind and tide. The entire group of monastic buildings are placed on a narrow rock-shelf against the final slope leading up to the summit ridge. They were thus sheltered by the ridge from the strong prevailing south-westerly winds, while at the same time they faced south-eastwards on to a narrow walled terrace which contained the monks' garden. From this terrace steps and pathways led down to the sea. On every part of the rock where it was possible to do so, stretches of retaining wall were built to hold back pockets of soil. Consequently, there are still remains of terraced cultivation on different parts of the rock. Possibly a few plants were cultivated in such precarious positions. The hermits most certainly possessed goats and lived on goats' milk and flesh. The cliffs naturally abound in birds, which together with their eggs were another source of food supply. Fish, too, were plentiful in the seas around so that a hard and frugal existence was just possible.[(1)] The remains of a souterrain on this inhospitable

(1) De Paor, L. "*A survey of Sceilg Mhichíl.*" J.R.S.A.I., 85 (1955), p. 174, and de Paor, M. & L., *Early Christian Ireland,* London, 4th impression (1964), pp. 52-56.

site probably reflects the austere discipline practised by the monks whereby, as an act of penance, one of them might subject himself to incarceration in one of these cold, narrow, dark, damp holes underground.

It is obvious that no modern settlement could ever be established at Sceilg Mhichíl, and it is interesting mainly in that it has retained so much of its original form. Strangely enough no settlement grew up around the monastery on Ardwall Isle either, although this would not have been impossible from the geographical point of view. On the contrary, settlements did arise around a very large number of the smaller hermitages of the Celtic saints scattered throughout Ireland, Scotland, Wales, Cornwall, the Isle of Man and Brittany, much in the same way as they did around some of the larger monasteries. The important factors in the case of the smaller sanctuaries were, first of all, their general accessibility or nodality, and, secondly, their attraction for pilgrims, especially in the Middle Ages. In many cases pilgrims gathered around the shrines of these holy hermits in large numbers, believing, as was the custom of the time, that the saint, although dead, could still work miracles from his tomb. The resultant settlement accretion is excellently summarized for us, in the case of the village of St. Day, two miles north-east of Redruth in Cornwall, by the famous Elizabethan cartographer and historian John Norden, who, writing about the year 1600, notes "St. Daye, a hamlet: there was sometime a chappell, now decayde, called Trinitye," [we notice how the original dedication to St. Day had been supplanted by one more acceptable to the medieval church] "to which men and women came in times paste from far in pilgrimage. The resorte was so greate, as it made the people of the countrye to bringe all kinde of provision to that place; and so longe it contynued to increase, that it grew to a kinde of market; and by that meanes it grew and contynueth a kinde of market to this daye, without further charter."[(1)]

In pursuing further the relationship of the Celtic Church to the settlement problems of the Dark Ages, the historical

(1) Quoted by Doble, G. H. in his *St. Day*, Cornish Saints Series, No. 32, p. 32

geographer has to consider to what extent the initial settlements of the Celtic saints were located near to the existing centres of settlement. Ralegh Radford states categorically that the larger monasteries were "in many cases situated near the more important settlements," while the hermits naturally "sought remote and lonely refuges."[(1)] Since he is dealing especially with Anglesey he cites Caergybi (Holyhead), Penmon, and Llangaffo as examples of large monasteries near to important settlements at the time of their establishment.

Before examining one of these examples in some detail it is worthwhile noting the extent to which the Celtic saints made use of what were certainly abandoned sites in their own day. Although no actual archaeological remains of an early ecclesiastical settlement survive at Caergybi, the parish church, bearing the saint's name, is located within the disused Roman fort. Likewise, Celtic saints established settlements in the ruins of Caerleon and Caerwent. At Caerleon the church of St. Cadoc is placed on the site of the former *praetorium* within the legionary fortress. In Brittany we have already referred to the interesting case of the island of Lavré. More recently, it is reported that the first church of St. Tegai, situated some three quarters of a mile away from the present village church bearing his name, was originally placed on a site where emergency excavations have revealed burial grounds of both Neolithic and Bronze Age dates. Almost by accident on this site there was revealed sixty rows of Christian graves together with the outline of a sixth century Celtic church, within which were the traces of a pit or grave which had at one time been surrounded by wooden props—undoubtedly the original shrine or grave of St. Tegai.[(2)] Possibly a second church of St. Tegai built of stone grew up on this site before a new position was sought (for some reason unknown) around which the present village of Llandegai has grown up.

We must return from this slight, but, nevertheless, important digression to the definite evidence that exists for the establish-

(1) Roy. Comm. Anct. Monuments, *Anglesey*. Introduction "Early Medieval Period," H.M.S.O. 1937, p. xci.

(2) 'Site found of Sixth Century Church.' *Daily Telegraph*, May 16th, 1967.

ment of a Celtic monastery near to a contemporary inhabited settlement. The site in question is that of Penmon in south-eastern Anglesey, established by St. Seiriol—a 6th century saint. About eighty yards north-east of the present ruins of the monastic church are the remains of a cell and a holy well. It is probable that St. Seiriol's original settlement was here. The double structure now enclosing the well represents the nave and chancel of this original chapel, and the adjoining oval hut his dwelling place (see Fig. 48). As time went on more monks

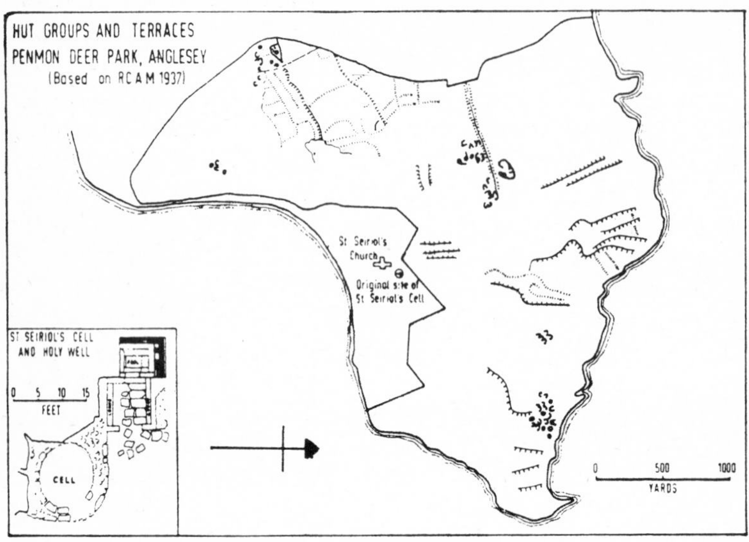

Fig. 48

would assemble at Penmon and they would be housed likewise in scattered cells, or groups of cells, of the type found at Nendrum and Tintagel—the whole being enclosed by a wall or bank-just as Nendrum was enclosed within the ramparts of the original cashel. In due course it is likely that St. Seiriol himself withdrew to an island retreat on Ynys Lannog, followed, doubtless, by later leaders of the monastery. As has already been noted there were hermits still living on the island in the days of Giraldus Cambrensis (see page 191). More significant for our present thesis is the fact that to the north and west of the site where St. Seiriol originally settled is Penmon Deer Park, an uncultivated roughly triangular promontory composed of limestone rock about half a square mile in extent. Scattered over this territory are several hut-groups and cultivation terraces (see Fig. 48). Altogether the remains of approximately fifty-eight huts can be detected, not including several rectangular and sub-rectangular enclosures. These remains are clearly indicative of a fairly large-size village of at least three hundred inhabitants. One of the huts was excavated in 1932 and the finds included a socket for holding an upright post in the centre, which in turn held up the roof; a very large number of stones used as pot boilers, found both inside the hut and outside; stone hammers; a large saddle quern and a rubbish heap of shells and bones. In addition, three metal objects were also found—a thin bronze plate, an iron socketed gauge, and, most interesting of all, a composite iron sickle, indicating the presence of cultivation, which was, doubtless, of a type similar to that usually found associated with Celtic Fields—an agriculture based on small fields tilled by a light plough.(1) Ralegh Radford thinks that the most intensive period of occupation of this site was contemporary with the Roman period and before the Irish settlers in these parts were driven off about 500 A.D.(2) Many villagers, doubtless, continued to inhabit the site for several centuries later. We have, therefore, at Penmon a clear example of a Celtic monastery being sited near to an important contemporary settlement.

The general thesis propounded by Ralegh Radford, and well illustrated at Penmon, has been considerably extended in recent years by the work of T. Jones-Pierce and G. R. J. Jones.(3) These workers have revolutionized our conception of the nature of early Welsh society based on the classical descriptions of Seebohm, T. P. Ellis and Vinogradoff. Jones-Pierce and G. R. J. Jones have destroyed the traditional picture of early Welsh society being tribal, pastoral and nomadic and

(1) Roy. Comm. Anct. Mon. *op. cit.*, p. 128.

(2) Roy. Comm. Anct. Mon., ibid, *Preface*, p. lxxviii.

(3) For a general statement see Jones, G. R. J., *Welsh Historical Review* Vol. 1, No. 2, 1961, p. 130.

unchanging over long ages. They envisage that in the period immediately following the departure of the Romans there emerged two major social groups—freemen and bondmen. At first it would appear that the freemen were but a small privileged minority supported by a sedentary bond majority. The bond-men lived in nucleated settlements (usually referred to as bond-vills), groups of which were attached to the residence, or *llys*, of the local lord to whom the bondmen rendered dues and services, as we read in the early Welsh Laws, codified, it is supposed, by Hywel Dda, in the late ninth century. In time, the bond-vills with their open fields were largely replaced by isolated farmsteads and enclosed fields. This process would seem to have been completed by the sixteenth century. Originally, the farmsteads of the free tribesmen were disposed in open order around the edges of their open arable fields. These fields, likewise, were enclosed by the sixteenth century.[1] Reverting to the author's major arguments, the existence of this aristocratic minority of freemen does not warrant a picture of an all-pervading tribalism, or, as is so often accepted, is there any justification for the equation of this alleged tribalism with pastoral nomadism. As far as the ground picture is concerned we are left with a rural scene involving a group of scattered hamlets attached to the *llys* of a local lord, and clusters of free tribesmen's holdings around an arable patch cultivated by them in common. In the early Dark Ages the *llys* was very often located within a reconditioned hill-fort, or in the ruins of a Roman villa, and the hamlets of the bondmen were outside, near to the good agricultural land. These settlements, therefore, tended to be near to the heavier soil areas which in many cases meant entry into forest clearings. In this way these newer concepts of early Welsh society are in keeping with universally accepted modern ideas concerning the movement of peoples into forested land in Western Europe at this time—a matter which has already been stressed.

G. R. J. Jones' views have not met with universal acceptance,

(1) Summary of a paper delivered to the British Association for the Advancement of Science—*Advancement of Science,* Vol. XV, No. 60, 1959.

more particularly from the archaeologists. Leslie Alcock[1], for example, claims that there is no proven archaeological evidence for the re-occupation of many of the hill-forts after about 400 A.D., and, particularly, for some of those specifically instanced by Jones. It is further argued that all hill-forts built at this time were small in size and weakly defended, and only very minor improvements were made to older ones. There is little evidence, therefore, according to Alcock, for Jones' picture of the lord living in his 'hill-fort *llys*' in great estate, dependent on the rich supply of serf-labour and serf-produced food at the hands of the bond-men. Alcock does, however, concede that it is possible that the seeds of the medieval system of bond hamlets, as described in the Welsh Laws, were sown in the ruins of the villa system, and adds that this is as far as reasonable inference can go. He has stated elsewhere that the bond-vills would appear to be in decay at the time of the Anglo-Norman conquest, but that we may infer that they flourished in the later Dark Ages and that their origin must be sought in the late Roman and immediate post-Roman centuries.[2] Thus, if we put the archaeological quarrel about the re-conditioning of the larger hill-forts aside, both writers seem to accept the presence of bond-vills in some stage of development in Wales in the immediate post-Roman centuries. Both are, likewise, in agreement that bond-vills were more in evidence before the year 1100 than after.

It is Jones, however, who suggests a link between the bond-vills and the settlements of the Celtic saints and he does so in no uncertain terms—"indeed every Celtic church appears to have been established in a bond hamlet, the only exceptions being occasional lonely hermitages."[3] His footnotes instance three examples: Clynnog Fawr in Caernarvonshire,[4] Heneglwys in Anglesey[5] and Llangyfelach in Glamorgan.[6]

(1) Alcock, Leslie, *Settlement patterns in Celtic Britain, Antiquity,* 1962, p. 51 ff.

(2) Alcock, Leslie, *Dinas Powys,* Appendix 3 p. 196. Univ. of Wales Press, Cardiff, 1964.

(3) Jones, G. R. J., *op. cit.,* pp. 341-2.

(4) R.C.A.M. Caernarvonshire, Vol. II, p. 216. 1962.

(5) Record of Caernarvon, pp. 26, 44.

(6) *Black Book of St. David's,* Ed. Willis Bund, 1902, pp. 285-9.

Jones' picture is valuable in that it helps to explain the very large number of Celtic churches that now appear isolated in the landscape (with possibly only the vicarage or a school nearby). This situation could have resulted easily from the general decay of the bond-vills in Wales, or the *clachan* settlements in Ireland. All isolated churches would certainly not be classed by G. R. J. Jones as "occasional lonely hermitages"—hermitages which in view of their poor siting had failed to attract further settlement around them. In his view many such isolated churches are isolated today because the original bond-vills or *maerdrefi* in which they were placed no longer exist.

The contention that in the first instance the Celtic saints established their cells close to existing settlements is further illustrated by studies based on the Isle of Man. All students who have studied the ancient land systems of the island emphasize the importance of treens and quarter lands. The treens may have been the original units, possibly family lands lying around a cluster of homesteads, rather like the Irish *clachan,* and they later became subdivided into quarterlands. Many think that parallels can be drawn with the land system of medieval Wales, to which reference has already been made, and rather more tenuously with land systems in the Highlands and Islands of Scotland.(1) It was the great Scandinavian scholar Marstrander who first suggested that every treen had, from the earliest days of Celtic Christianity at least one *Keeill* or chapel.(2) This has been generally accepted by most scholars even though it is by no means certain that all the *Keeills* are of pre-Norse date. Elwyn Davies has shown the distribution of treens (omitting abbey lands, baronies and larger intacks), while Marstrander has prepared a map showing the general distribution of Manx *Keeills*. These maps have been reduced to the same scale and superimposed to produce Fig. 49, which does demonstrate fairly clearly Marstrander's general contention. A reasonable inference is, therefore, that the wandering Celtic monks both

(1) Davies, Elwyn, *"Treens and Quarterlands. A study of the Land System of the Isle of Man." Trans. Inst. of British Geogr.* Vol. 22, 1957, pp. 97 ff.

(2) Marstrander, C., *Treen og Keill et førnorsk jorddelingsprinsipp pa de Britiske Øyene* (Treen and Keill, a pre-Norse land system in the British Isles) English summary, *Norsk Tidsskrift for Sprogvidenskap* 6 (1932) and 8 (1937).

in the Isle of Man, and elsewhere, first attempted to contact the local lord, or petty chieftain, and sought not only his conversion, but ultimately, his permission to settle somewhere on his estate. The famous story of St. Columba visiting the Pictish King Brude in his hill-fort near Inverness, and his confrontation with the king's druids, is by no means irrelevant in this context.

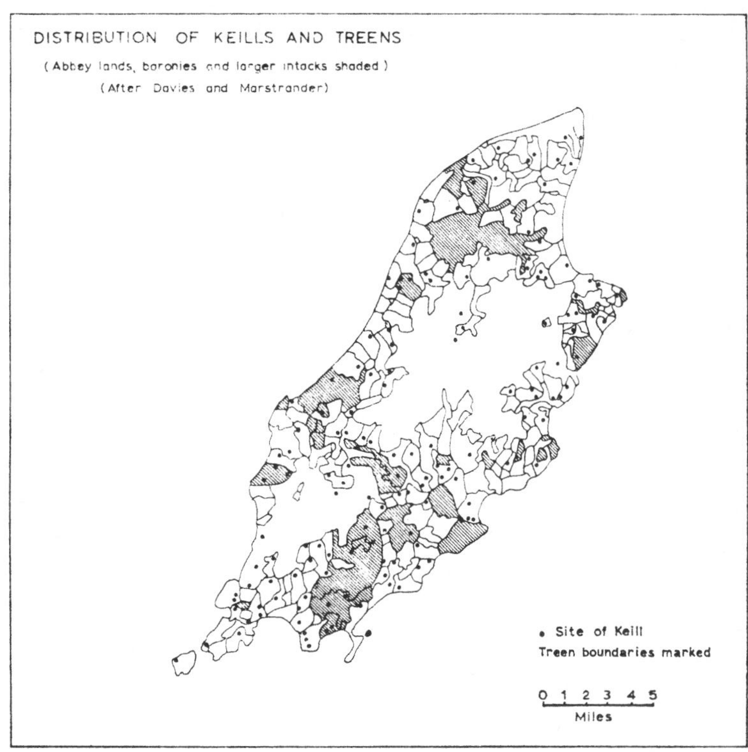

Fig. 49

All students of settlement must be concerned with siting, and nowhere is the study more rewarding than when we are concerned with the settlements established by the Celtic saints. Geomorphological studies in recent years in Wales, the Southwest peninsula, Brittany, Ireland, the Isle of Man and the Highlands, Islands and Uplands of Scotland have emphasized that what stands out most prominently in their relief pattern are the plateau surfaces superimposed upon one another, giving a series of "flats" and "breaks of slope." Very often, the uppermost surface carries great monadnocks, or superstructures, like those of Snowdonia in Wales or Dartmoor in Devon.[1] Many of these surfaces are tilted seawards and are, of course, much dissected by the present drainage cycle. Many areas are also considerably modified by Quaternary glaciation, giving fjiorded coasts, U-shaped valleys and other well-known features; while in Ireland, Wales, Cornwall and Brittany recent negative coastal movements have given rise to extensive estuarine areas with tidal creeks extending deeply into the tapering land-mass. In addition, many island clusters frequently stand out offshore. No geographer can escape, therefore, the overall impression of a systematic staircase morphology giving a physiographical escalation, beginning with islands offshore and moving on to coastal lands of great diversity, some with high cliffs and raised beaches, others with fjiords, or the gentler topography of ria type, while yet other coastlands may be made up of sandy stretches alternating with dune formations. Leaving the coastal zone we enter the valleys proper, and from their flood plains and floors pass upwards to their slopes, and on to the valley-heads and intervening spurs, and, finally, on to the hilltops themselves. It will be convenient to think of this simple arrangement not only as a reflection of the physical landscape throughout the Celtic lands, but also as a transect on which to pinpoint the variety of sites used by the Celtic saints, for the establishment of their settlements.

We can begin with island sites. It can, indeed, be claimed that while asceticism in the Eastern Mediterranean was marked by a movement into the desert, in the West it was marked by the creation of innumerable island sanctuaries.

In Britain almost all the islands around the coast have chapels or churches on them dedicated to some Celtic saint. The most important is Iona, founded by St. Columba, the

(1) There is a copious literature on this subject which it would be irrelevant to outline here, but *The Relief and Drainage of Wales* by Professor E. H. Brown, University of Wales Press, Cardiff, 1957, is a good text treating this theme in Wales, and can be considered representative of this type of literature.

earliest island sanctuary in the British Isles of which we have record, but the most impressive is certainly Sceilg Mhichíl (Skelling Michael), the bare and precipitous rock in the Atlantic whose monastic buildings we have already described. Inishmurray, North Rona, Sula Sgeir, Bardsey, Lindisfarne (Holy I.), Caldy and Ynys Seiriol (off Anglesey) are amongst scores of others that could be named. It is thought that these island sanctuaries arose in two ways. Many saints would make a first landing on some island offshore before proceeding inland to found a larger and more important monastery. A well known example of this has already been referred to in the case of St. Paulinus (St. Pol de Léon) who settled on the Ile Batz on the northern coast of Brittany after journeying from South Wales, and before establishing his famous monastery on the mainland. Conversely, the larger monasteries near the coast frequently established a solitary retreat on some island out to sea to which the religious could retire for periods of silence. This may well have been the relationship between Penmon and Ynys Seiriol off the Anglesey coast.

The coastlands of Brittany, like those of Western Britain, are studded with islands and present no exception to the general rule. It is convenient for purposes of illustration to look in a little greater detail at the famous Bréhat archipelago, off the north coast, and then at the island communities on the Morbihan coastlands. Reference has already been made to both groups. The little archipelago of Bréhat lies in the Gulf of St. Malo and is distinguished by the fact that on many of the islands we have traces of Celtic sanctuaries closely resembling those of Britain (Fig. 50a). The names of the saints who settled here are well-known and have numerous dedications on the mainland. Two of the islands are of special interest, the Ile Modez (St. Maudez had a widespread cult in Brittany) and the Ile Lavré (St. Budoc [Bothmael]). The most important feature concerning the latter is the location of the Celtic monastery within the ruins of a 4th century Roman villa. All objects found on the site, although few in number, confirm the occupation and repair of the ruins by Breton immigrants in the 5th century. Nearby are the remains of eight round cells in a row and signs also of many others.[1] The monastic plan corresponds closely with those of the Syrian *lauras,* which date from the fourth and fifth centuries. The island probably owes its name to the word *Laura,* so that it is highly probable that we are here in the closest touch with one of the earliest Christian sanctuaries in the West.

The much indented coast of Le Morbihan with its drowned river valleys, its peninsulas and offshore islands, offered ideal sites for the Celtic recluse. The secluded islands within the Morbihan itself and those in the Rivière d'Etel proved especially attractive to the saints, while the larger islands off the coast became well-known retreats. St. Gunthian settled on the Ile de Groix before proceeding to the foundation of the monastery of d'Anaurot, very often called St. Groix de Quimperlé, on the mainland. St. Tudy had establishments on the Ile de Groix and on Belle Ile off this coast. St. Gourstin retired to Ile de Hoedic, while St. Guémael, the second abbot of Landévennec, went to the Ile de Groix in search of solitude.

It is, however, the islands in the Rivière d'Etel—Ile de S.Cado and the larger island of Locoal (the resort of St. Gudwal) that are the most interesting of this group (Fig. 50b). Ile de S.Cado is a small island on the southern side of the Rivière d'Etel and contains a chapel of the saint. Near to the shore, and separated from the sea at high tide only by a wall, is the saint's well. The island is connected with the village of St. Cado on the mainland by a causeway carrying two bridges. The first mention of this island is in a series of charters in the Cartulary of the Abbey of Quimperlé, the earliest of which was written about 1009. Locoal, the larger island in the Rivière d'Etel, is referred to in a charter of 1037 as 'insula sancti Gutuali.' Like the Ile de S.Cado the Ile de Locoal is joined to the mainland by a short causeway and bridge. Beneath the hill on which the church stands and close to the shore is the holy well of St. Gudwal. From his island retreat Gudwal founded other establishments on the mainland, in one of which he died, but his body was taken back to Locoal. When the Northmen occupied

(1) De La Borderie, *Histoire de Bretagne,* Vol. I, p. 295 ff.

Brittany in 919 a great exodus of the relics of the principal Breton saints took place and St. Gudwal's body was taken to Picardie and then to Flanders. Some brief facts about him were handed down either in writing, or by oral tradition, to those who received the guardianship of the relics. These facts later formed the basis of the discursive *Life of St. Gudwal* written by a monk in the Abbey of Ghent.[1] Likewise, L'Isle aux-Moines, one of two principal islands in the Gulf of Morbihan, and the

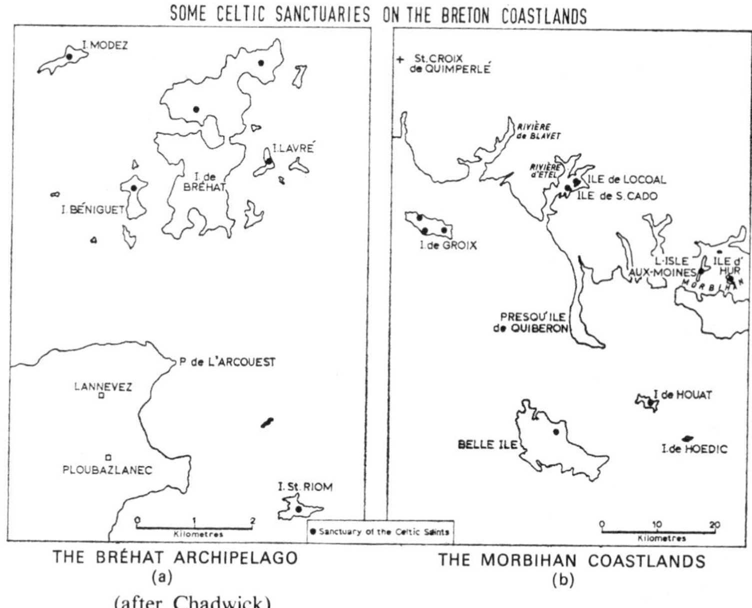

(after Chadwick)

Fig. 50

Ile d'Hur in the same bay offered ideal sites for Celtic sanctuaries in the Age of the Saints.

We can now turn to a consideration of Celtic chapels located on coastal margins. Frequently, a wandering saint tossed by the waves and at the mercy of the wind and the tide, would draw up his frail craft onto the beach and offer a prayer for a safe landing, or ask a blessing for a difficult journey overland. Later, a tiny

(1) Doble, G. H. *The Saints of Cornwall,* Part I. *Saints of the Land's End District:* St. Gudwal, Patron of Gulval. Chatham, 1960, pp. 61-78

chapel might be erected where the saint had prayed near to the waters' edge. Other *peregrini* having dragged their craft ashore often found bare cliffs above them. They would climb to the top and pray, and later a chapel would be erected at the sacred spot. Others would enter a steep-sided river valley and establish their settlements on the valley floor, usually beyond a bend in the valley where they could remain unseen from the sea, and, consequently, receive at least a chance of protection from pirates and other marauders. Six examples of such sites will be selected along the Welsh coast for illustrative purposes: two chapels immediately on the shore; two others on cliff sites overlooking the shore; and a further two some distance up steep-sided valleys and in presumably sheltered positions.

A well-known coastal chapel is that known as St. Patrick's chapel on the shore at Whitesands Bay near St. David's in Pembrokeshire. Here a rectangular mound stood in a field known as Parc-y-capel close to the shore. The field terminates to the westward in a low cliff barely ten feet high which abuts immediately onto the sandy beach. Cliff and field form part of the northern edge of the tract of blown sand which covers the boulder clay lying on the upper Cambrian rocks of the western half of the bay, behind which there is a shallow valley (Fig. 51.1). The mound was excavated in 1924 and revealed the outline of a rectangular chapel of the single cell type, wider at its eastern than at its western end. Human remains were discovered below the west wall and beneath a black layer of earth (which probably indicates the floor level of the chapel). It seemed evident that others, too, had been buried beneath the chapel floor.(1) This, of course, is a well-known feature of Celtic chapels of this type. It would appear that as far back as the close of the reign of Queen Elizabeth I the building unearthed at Parc-y-capel was known as 'St. Patrick's chapel', and there is much evidence that Whitesands Bay, or Porth Mawr, was extensively used by pilgrims and others on their

(1) Bager, A. B. and Green, F., *'The Chapel traditionally attributed to St. Patrick, Whitesands Bay, Pembrokeshire'*. *Arch. Camb.* Series 7, Vol. 5, 1925, pp. 87-120.

way to and from Ireland. We have already met with this harbour in connection with the story of the journey of Marchell, mother of Brychan Brycheiniog, to Ireland. Likewise, there was much intercourse between the Irish saints and St. David's, as shown by statements in the *Lives* of Aidan of Ferns, Ailbe, Declan of Ardmore, Findbar, Finnian of Clonard and others—all of whom resorted to *Cill Muni.*(1) Later, Irish pilgrims on their way to the shrine of St. James at Compostella used this route(2)—a factor which might help to explain the association of the chapel with St. Patrick.

As another example of an ancient Celtic church located near to the shore it is worth examining Llandanwg old church in Merioneth (Fig. 51.2). It stands on a shingle and dune spit facing Morfa Dyffryn. The Morfa is made up of extensive sandflats attached to the old coast and fringed on the outer side by dunes. Much boulder clay and morainic material exists along the coast, supplying boulders and course shingle which has spread over all the beach. This shingle travels northwards and forms the shingle-and-dune spit on which the church stands. The high-water mark of ordinary tides lies close by. This old church (the present parish church is located in Harlech) does not appear to have been built when the sea was quite so close to it as it is now, even though it is described in a Terrier dated 29 July 1776 as lying "on a sandy bank adjoining the sea shore."(3) We have no known record which describes its position relative to the sea when it was built. It is now disused, and but for clearing, would be almost covered by the drifting sand. Of St. Tanwg himself we know nothing, but we should not overlook the fact that the church contains two early inscribed stones which take us back to the very beginnings of Christianity on these shores. One of these stones built into the east window of the chancel, as a lintel, dates from the 5th century, while the other is a fragmentary rough pillar-stone inscribed in small Roman capitals. It has an unusual formula

(1) Wade-Evans, A. W., *Life of St. David,* Oxford, 1923, pp. 34-46.

(2) Hartwell-Jones, G. W., *Celtic Britain and the Pilgrim Movement.* Proc. Roy. Soc. Cymmrodorion, 1912.

(3) See *Arch. Camb.* 1935, pp. 70-2 and *Harlech Studies presented to Dr. Thomas Jones, C.H.*, Cardiff, 1936, p. 121.

which was, nevertheless, employed in early Christian epitaphs of the 4th century A.D. and later, both in Italy and Gaul, and was apparently derived from Roman pagan usage. This second stone can be dated to the 6th century A.D. and is now inside the church mounted on the sill of the south window of the chancel.[(1)] It is unlikely that these early Christian stones were ever inside the earliest church on this site, but they might very well have stood in an early Christian cemetery nearby, in which St. Tanwg located his cell, possibly at a somewhat later date than that represented by the stones themselves.

On a northern facing hollow called Pant-yr-Eglwys, some 350 feet above sea-level, among the cliffs forming the magnificent Carboniferous Limestone headland of the Great Orme, overlooking modern Llandudno, is found the little church of St. Tudno (Fig. 51.3). It now consists of a nave and chancel forming a long rectangle without structural division, with a north porch and vestry. The building retains fragments of 12th century or early 13th century work but there are more recent additions.[(2)] The dedication is obviously to a local saint, as this is the only church of which Tudno is patron. The saint's well—Ffynnon Tudno is about a hundred yards to the east of the church and still flows. The limestone rock on the shore below has several caves and fissures within it, one of which, known as Ogof Llech is supposed to have been occupied by St. Tudno as a cell or retreat. We should remember in this context that caves, like islands, abound as personal retreats of the Celtic saints.[(3)] Here we seem to have the primitive settlement picture complete—the cave at the water's edge—the original church with its holy well nearby—situated in a sheltered hollow among the steep cliffs above.

A similar site is that of St. Celynnin's church between Tywyn and Fairbourne on the Merioneth coast. The detail is not quite so fully represented here, but like so many other examples of this type, the church itself stands immediately

(1) Nash-Williams, V. E., *op. cit.*, No. 278 and 279 and Bowen, E. G., *History of Merioneth*. Dolgellau, Vol. I, 1967, p. 289.

(2) R.C.A.M., *Caernarvonshire*, Vol. II, p. 210, 1962.

(3) Baring-Gould, S. and Fisher, J., *op. cit.*, Vol. IV, pp. 268-9.

above the sea shore on the steep cliffs to the south of Fairbourne (Fig. 51.4). The cliffs on this coast have been severely undercut by waves and the beach consists of coarse boulders difficult to traverse. The lower Palaeozoic rocks do not easily form caves such as those in the Carboniferous Limestone. St. Celynnin's church itself is like that of St. Tudno's—a simple parallelogram consisting of an undivided nave and chancel—the building, as we have it, dating from the late 12th to the early 13th century. As is the case at Llandanwg, and with St. Tudno's church on the Great Orme, and several others in this class—new churches have had to be built nearer to the present centres of population. The erection of a new church in the village of Llwyngwril has led in this case to the disuse of St. Celynnin's church except during the summer months.

South of New Quay in Cardiganshire, the coast is formed of dark cliffs of shales and mudstones broken in several places by deep and narrow valleys usually with sandy beaches or bays at their seaward ends. It was in one such valley that St. Carantoc, in the sixth century, located one of his important settlements. We have had occasion earlier to note that St. Carantoc appears to have been a member of a famous band of pilgrims whose settlements were most frequently in coastal locations from North Wales to Brittany. His church at Llangrannog is so placed as to benefit to the full from the protection of the Ynys Lochdyn peninsula, built of massive grits and mudstones of Lower Palaeozoic age. In places the cliffs of thin bedded grits reach up to 300 feet, while the high ground behind the church, forming the core, as it were, of the peninsula, reaches to above 500 feet. The Nant Hawen flows in one of the typical deep and narrow valleys ending in a sandy beach. It should be noticed, however, that after flowing in a general E–W direction towards the sea it turns near the church onto a E.S.E–W.N.W., and finally onto a S.E.–N.W. course towards the sea (Fig. 51.6). This change of course together with the general protection afforded by the Ynys Lochdyn peninsula to the north and the ridge of high ground rising to above 300 feet south of the Hawen valley, is sufficient to make St. Carantoc's church invisible from the open sea—a distinct advantage in the Age of the Saints.

Possibly the best known and most clearly illustrated example of this type of coastal site is that of Dewi's original 'podum'

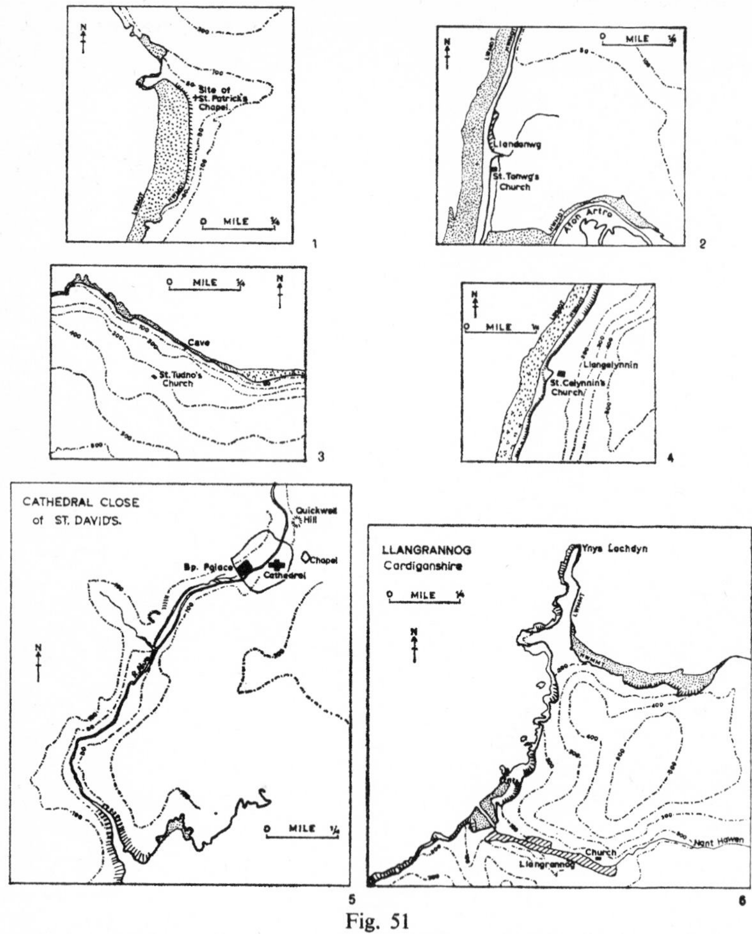

Fig. 51

Sites of Celtic Churches along the Welsh coast.

(presumably where the Cathedral church of St. David's now stands) in the valley of the Alun in north-west Pembrokeshire (Fig. 52). The land forming the Dewisland peninsula is, broadly speaking, a plateau surface some 200 feet in general elevation.

Nearly all the prominent features, however, are of igneous origin—the dolorites of Penbiri and Carn Llidi standing up as great monadnocks above the plateau surface. The area has a heavy drift cover reaching down to and below sea-level in the Melgan and Whitesands Bay areas, but everywhere there is a

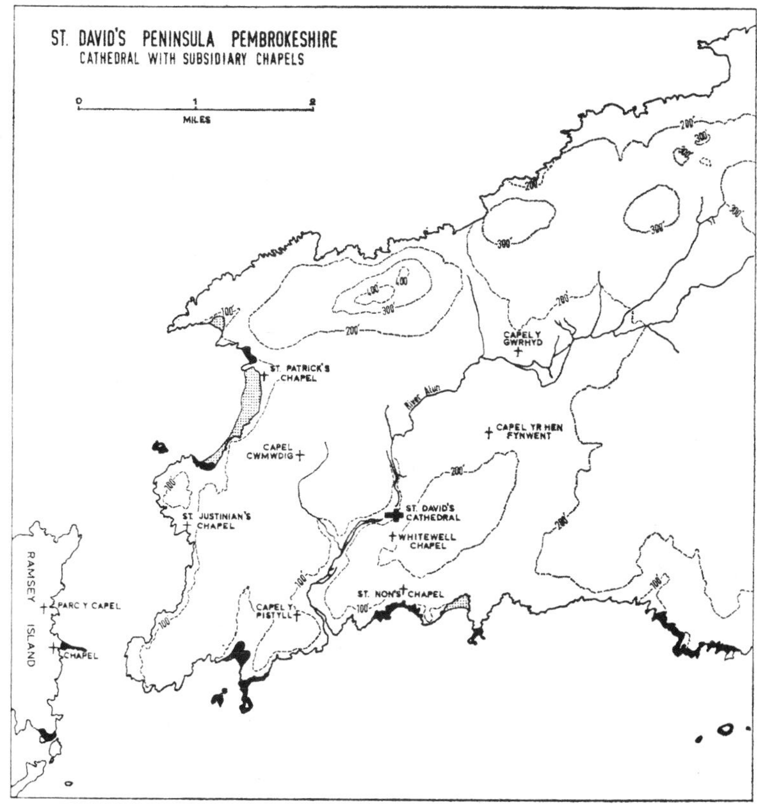

Fig. 52

tendency for the drift to fill up any natural hollows in the peneplain. The river system is most likely early Pliocene in age, or may even be dated before this. In any case, the streams were rejuvenated by a pre-glacial uplift so that their courses are now incised into the plateau surface. The river Alun is of particular interest, flowing in its upper reaches in an E.N.E.–W.S.W. direction, then, as it approaches the rejuvenation head, or 'knick point' of the valley (about half a mile to the north of St. David's), it turns in a general N.–S. direction, then back again to a N.E.–S.W. alignment, and finally makes another sharp bend about a quarter of a mile from its mouth, completing its course in a N.W.–S.E. direction. From the rejuvenation head to the sea the river flows in a deeply incised narrow valley (see Fig. 52 and Fig. 51.5). This narrow winding dell stands out in sharp contrast to the upper portion of the valley on the plateau surface—a difference which seems to have been noted throughout the ages, as the lower portion is always referred to as the *Nant, Vallis* or *Vale*. It is in the upper portion of this narrow dell that the cathedral now stands, on the site where, presumably St. David located his original cell, carefully hidden below the plateau surface, on the one hand, and yet able to maintain direct access to the sea—the chief highway of movement in the Age of the Saints—on the other. At the same time his settlement (like that of St. Carantoc at Llangrannog and many others in similar positions) was completely hidden from all who sailed around these shores. In Rhygyfarch's *Life* of St. David, written early in the 11th century, we are told that the saint established his cell in the *Vallis Rosina*. Wade-Evans[(1)] correctly noted that this term was never intended to apply to the whole of the river Alun, but only to its lower rejuvenated section. Neither is the word *Rosina* a Latin form of the Welsh *rhosyn* (rose) to give the English equivalent—'Vale of Roses,' as is so frequently thought, but derives from an older word *rhosan* (which appears to be a diminutive of *rhos*) meaning "a little swamp." The ancient site was, therefore, located in 'the valley of the little bog.' Rhygyfarch adds that the Welsh people generally call the valley *Hodnant* or *Hoddnant* i.e. *'vallis prospera'*—'a favourable valley.' This term is no longer used, but it might well have retained an echo in Rhygyfarch's day of its special appeal to the original founder of the settlement. When the present Cathedral, built largely by Peter de Leia (bishop 1176-1203) was erected on the site, it became necessary to excavate into

(1) Wade-Evans, A. W., *The Life of St. David,* S.P.C.K., London, 1923, esp. p. 67.

the steep valley side to the eastwards to accommodate such a large structure. In so doing de Leia tapped the spring which fed the moisture to the little bog on the valley floor thereby creating special problems for the heavy tower of the Cathedral which rested on such precarious foundations. The full medieval picture (although strictly beyond our terms of reference in this work) is completed when we note that the roof of the cathedral tower is just level with the plateau surface on either side of the valley, thus rendering the cathedral invisible until the traveller is immediately on top of it. Fig. 52 shows also the sites of the large number of medieval chapels (some of which may even date back to the days of the Saints) that are located near the many bays and inlets around the peninsula. They are all tributary to the Cathedral, and as George Owen, the distinguished historian of Pembrokeshire, put it nearly 360 years ago "there were formerly several chapels about St. David's, which all belonged to the mother church, dedicated to several saints. . . . all the chapels are near the seaside and adjoining to the places where those that come by sea commonly landed. They were placed here to draw the devotion of the seamen and passengers when they first came ashore: other pilgrims us'd likewise to come to them.(1)" In this way, seaways, settlements and saints are intimately associated in these western lands, and the pattern of things laid down in the Dark Ages would appear to have continued, little changed, into the centuries that lay ahead.

Next we must consider the strong attachment shown by the Celtic saints for extensive estuarine areas. The simple reason in this case being that estuaries provided one of the most obvious entries into the interior in the days when the sea was the main thoroughfare for travellers and transpeninsular routes were extensively used. The south-west peninsula of Britain is an obvious region for illustrative purposes. From the point of view of the cycle of shoreline evolution, the coastlands of the south-west are in a distinctly youthful stage. On the other hand, the rocks of which the peninsula is formed are, for the most part, hard and old. This helps to account for the present

(1) Browne Willis, *Survey of the Cathedral Church of St. David's*, 1717, p. 52, copying a memorandum of George Owen (d. 1613).

indented nature of the coastline together with the fact that the river valleys (formed in late geological times) are both deep and narrow. It is, however, the fluctuations in sea-level during the glacial period that have put the final touches to the scene. The rapid rise in the level of the sea following upon the final with-

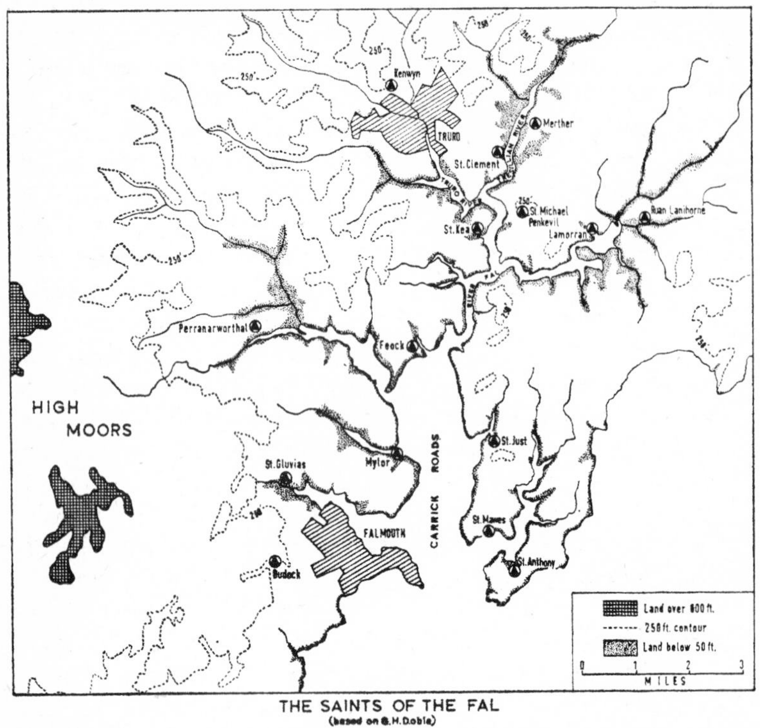

THE SAINTS OF THE FAL
(based on G. H. Doble)

Fig. 53

drawal of the ice sheets in north-western Europe submerged the lower reaches of most of the valleys in the south-west peninsula to produce the magnificent ria coastline we see today. The Fal, the Camel, the Taw and the Torridge and other rivers flowing into Carrick Roads, Plymouth Sound, or Salcombe Harbour are well-known examples. Finally, we should not overlook the fact that since a richly indented ria coastline occurs on both the northern and the southern shores of the peninsula, transpeninsular movement, utilizing recognized trackways over the rough intervening moorland, became a marked feature of this area in both pre-and proto-historic times. Fig. 53 shows the location of the main settlements of the Celtic saints along the estuary of the Fal. This area involves one of the partially drowned river systems just described, with an array of inlets—all fully tidal. The large number of ancient churches standing near the water's edge is unmistakable. St. Gluvias, Mylor, St. Koa, St. Clements, Lanmorran, Ruan Lanihorne, St. Just in Roseland, St. Mawes and St. Anthony all lie about 50 ft. above the water; while Perranworthal, Merther and Feock lie between 50 ft. and 100 ft., all possessing immediate access to the sea. Others like Budock, Kenwyn and St. Michael Penkevil are on sites offering commanding positions not far from the river. Such a general location of churches is related not only to the importance of the estuaries as lines of movement, but also to the fact that during the Age of the Saints, the valley sides of most Cornish rivers were clothed in damp oakwood forest, while rough land characterized the moorlands above 600 ft. Doble[(1)] has drawn attention to the vivid picture of conditions existing in the South-west peninsula in the Age of the Saints preserved in the early *Life* of St. Samson of Dol. The saint journeyed from South Wales across the peninsula into Brittany in the sixth century. In this *Life* we get glimpses of the estuarine areas on either side of Cornwall covered with little Christian monastic settlements, while the interior of the country (where St. Samson encountered people worshipping 'around a great pillar') remained barbarous and pagan.[(2)] Estuarine locations, therefore, rank very highly in the list of sites favoured by the wandering saints, not only in the South-west peninsula but generally throughout the whole of north-western Europe.

Thus far we have been considering settlements on islands,

(1) Doble, G. H., The Saints of Cornwall, Part II, *"The saints of the Fal and its Neighbourhood,"* Oxford, 1964, pp. 15-16.

(2) See Bowen, E. G., *The Travels of St. Samson of Dol. Aberystwyth Studies,* xiii, 1934, p. 71 and also Bowen, E. G., *"The Seas of Western Britain —studies in historical geography,"* in *Geography at Aberystwyth,* Univ. of Wales Press, Cardiff, 1968, p. 165.

those by the sea-shore and those along the estuaries, but we must not forget that the Celtic saints also moved far inland. It has not hitherto been fully appreciated that their inland settlements may have been conditioned by geological as well as by relief conditions, very much in the same way as secular settlements have been. With a view to rounding off this survey it is convenient to illustrate this point by examples taken at random from the two major territories of the Celtic Lands—Ireland and Scotland— from which examples have not hitherto been selected in this chapter.

The relationship of early Celtic monastic settlements to the geological outcrops of Co. Clare is worthy of special attention. The essential point has already been appreciated by Aubrey Gwynn and D. F. Gleeson in their history of the diocese of Killaloe.[(1)] They point out that most of the early Celtic churches in what is now Co. Clare are to be found on the higher limestone deposits in the eastern part of the county. They draw particular attention to the rich limestone country around Ennis where there is a cluster of monastic houses, many, but not all, of which can be traced back to early pre-Norman times. Dysert O'Dea, Rathblathmaic, Dromcliffe, Inchicronan and Quin all belong to this area. In sharp contrast to the richer limestone land we have the peninsula of West Clare made up of flagstones and shales of the Millstone Grit and Coal Measures with only a few churches of historic interest. Likewise, the Slieve Aughty and the Slieve Bernagh mountains made up of Silurian and Old Red Sandstone rocks, together with narrow outcrops of Carboniferous slates and sandstones, have very few ancient Christian sites. The lands of primary and secondary rocks stand out in sharp contrast to the limestone areas. An attempt has been made on Fig. 54 to sketch in the major geological outcrops from the maps of the Irish Geological Survey and superimpose upon them the early Celtic Christian sites from the map of Monastic Ireland published by the Ordnance Survey Department in Dublin.[(2)] A general correlation

(1) Gleeson, D. F. and Gwynn, A., *A History of the Diocese of Killaloe,* Vol. I, Dublin, 1962.
(2) Léarscáilíocht Éireann. *Map of Monastic Ireland.* 2nd Edit. O.S. Dublin 1965.

between the limestone terrain and the greater concentratiou of these Celtic monasteries is obvious, but it should be remembered that other factors entered in, factors which have already been discussed. The area abounds in estuarine and island sites. Who can overlook the importance of the Aran islands, or the smaller islands off the West Clare coast in the days of the Saints, to say nothing of Scattery Island (near to the mouth of the Shannon) on which St. Senan's famous cell is found? His influence must have dominated the whole of western Clare.

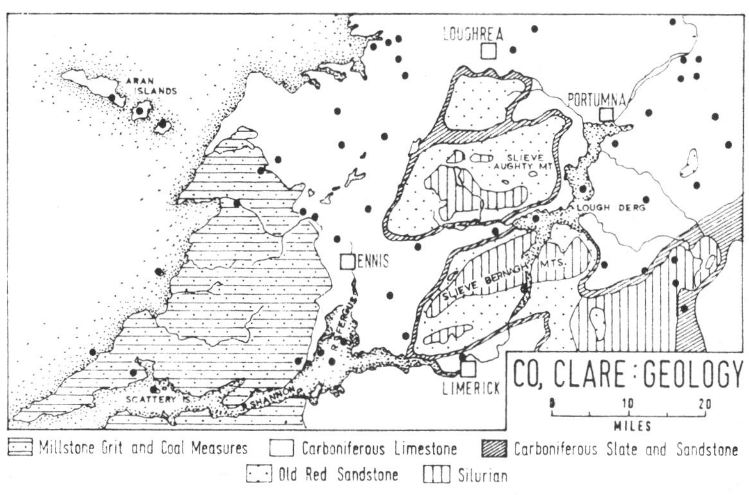

Fig. 54

Early Celtic Settlements in relation to geological outcrops in Co. Clare.

Then, there are the island sites in Loch Derg and in the estuary of the Fergus, where we have Canon's Island, Feenish and Inishoe. It is true that little or nothing is known of the history of many of these churches before the 12th century, but some have ruins surviving from the Early Christian period and must, therefore, be considered to be Early Christian in origin.[1]

Finally, Fig. 55 shows the settlements of Irish saints in southern Scotland. Once again we have no reason to assume that all the dedications shown belong to the Celtic Christian period —indeed, many of them almost certainly date from the Middle

(1) Leask, H. G., *Irish churches and Monastic Buildings,* Vol. I, 1955.

Ages. Nevertheless, the resultant overall pattern is exactly what one would have expected from an Irish-based culture entering southern Scotland. The settlements on the islands, especially those of Bute and Arran are in obvious locations, while the river valleys, especially that of the Clyde, stand out as major lines of entry. The main purpose of this final section is to show that when we consider settlement problems associated with the Celtic saints, relief as well as geological and other considera-

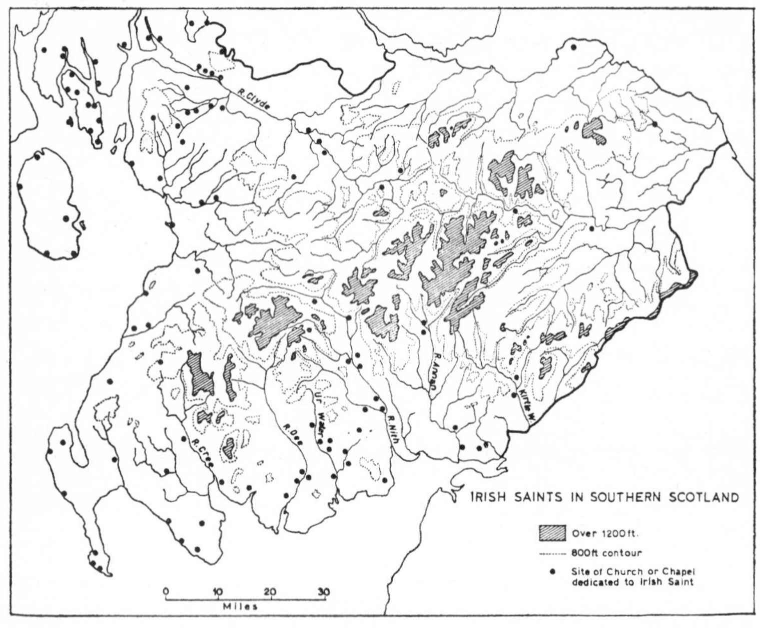

Fig. 55

tions must be taken into account. Saints with Irish associations have been selected merely to keep the picture as simple as possible.

The Southern Uplands of Scotland illustrate very clearly the systematic staircase morphology of tilted erosion surfaces separated from each other by marked breaks of slope, already noted as typical of much of Western Britain. The present drainage pattern has, of course, greatly fractionated these surfaces giving the landscape features we see today. It has been suggested[1] that by selecting any single valley set in this 'physiographic staircase' a number of site categories can easily be distinguished, such as hilltop, spur, valley-head, valley-slope, valley-floor and coastal. Any detailed study of a large valley cut deeply into the staircase, such as that of the Nith in the Kirkconnel country, or that of the Annan in the Beattock country, shows Celtic churches occupying most of these site categories. One of the important overall features shown on the map is the number of churches located on valley-head sites, a point well illustrated in the case of the valleys just mentioned. With the mass of the population occupying the upper moorlands in late pre-historic and proto-historic times this is taken to imply that an attack on forested land was being made, and that a general valley-ward movement of population was under way. A further, and possibly more reliable, inference from the map is that the occupation of land on valley floors was well established by medieval times (the latest date to which the distribution shown can be assigned). Nevertheless, we must not overlook the fact, so frequently mentioned in this study, that the Celtic saints in highland Britain may well have been the pioneers in the Dark Ages of a "movement into forested land"—a movement which probably did not reach its fullest extent until the Middle Ages. This movement represents the counter-part in highland Britain of an achievement usually accredited to the Anglo-Saxon settlers in lowland Britain.

(1) Ravenhill, W. L. D. *"Cornwall and Devon"* in "Rural Settlement in Ireland and Western Britain"—Report of a Symposium (Ed. E. E. Evans). *The Advancement of Science*. Vol. xv, No. 60, 1959, p. 343.

BIBLIOGRAPHY AND GENERAL REFERENCES

Abbreviations

A.A.A.L.	*Annals of Archaeology and Anthropology, University of Liverpool*
An. Boll.	*Analecta Bollandiana*
Ant.	*Antiquity*
Ant. Journ.	*Antiquaries Journal, London*
Arch.	*Archaeologia, London*
Arch. Ael.	*Archaeologia Aeliana*
Arch. Camb.	*Archaeologia Cambrensis*
Arch. Journ.	*Archaeological Journal*
B.B.C.S.	*Bulletin of the Board of Celtic Studies*
Cerd.	*Ceredigion,* Journal of the Cardiganshire Antiquarian Society
E.H.R.	*English Historical Review*
H.B.S.	*Henry Bradshaw Society*
H.S.C.W.	*The Historical Society of the Church in Wales*
I.H.S.	*Irish Historical Studies*
J.B.A.A.	*Journal of the British Archaeological Association*
J.E.H.	*Journal of Ecclesiastical History*
J.R.S.A.I.	*Journal of the Royal Society of Antiquaries of Ireland*
P.B.A.	*Proceedings of the British Academy*
P.P.S.	*Proceedings of the Prehistoric Society,* Cambridge
P.R.I.A.	*Proceedings of the Royal Irish Academy*
R.C.A.M.	*Royal Commission on Ancient Monuments* (Wales)
S.H.	*Studia Hibernica,* Dublin
S.H.R.	*Scottish Historical Review*
T.C.H.S.	*Transactions of the Caernarvonshire Historical Society*
T.C.W.A.A.S.	*Transactions of the Cumberland & Westmorland Archaeological and Antiquarian Society*
T.D.G.N.H.A.S.	*Transactions of the Dumfriesshire & Galloway Natural History and Antiquarian Society*
T.H.S.C.	*Transactions of the Honourable Society of Cymmrodorion,* London
T.L.C.A.S.	*Transactions of the Lancashire & Cheshire Antiquarian Society*
T.P.I.B.G.	*Transactions and Papers of the Institute of British Geographers*
T.R.H.S.	*Transactions of the Royal Historical Society*
W.H.R.	*Welsh History Review,* Cardiff
Y.C.	*Y Cymmrodor,* London

Adamnan, *Vita S.Columbae,* Ed. William Reeves, Dublin 1857.

Anderson, A. O. 'Ninian and the Southern Picts,' S.H.R. xxvii, 1948.

Anderson, A. O. and M. O. *Adomnán's Life of Columba,* Edinburgh & London 1961.

Anderson. J. *Scotland in Early Christian Times,* 2 vols., Edinburgh 1881.

Alcock, Leslie *Dinas Powys,* Cardiff 1963.

Annals of the Four Masters (Ed. J. O'Donovan, Dublin 1848-51) together with those of monasteries and other districts in Ireland.

Arnold-Forster, F. E. *Studies in Church Dedications,* 3 vols., London 1899.

Ashley, A. *The Church in the Isle of Man,* London & York 1958.

Barbier, M. P. *Le Trégor Historique et Monumental,* Saint-Brieuc, 1960.

Baring-Gould, S. and Fisher, J. *The Lives of the British Saints,* I-IV, London, 1907-13.

Bede, The Ven. *Historia ecclesiastica gentis Anglorum,* Ed. C. Plummer, Oxford, 1896.
Bieler, L. *The Life and Legends of St. Patrick,* Dublin, 1949.
Binchy, D. A. 'Patrick and his Biographers,' S.H. 2, Dublin 1962.
Bowen, E. G. 'The Travels of St. Samson of Dol,' *Aberystwyth Studies,* xiii, 1934.
Bowen, E. G. 'The Travels of the Celtic Saints,' Ant. xviii, 1944.
Bowen, E. G. 'The Settlements of the Celtic Saints in South Wales,' Ant. xix, 1945.
Bowen, E. G. 'The Saints of Gwynedd,' T.C.H.S., 1948.
Bowen, E. G. 'The Celtic Saints in Cardiganshire,' Cerd. I, 1950.
Bowen, E. G. *The Settlements of the Celtic Saints in Wales,* Cardiff, 1954.
Bowen, E. G. 'Archaeoleg a'n Llenyddiaeth Gynnar,' *Llên Cymru,* Cyf. 8, Rhif 3 a 4, 1965.
Bowen, E. G. 'The Seas of Western Britain: Studies in Historical Geography' in *Geography at Aberystwyth,* Jubilee Volume (Ed. Bowen, Carter & Taylor), Cardiff, 1968.
Bromwich, R. *Trioedd Ynys Prydain (The Welsh Triads),* Cardiff, 1961.
Brown, E. H. 'Erosion Surfaces in North Cardiganshire,' T.P.I.B.G. 16, 1950.
Bu'lock, J. D. 'The Lost Kingdom of Teyrnllwng,' T.L.C.A.S. lxvi, 1956.
Bu'lock, J. D. 'Early Christian Memorial Formulae,' Arch. Camb. cv. 1956,
Bury, J. B. *The Life of St. Patrick and his place in History,* London, 1905.
Carney, J. *The Problem of St. Patrick,* Dublin, 1961.
Chadwick, H. M. (Ed. N. K. Chadwick), *Early Scotland,* Cambridge, 1949.
Chadwick, N. K. (Ed.) *Studies in Early British History,* Cambridge 1954 and 1959.
Chadwick, N. K. (Ed.) *Celt and Saxon: Studies in the Early British Border,* Cambridge, ,1963.
Chadwick, N. K. (Ed.) *Studies in the Early British Church,* Cambridge, 1958.
Chadwick, N. K. 'St. Ninian. A preliminary study of Sources,' T.D.G.N.H.A.S., xxvii, 1959.
Chadwick, N. K. *The Age of the Saints in the Early Celtic Church,* (Oxford), 1961.
Chadwick, N. K. *Celtic Britain.* Ancient Peoples and Places, London, 1963.
Chadwick, N. K. *The Colonization of Brittany from Celtic Britain.* Sir John Rhŷs Memorial Lecture, 1965. From P.B.A. Vol. LI.
Chadwick, Owen 'The evidence of dedications in the Early History of the Welsh Church' *Studies in Early British History,* Cambridge, 1954.
Chaguolleau, J. *Les Iles de l'Armor,* Paris, 1951.
Charlesworth, M. P. *The Lost Province,* Cardiff, 1949.
Childe, V. G. *The Prehistory of Scotland,* London, 1935.
Childe, V. G. *Scotland before the Scots,* London, 1946.
Childe, V. G. *The Prehistoric Communities of the British Isles,* 2nd Edit., London, 1947.
Childe, V. G. *The Prehistory of European Society,* Pelican Book, London, 1958.
Chope, R. P. *The Book of Hartland,* Torquay, 1940.
Clapham, A. W. 'The origins of Hiberno-Saxon Art,' Ant. viii, 1934.
Clark, Grahame 'The Prehistory of the Isle of Man,' P.P.S., 1935.
Collingwood, R. G. & Myres, J. N. L. *Roman Britain and the English Settlements,* Oxford, 1936.
Contributions to a Dictionary of the Irish Language, R.I.A., Dublin 1942-1966.
Couffon, R. 'Limites des cités gallo-romaines et fondation des évêchés dans la péninsule armoricaine,' *Bull. et Memoires de la Soc. d'Emulation des Côtes-du-Nord,* lxxiii, 1942.
Crawford, O. G. S. 'Western Seaways' in *Custom is King,* Oxford, 1936.
Daniel, G. E. 'Who are the Welsh?'. Sir John Rhŷs Memorial Lecture. P.B.A. xl, 1954.

Daniel, G. E. 'The Dual Nature of the Megalithic Colonization of Prehistoric Europe,' P.P.S., New Series, Vol. 6 and 7, 1940-1.
Davies, E. 'Treens and Quarterlands: A study of the Land System of the Isle of Man,' T.P.I.B.G., 22, 1957.
Davies, J. Conway 'Episcopal Acts relating to Welsh Dioceses 1066-1272,' *Hist. Soc. of the Church in Wales*. Introduction, Vols. I & II, 1946-48.
Davies, M. 'The diffusion and distribution pattern of the Megalithic Monuments of the Irish Sea and North Channel coastlands,' Ant. Journ. xxvi, Nos. 1 and 2, 1946.
Decuil *De Memoria orbis terrae* (Ed. Parthney, 1894).
De la Borderie, A. *Histoire de Bretagne,* Paris, 1887.
De Paor, M. and L. *Early Christian Ireland,* London, 1958 and 1964.
De Paor, L. 'A Survey of Sceilg Mhíchíl' J.R.S.A.I. 85, 1955.
Dewick, E. S. and Frere, S. (Eds.) *Leofric Collector,* Vol. II, H.B.S., lvi, 1918.
Dillon, Myles *Catalogue of Irish Mss. in the British Museum* (Revised), London, 1953.
Dillon, Myles and Chadwick, N. K. *The Celtic Realms,* London, 1967.
Dimock, J. F. (Edit.), Giraldus Cambrensis, *Itinerarium Kambriae et Descriptio Kambriae,* London, 1908.
Doble, G. H. (Ed.) *Exeter Martyrology,* H.B.S., Vols. xxxviii and lxxix, 1909-1940.
Doble, G. H. The *Cornish Saints Series* Nos. 1-48, 1923-1944.
Doble, G. H. *Saint Brioc,* Exeter, 1928.
Doble, G. H. *Saint Budoc,* Shipston-on-Stour, 1937.
Doble, G. H. *Saint Iltut,* Cardiff, 1944.
Doble, G. H. *Saint Paul de Léon,* Lampeter, 1941.
Doble, G. H. 'The Relics of St. Petroc,' Ant. xxi, 1939.
Doble, G. H. 'St. Congar,' Ant. xix, 1945.
Doble, G. H. The *Welsh Saints Series* Nos. 1-5. 1942-1944,
Doble, G. H. *The Saints of Cornwall,* Chatham, 1960
Part I Saints of the Land's End District.
,, II Saints of the Lizard District.
,, III Saints of the Fal.
Doble, G. H. *Saint Winwaloe,* Cornish Saints Series, 2nd Edit., Shipston-on-Stour, 1940.
Doble, G. H. and Kerbirion, L. *Les Saints Bretons,* Brest, 1933.
Dom Plaine 'Vita S. Mevenni abbatis in Britannia Armoricana,' An. Boll., iii, 1884.
Downes, A. 'The Cultural regions of prehistoric and protohistoric Britain, M.A. Thesis, University of Wales. Unpublished.
Duchesne, L. *L'Eglise au VIe siècle,* Paris, 1925.
Duckett, E. *The Wandering Saints,* London, 1959.
Du Gleuzion, J. R. 'De quelques sources de la Vie de Saint Guénolé,' Soc.d' Êmul. des Côtes-du-Nord. Bull. et Mémoires, lxxxviii, 1960.
Duine, F. M. *Memento des sources hagiographiques de l'histoire du Bretagne. I. V^e^ au Xe siècle,* Rennes, 1918.
Duke, J. A. *The Columban Church,* Oxford, 1932.
Edwards, W. 'The Settlement of Brittany,' Y.C., xi, 1892.
Evans, D. Simon. *'Buchedd Dewi,'* Cardiff, 1959.
Evans, E. E. 'Prehistoric Geography' in *The British Isles: a systematic geography,* (Ed. Watson, G. J. W. and Sissons, J. B.), London, 1964.
Evans, E. E. *Prehistoric and Early Christian Ireland. A Guide,* London, 1966.
Evans, J. G. (Edit.) *The Book of Taliesin* 'Armes Prydein Vawr,' Oxford, 1910.
Evans, J. G. and Rhŷs, J. (Editors) *Liber Landavensis.* The text of the Book of Llan Dav, Oxford, 1893.

Fahy, D. 'When did Britons become Bretons?' A note on the Foundation of Brittany, W.H.R., ii, 1964.
Fleure, H. J. & Roberts, E. J. 'Archaeological Problems of the West Coast of Britain' Arch. Camb., Vol. 70, 1915.
Falc'hun, F. *L'Histoire de la langue bretonne d'après la géographie linguistique,* Rennes, 1951.
Fawtier, R. *La Vie de Saint Sampson,* Paris, 1912.
Ferguson, W. *Pelagius,* Cambridge, 1956.
Fisher, J. 'Welsh Church Dedications,' T.H.S.C., xv, 1906-07.
Fitzgerald, W. *The Historical Geography of Early Ireland,* Geog. Teacher Supplement, No. 1, London, 1925.
Flower, R. 'The Two Eyes of Ireland.' Report of the Church of Ireland Conference, Dublin, 1932.
Foster, I. Ll. and Daniel, G. E. (Eds.) *Prehistoric and Early Wales,* London, 1963.
Fox, Aileen 'Early Christian Period.' *A hundred Years of Welsh Archaeology,* Camb. Arch. Assoc., 1946.
Fox, Sir Cyril *The Personality of Britain,* 4th Edition, Cardiff, 1943.
Fox, G. E. and Hope, W. H. St. J. 'Excavations on the site of the Roman city of Silchester, Hants. in 1893,' Arch. liv, 1894.
Frere, S. S. (Ed.) *Problems of the Iron Age in Southern Britain,* London, 1960.
Gildae, De Excidio Britanniae (Ed. and Trans. by Hugh Williams), London, 1899.
Giot, P. R. *Brittany,* London, 1960.
Gleeson, D. F. and Gwynn, A. *A History of the Diocese of Killaloe,* Vol. I, Dublin, 1961.
Gougaud, Dom L. *Christianity in Celtic Lands,* London, 1932.
Gougaud, Dom L. *Les saints irlandais hors d'Irlande,* Louvain, 1936.
Graham, T. H. B. and Collingwood, W. G. 'Patron Saints of the Diocese of Carlisle,' T.C.W.A.A.S., 1925.
Griffiths, G, and Owen. H. P. 'The earliest mention of St. David,' B.B.C.S., 1957.
Grimes, W. F. *Guide to the collections illustrating the Prehistory of Wales,* Nat. Mus. of Wales, Cardiff, 1939.
Grimes, W. F. (Ed.) *Aspects of Archaeology in Britain and Beyond,* Essays presented to O. G. S. Crawford, London, 1951.
Griscom, A. (Edit.) *Historia Regum Britanniae,* (Geoffrey of Monmouth), London, 1929.
Grosjean, P. (Edit.) *Acta Sanctorum. A travers trois siècles,* L'ouvre des Bollandistes 1615-1915, Bruxelles, 1920.
Grosjean, P. 'Gloria postuma St. Martini Turonensis apud Scottos et Britannos' An. Boll., lv, 1937.
Grosjean, P. 'Life of St. Cadoc,' An. Boll., lx, 1942.
Grosjean, P. 'Notes d'hagiographie celtique,' An. Boll., lxiii, 1945.
Grosjean, P. 'Bulletin des Publications Hagiographiques', An. Boll., lxix, 1951.
Grosjean, P. 'Notes d'Hagiographie Celtique 15-17' An. Boll., lxix, lxx, lxxii, 1951, 1952 and 1954.
Grosjean, P. 'Edition et commentaire du Catalogus sanctorum Hiberniae', An. Boll., lxxiii, 1955.
Grosjean, P. 'Edition et commentaire du Catalogus Sanctorum Hiberniae secundum diversa tempora ou Detribus Ordinibus Sanctorum Hiberniae,' An. Boll., lxxiii, 1955.
Gwynn, J. (Edit.) *Beati Martini Vita,* (Sulpicius Severus). Royal Irish Academy, 1913.
Harden, D. B. (Ed.) *Dark Age Britain,* Studies presented to E. T. Leeds, London, 1956.
Harris, S. M. 'Was St. David ever canonized?' *Wales,* No. 4, 1944.
Harris, S. M. 'Note on a Llanbadarn Fawr Kalendar,' Cerd. II, 1952.
Harris, S. M. 'Kalendar of the Vitae Sanctorum Wallensium,' *Wales,* ix, 1953.

Hawkes, C. F. C. 'The British Hill-Forts,' Ant., v, 1931.
Hawkes, C. F. C. 'The ABC of the British Iron Age,' Ant.. xxxiii, 1959.
Hencken, H. O'N. *Archaeology of Cornwall and Scilly,* County Archaeology Series, London, 1932.
Henry, F. 'Early Monasteries, Beehive Huts, etc,' P.R.I.A., 58, Section C No. 3, 1957.
Hillygarth, J. N. 'Visigothic Spain and Early Christian Ireland,' P.R.I.A., 62, 1962.
Hogan, E. *Onomasticon Goedelicum Locorum et Tribum Hiberniae et Scotiae,* Dublin and London. 1910,
Hogg, A. H. A. *'The Date of Cunedda',* Ant., xxii, 1948
Hogg, A. H. A. 'The Votadini' in *Aspects of Archaeology in Britain and Beyond,* London, 1951.
Hornis, G. (Edit.) *Sulpicii Severi Presbyteri Opera Omnia,* London, 1665.
Horstman, C. (Ed.) *Nova Legenda Anglia,* Oxford ,1901.
Hughes, H. 'Ynys Seiriol,' Arch. Camb., New Series I, 1901.
Hughes, K. 'Cult of St. Finnian,' I.H.S., ix, 1954.
Hughes, K. '*Lives* of St. Finnian of Clonnard,' E.R.H., 1954.
Hughes, K. 'An Irish Litany of Irish Saints compiled c.800,' An. Boll., lxxvii, 1959.
Hughes, K. The changing theory and practice of Irish Pilgrimage,' J.E.H., xi, 1960.
Hunter-Blair, P. 'The origins of Northumbria,' Arch. Ael., xxv, 1947.
Jackson, K. H. 'Notes on the Ogham Inscriptions of Southern Britain' in *The Early Cultures of N.W. Europe* (H. M. Chadwick Memorial Studies), Cambridge, 1950.
Jackson, K. H. 'The Britons of Southern Scotland,' Ant. ,xxix, 1955.
Jackson, K. H. 'The Sources for the Life of St. Kentigern', *Studies in the Early British Church,* Cambridge 1958.
Jackson, K. H. *Language and History in Early Britain,* Edinburgh, 1953.
James, J. W. *A Church History of Wales,* London, 1945.
James, J. W. *Rhygyfarch's Life of St. David,* Cardiff, 1967.
Johns, C. N. 'The Celtic Monasteries of North Wales,' T.C.H.S., xxi, 1960.
Jones, G, Hartwell 'Celtic Britain and the Pilgrim Movement,' Y.C., xxiii, 1912.
Jones, G. R. J. 'Basic Patterns of Rural Settlement in North Wales,' T.P.I.B.G., 19, 1953.
Jones, J. Morris and Rhŷs, J. (Editors) Llyvyr Ankyr *Llandewivrevi,* Oxford, 1894.
Kenney, J. F. *The sources for the Early History of Ireland,* I, Ecclesiastical, New York, 1929.
Killanin, Lord and Duignan, M. V. *The Shell Guide to Ireland,* Dublin, 1962.
Kinvig, R. H. *A History of the Isle of Man,* 2nd Edit., Liverpool, 1950.
Kirby, D. P. 'Bede's Native Sources for the Historia Ecclesiastica' *Bull:John Ryland's Library* 48, 2, 1966.
Lawlor, H. C. *The Monastery of St. Mochaoi of Nendrum,* Belfast, 1925.
Largillière, J. *Les Saints et l'organisation chrétienne primitive dans l'Armorique Bretonne,* Rennes 1925.
Latouche, R. *Mélanges d'Histoire de la Cornouaille,* Ve–XIe siècle, Paris, 1911. especially Appendix III 'La plus ancienne vie de Saint Guénolé.'
Léarscáilíocht Éireann, Map of Monastic Ireland, Ordnance Survey, Dublin, 2nd Edit., 1965.
Leask, H. G. *Irish Churches and Monastic Buildings,* Vol. I, Dundalk 1955; II 1958; III 1960.
Le Grand, A. *Vies des Saints de la Bretàgne Armorique,* (Paris), 1636.
Leland, J. *The Itinerary of John Leland in or about the years* 1535-1543, 5 vols. Ed. Lucy T. Smith, London, 1964.
Lethbridge, T. C. *Herdsmen and Hermits—Celtic Seafarers in the Northern Seas.* Cambridge, 1950.

Levison, W. 'An eighth century poem on St. Ninian,' Ant., xiv, 1940.
Lewis, A. R. *The Northern Seas,* Princeton, 1958.
Lewis, C. W. *'Agweddau ar Hanes Cynnar yr Eglwys yng Nghymru',* Llên Cymru, vii. Rhif 3 a 4, 1963.
Lloyd, Sir J. E. *A History of Wales,* I & II, 3rd Edit., London, 1939.
Lot, F. *Nennius et l'Historia Brittonum,* Paris, 1934.
Loth, J. *L'Émigration bretonne en Armorique,* du Ve au VIIe siècle de notre ère, Paris (1883).
Loth, J. *Les Noms des Saints Bretons,* Paris, 1910.
Macalister, R. A. S. *Corpus Inscriptionum Insularum Celticarum,* Vols. I & II, Dublin, 1945-49.
Mackinder, Sir H. J. *Britain and the British Seas,* Oxford, 1902.
Mackinley, W. *Ancient Church Dedications in Scotland,* Vols. I & II, Edinburgh, 1914.
MacQueen, J. *St. Nynia: A study based on literary and linguistic evidence.* Edinburgh & London, 1961.
Marstrander, C. *Treen og Keeill,* Norsk Tidsskrift for Sprogridenskap viii, 1937, with English summary. See also article in Journ. of Manx Museum, iv, 1938.
Megaw, B. R. S. & E. M. 'The Norse Heritage in the Isle of Man' in *The Early Cultures of N.W. Europe* (H. M. Chadwick Memorial Studies), Cambridge, 1950.
Megaw, B. R. S. 'Who was St. Conchan? A consideration of Manx Christian origins,' Journ. Manx Museum, vi, No. 79, 1962-63.
Merlet, R. 'L'émancipation de l'église de Bretagne,' *Le Moyen Age,* 2nd series ii, Paris, 1898.
Merlet, P. 'Le formation des diocèses et des paroisses en Bretagne, période antérieure aux immigrations bretonnes,' *Mém. de la Soc. d'Histoire et d'Archéologie de Bretagne,* xxx, 1950, *ibid* xxxi, 1951.
Morris, R. H. (Edit.) *Parochialia* (Edw. Lhwyd), Cambrian Archaeological Association Supplements. 1909-11.
Myres, J. N. L. 'Britain in the Dark Ages,' Ant. ix, 1935.
Nash-Williams, V. E. 'Excavations at Llantwit Major, Glamorgan, 1937,' Arch. Camb., xcii, 1937.
Nash-Williams, V. E. 'Some dated monuments of the Dark Ages in Wales,' Arch. Camb., xciii, 1938.
Nash-Williams, V. E. 'Excavations of the Roman Villa at Llantwit Major, Glamorgan, 1938,' Arch. Camb., xciii, 1938.
Nash-Williams, V. E. *The Early Christian Monuments of Wales,* Cardiff, 1950.
Nennius, *Historia Brittonum* (Ed. Th. Mommsen in *Chronica Minora Saeculi* iv–vii (Berlin) 1898.
Nock, Sir F. C. (Ed.) *Vita Sancti Fructuosi,* Washington, 1946.
O'Dell, A. C. and Walton, K. *The Highlands and Islands of Scotland,* Regions of the British Isles, London and Edinburgh, 1962.
O'Donovan, J. Ordnance Survey Letters: MSS in National Museum of Ireland, Dublin.
O'Hanlon, J. (Edit.) *Lives of the Irish Saints,* Dublin, 1875, ff.
O'Rahilly, C. *Ireland and Wales,* London, 1924.
O'Riordáin, S. P. 'Roman material in Ireland,' P.R.I.A., Vol. 51, 1947.
Owen, H. (Edit.) *The Description of Pembrokeshire* (George Owen) 4 parts, Cymmrodorion Record Series, London, 1892-1936.
Palmer, A. E. 'Notes on the Early History of Bangor-is-coed,' Y.C., x, 1889.
Peake, H. J. E. and Fleure, H. J. *The Corridors of Time,* Vols. i–ix, Oxford, 1927-1936.
Piggott, Stuart 'South-east Scotland—Prehistoric Settlement,' British Association Handbook, Edinburgh, 1951.
Plummer, C. *Vitae Sanctorum Hiberniae,* Oxford, 1910.
Plummer, C. *Irish Litanies,* London, 1925.

Powell, T. G. E. 'The Celtic Settlement of Ireland' in *The Early Cultures of N.W. Europe* (H. M. Chadwick Memorial Studies), Cambridge, 1950.

Radford, C. A. R. 'Tintagel: The Castle and Celtic Monastery,' Ant. Journ., xv. 1935.

Radford, C. A. R. 'The Early Christian Monuments of Scotland,. Ant., xvi, 1942.

Radford, C. A. R. 'Excavations at Whithorn,' Ant., 1949.

Radford, C. A. R. 'Imported Pottery found at Tintagel, Cornwall' in *Dark Age Britain* (Ed. D. B. Harden), London, 1956.

Radford, C. A. R. 'The church in Somerset to 1100,' Proc. Soc. Antiq. Som. cvi, 1962.

Rébillon, A. *Histoire de Bretagne*, Paris, 1957.

Rees, R. *An Essay on the Welsh Saints*, London, 1836.

Rees, William *An Historical Atlas of Wales*, Cardiff, 1951. Reprinted 2nd edition 1966.

Rees, W. J. *Lives of the Cambro-British Saints*, 1853 (with numerous emendations noted by Kuno Meyer in Y.C., xiii, 1900).

Reeves, W. *Ecclesiastical Antiquities of Down, Connor and Dromore, consisting of a Taxation of those Dioceses compiled in the year MCCCVI*, with notes and illustrations, Dublin, 1847.

Reeves, W. *The Life of St. Columba*, Dublin, 1857.

Reeves, W. *The Culdees of the British Islands*, Dublin, 1864.

Richards, Melville 'The Irish Settlements in South-west Wales,' J.R.S.A.I., xc, Part II, 1960.

Richards, R. and Lloyd, R. G. 'The Old Church of Llandanwg,' Arch. Camb., xc, 1935.

Richards, R. 'Ardudwy and its Ancient Churches' in *Harlech Studies*, Cardiff, 1938.

Royal Commission on Ancient Monuments: County Reports—England, Wales and Scotland, as published.

Ryan, J. *Irish Monasticism, Origins and Early Development*, Dublin, 1931

Ryan, J. (Ed.) *St. Patrick*, Thomas Davies Lectures, Radio Éireann, Dublin, 1958.

Ryan, J. (Ed.) *Irish Monks in the Golden Age*, Dublin and London, 1963.

Scott, Sir Lindsay, 'The Problem of the Brochs,' P.P.S., xiii, 1947.

Scott, Sir Lindsay 'Gallo-British Colonies,' P.P.S., xiv, 1948

Simpson, W. D. *The Celtic Church in Scotland*, Aberdeen University Studies, No. III, 1935.

Shaw, R. C. *Post-Roman Carlisle and the Kingdoms of the North-West*, 2nd Edit, Preston, 1964.

Shaw, R. C. 'Prolegomena to a re-appraisal of Early Christianity in Man relative to the Irish Sea Province, *Proc. Isle of Man Nat. Hist. and Antiq. Soc.*, VII, I, 1967.

Stallibrass, B. 'Recent Discoveries at Clynnogfawr,' Arch. Camb., xiv, 1914.

Steers, J. A. *The Coastline of England and Wales*, Cambridge, 1946.

Stenton, Sir F. M. 'The Historical Bearing of Place Name Studies: England in the Sixth Century,' T.R.H.S. (Series 4), xxi, 1939.

Stevens, C. E. 'Magnus Maximus in British History,' *Études Celtiques*, III, 1938.

Stevens, C. E. 'Gildas Sapiens,' E.H.R., 56, 1946.

Stokes, Whitley (Ed.) *The Lives of the Saints from the Book of Lismore*, Oxford 1890.

Taylor, T. *The Life of St. Samson of Dol* (London), 1925.

Thomas, C. *Archaeology in Cornwall* 1923-38, Twenty-fifth Anniversary Number. Proceedings of the West Cornwall Field Club, Vol. 2, No. 2, 1957-58.

Thomas, C. 'Ardwall Isle: the Excavations of an early Christian site of Irish type,' T.D.G.N.H.A.S., 3rd Series, xliii, 1966.

Thomas, R. J. *The Brychan Dynasty in East Glamorgan*, Cardiff, 1936.

Thompson, E. A. 'The Origin of Christianity in Scotland,' S.H.R., xxxvii, 1958.
Toulmin-Smith, L. (Edit.) Itinerary (J. Leland), I-IV, 1907-10.
Towill, E. G. 'St. Machaoi of Nendrum,' *Ulster Journ. of Archaeology,* 3rd Series, 27, 1964.
Toynbee, J. M. C. 'Christianity in Roman Britain,' J.B.A.A., 3rd Series, xvi, 1953.
Varley, W. J. 'Further Excavations at Maiden Castle, Bickerton, 1935,' A.A.A.L., xxiii, 1936.
Wade-Evans, A. W. 'Parochiale Wallicanum,' Y.C., xxii, 1910.
Wade-Evans, A. W. *Life of St. David,* London, 1923.
Wade-Evans, A. W. 'Beuno Sant,' Arch. Camb., lxxxv, 1930.
Wade-Evans, A. W. *Welsh Christian Origins,* Oxford, 1934.
Wade-Evans, A. W. (Edit.) *Vitae Sanctorum Britanniae et Genealogiae,* Cardiff, 1944.
Wainwright, F. T. (Ed.) *The Northern Isles,* Edinburgh, 1962.
Walker, G. S. M. *Sancti Columbani Opera,* Dublin, 1957.
Watson, W. J. *History of the Celtic Place Names of Scotland,* Edinburgh, 1925.
Watson, W. J. 'The Cult of St. Cadoc in Scotland,' *Scottish Gaelic Studies,* II, 1927.
Waquet, P. *Histoire de la Bretagne,* Paris, 1958.
Wheeler, R. E. M. 'Hill-forts of Northern France—a note on the expedition to Normandy, 1939,' Ant. Journ., xxi, 1941.
Wheeler, R. E. M. & Richardson, K. M. *Hill-forts of Northern France,* Oxford, 1957.
Williams, Hugh 'The Christian Church in Wales,' T.H.S.C., 1893-4.
Williams, H. (Edit.) *De Excidio Britanniae* (Gildas) Fragmenta, Liber de Paenitentia accedit et Lorica Gildae, Cymmrodorion Record Series, No. 3, London, 1899-1901.
Williams, Hugh *Christianity in Early Britain,* Oxford, 1912.
Williams, Sir Ifor *Canu Aneirin,* Caerdydd, 1938.
Williams, Sir Ifor *Enwau Lleoedd,* Cyfres Pobun V, Lerpwl, 1945.
Williams, Sir Ifor *'Hen Chwedlau,'* T.H.S.C., 1946-47.
Williams, Sir Ifor 'Wales and the North,' T.C.W.A.A.S., li (New Series), 1952.
Williamson, E. W. *'Vespasian A xiv,'* Arch. Camb. C1, Pt 2, 1951, pp. 91-105.
Wilson, P. A. 'Romano-British and Welsh Christianity: Continuity or Discontinuity,' Pts. I & II, W.H.R., Vol 3, 1966, Nos. 1 and 2.
Wormald, F. *English Kalendars before A.D.* 1100, H.B.S., Vol. lxxii (1934).
Zimmer, H. *The Celtic Church in Britain and Ireland,* Trans. by A. Meyer, London, 1902.

INDEX

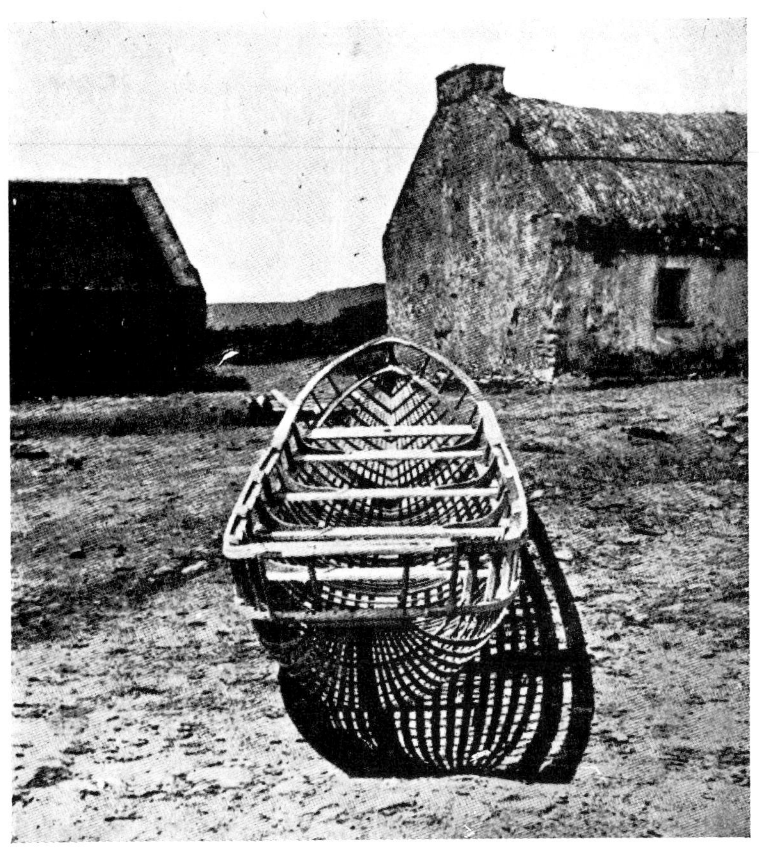

Photo, James Hornell

Plate I

Framework of a Dingle Curragh

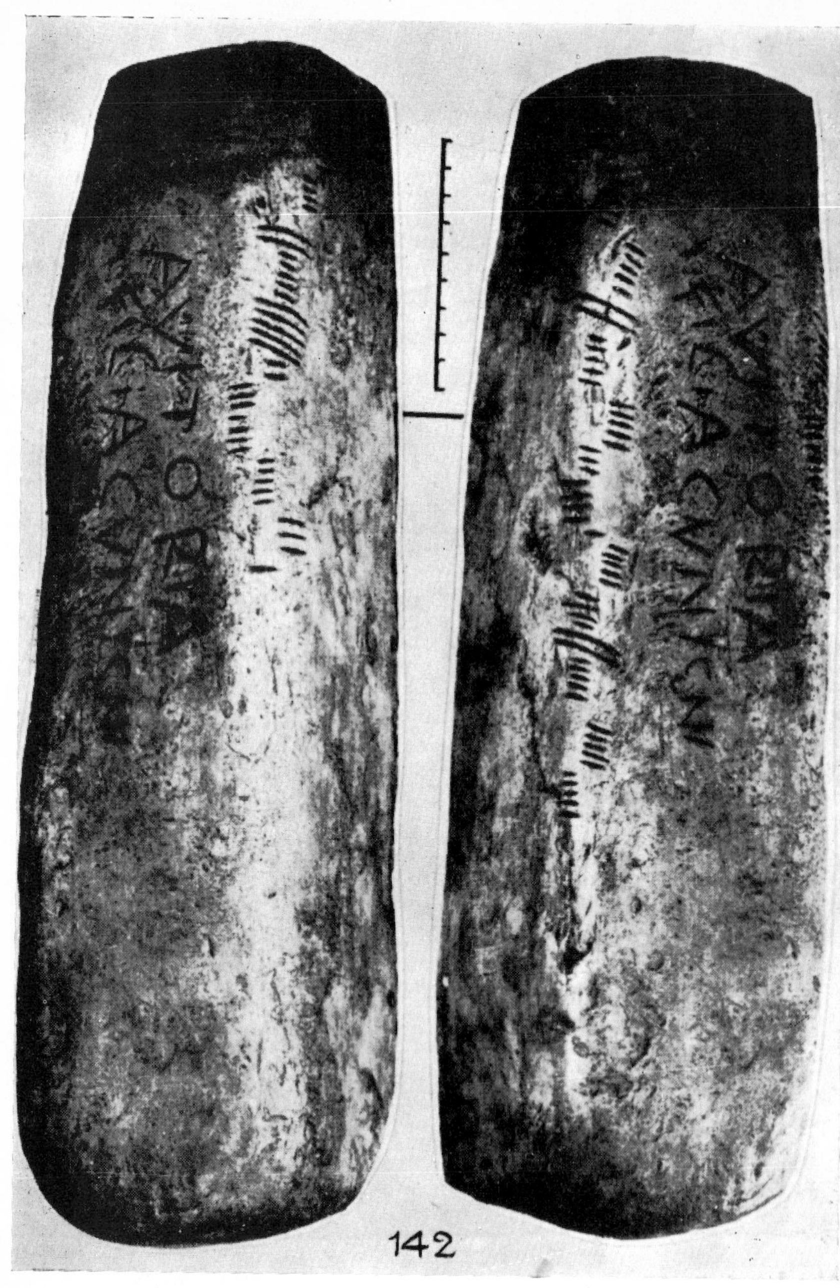

Photo, Nash-Williams

Plate 2

Bilingual Stone (Latin and Ogham) from Eglwys Gymyn, Carmarthenshire

Plate 3

Early Christian Inscribed Stone from Penmachno, Caernarvonshire, set up in the time of Justinus the Consul

Photo, Nash-Williams

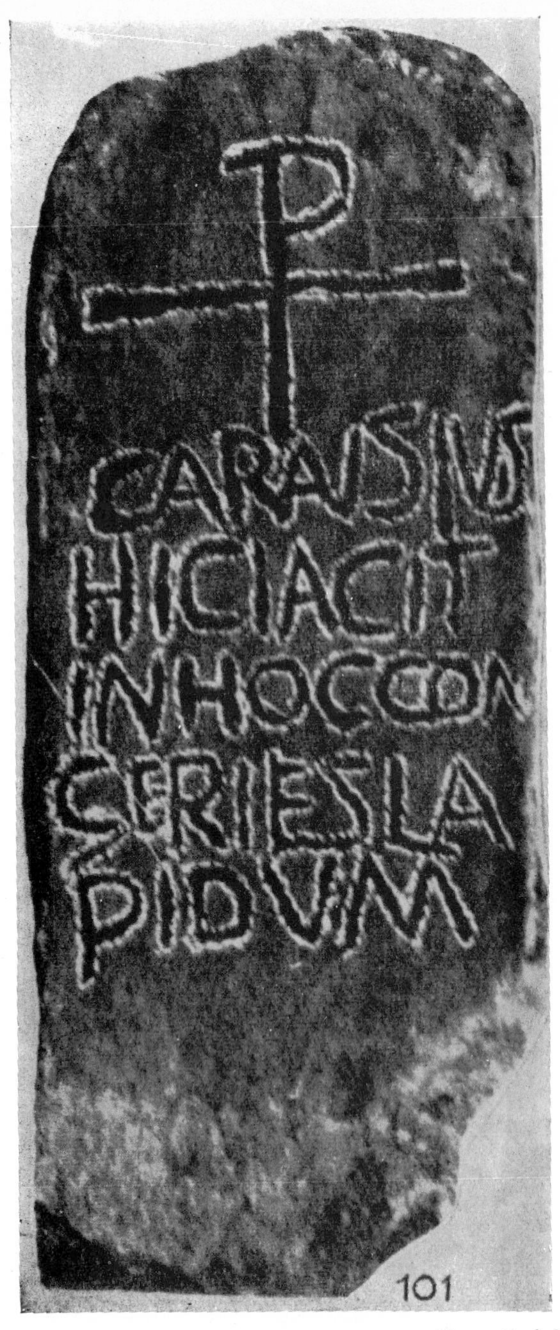

Photo, Nash-Williams

Plate 4

Early Christian Inscribed Stone with HIC IACIT a formula
Penmachno churchyard, Caernarvonshire

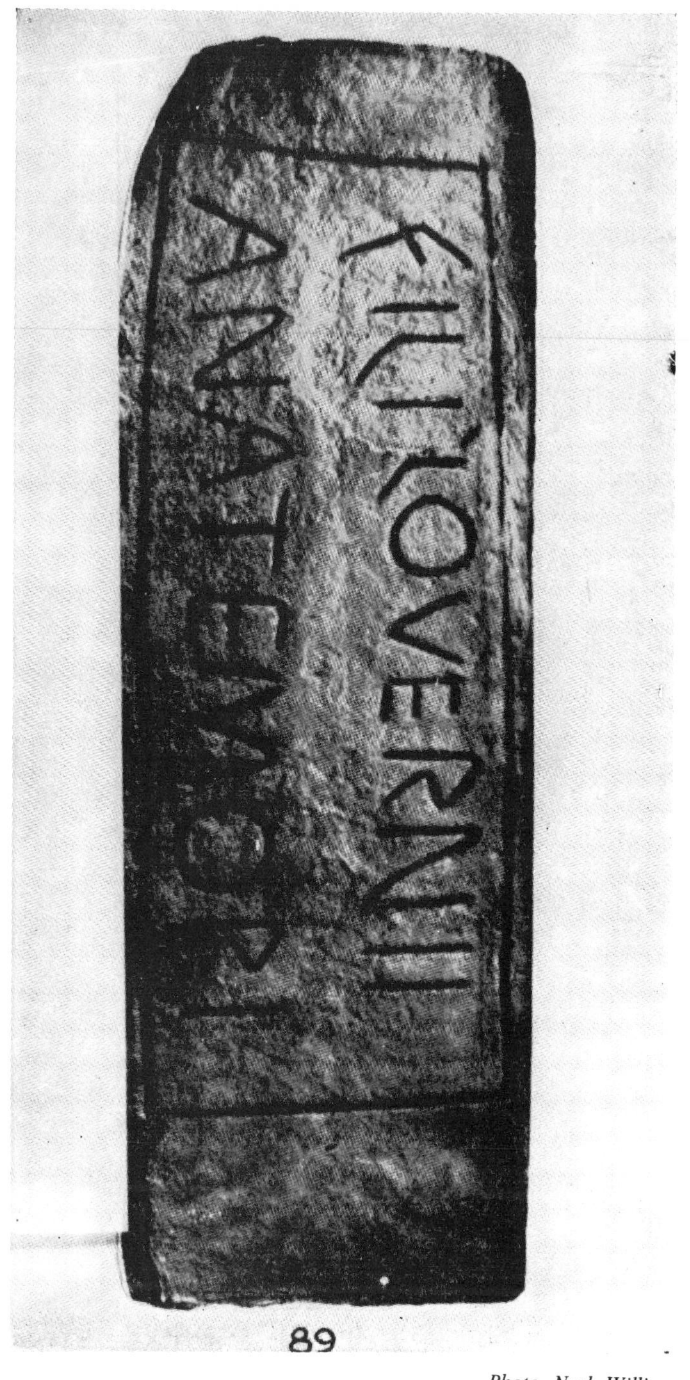

Photo, Nash-Williams

Plate 5

Early Christian Inscribed Stone with FILIUS formula Llanfaglan Church, Caernarvonshire

Reproduced by permission of the British Library Board

Plate 6

Initial from Lindisfarne Gospels. 8th Century
(Cotton MS. Nero D.IV.f.90)

Photo, J. K. St. Joseph

Plate 7

The monastery of Clonmacnoise from the air

Plate 8

A Manx Keeill at Lag ny Keililley

(after Baring-Gould & Fisher)

Plate 9

St. Samson sailing towards Armorica (from 13th Century window in the Cathedral of Dol.)

Reproduced by permission of the Commissioners of Public Works in Ireland

Plate 10

Head of Muiredach's Cross, Monasterloice, Co. Louth
Early 10th Century

Plate 11

Iona Cathedral as it was in 1850 with ruins of Benedictine Monastery and Nunnery (1203). (H.D. Graham: "Antiquities of Iona", 1850)

Reproduced by permission of the Commissioners of Public Works in Ireland

Plate 12

Round Tower and St. Declan's Church, Ardmore

(after Baring-Gould & Fisher)

Plate 13

Ile de S. Cadou, near Belz, Brittany

Photo, W.W. Harris

Plate 14

The Church of St. Celynin, Llangelynin

Plate 15

St. David's Cathedral in the valley of the Alun

(Cambridge University Collection: copyright reserved)